Dr (Col) Harikrishnan is a laparoscopic surgeon and endoscopist by profession, with a passion for writing, be it professional articles, travelogues, book reviews, music reviews or stories. He is a self-styled musicologist, with a huge personal collection of music and music-related books. This is his first full-length book based on personal experiences as a young soldier. He lives with his wife in Bangalore, and spends summers in London, where his son and daughter have settled. He is currently working on a book about his pet dog, Rufus.

The Three Muscat Years
by Dr (Col) KM Harikrishnan
Paperback Edition

First Published in India in 2022
by Inkfeathers Publishing, New Delhi 110095

Copyright © Dr (Col) KM Harikrishnan 2022
Illustrations © Sanjana A. Sridharan
Edited by Uma Bokil

All rights reserved.
ISBN 9789390882588

www.inkfeathers.com

THE THREE MUSCAT YEARS

ADVENTURES OF A YOUNG FAUJI

AND HIS FRIENDS

Dr (Col) KM Harikrishnan

Inkfeathers Publishing

www.inkfeathers.com

THEY LOVED THE BOOK

Dr Gopal Sankaran, MD, DrPH, MNAMS, CHES*
Professor of Public Health, West Chester University, USA

'With his debut book, *The Three Muscat Years: Adventures of a young fauji & his friends*, Col (Dr) Harikrishnan has hit a six! His evolving life as a budding surgeon in Army Medical Corps, on deputation to the Sultanate of Oman in the eighties, is a tale that is hilarious and heartwarming. People, places, and events are brought to life through a thoughtfully narrated prose infused with humour and compassion. A must read for all those serving in the defence and healing professions, and just about anyone that wishes to curl up with a can't-put-down book!'

Maj Gen RPRC Naidu, AVSM, VSM, Bangalore

'This book by Dr Harikrishnan is perhaps one of the most unputdownable books I have read for some time. It looks very autobiographical, of a time in his life when he was still in his formative years in the army as a doctor. Coming from a relatively humble background, a foreign posting at so early a stage must have been a bonanza for him, at least financially. His excitement at the prospect is very tangible, and he takes the reader along with him in his joy. The reviewer has had the good fortune of knowing the writer at a stage earlier than the period of the narrative, and he had the making of one who would go far professionally and socially. His interests were varied, from extensive reading, a passion for Carnatic music, cricket, and a distinct flair for the use of the English language to an almost classic demonstration of Dale Carnegie's advice for making friends. His moral and ethical principles were always a highlight of his character. His very family-centric personality is so well etched in the narrative. His middle-class father is the central figure in the making of his intellectual and moral fibre as well as his love for the language.

The book outlines the very interesting and convincing saga of the universality of human goodness in whichever conditions and company one is thrown together. With the kind of book that the author has written, one looks forward to a sequel which would perhaps depict a more mature stage in his life in this beautiful land.'

Dr Ramachandran Ramani, MBBS, MD, MNAMS
Emeritus Professor of Anaesthesia, University of Florida, Gainesville, USA

'Surgeons and anesthesiologists rarely ever complement each other. And here we have a brilliant writing by a surgeon, (ex-Col in the AMC, a well-informed person, and a great friend) which I thoroughly enjoyed reading. This book "Three Muscat Years" describing Dr Krishnan's time in Muscat (40 years ago) early in his career working for the Omanian Armed Forces expresses his sense of humour. His choice of words is commendable, and his ability to describe events in detail seems to be so natural to him. Every word of the comment of one of his commanding officers, 'Dr Krishnan can charm anyone under 5 minutes,' is evident in this writing. This book touches upon the peaks and troughs of starting out in medicine in a new country and in newfound love, with authenticity, charm, and gentle humour that makes it a must-read!'

Dr. Raghupathy Sarma, Emeritus Professor of Biochemistry
Stony Brook University

'I am delighted to write this brief account of my impressions of "The Three Muscat Years" by Colonel Harikrishnan. The present book is a pleasure to read. A fascinating recollection that is both easy to read and also detailed and nostalgia evoking. This book will delight anyone who wants to hark back to the first days in a new career, new country, new surrounds… It is extremely fascinating, from start to finish; difficult to stop reading. Hari's ability to recall even the most trivial events that happened nearly forty years ago is quite remarkable. He also has a unique style of narrating any incident however frivolous. I am looking forward to reading about his life in England and his second stay in Muscat.'

To my late sister Lalitha, who *ought* to have stayed on to see this book in print. This is for you, first and foremost, dear sis. Forgive my procrastination. For my part, I forgive your impatience to reunite with Appa and Amma.

To the Indian Army, the finest military force in the world. Thanks for the experiential lessons in humanity which no book can come close to imparting.

This book claims to be no less or no more than what it exactly is: a fictionalised version of my memoirs. They relate to a period in my life, short in span, but long in learning. I have deliberately distorted some facts to suit my narration. There has been no intention to hurt, malign, or show in a bad light any person or people. No advantage has been or will be taken of anything that has been said or claimed in this book. It has been written purely to entertain.

Contents

The Second Muscat Year

The Third Muscat Year

Preface

With Malice Towards None

In early 2020, the SARS-CoV-2 virus struck, and life was turned upside down for millions of us. I was already well past the standard retirement age. My wife had been periodically reminding me to slow down. Even as I was forced by my age to reduce my clinical and administrative responsibilities, another signal came from within me. No, not in a spiritual sense. It was just my prostate that had been clamouring for attention for some years. I was diagnosed with prostate cancer, something I, in my arrogance as a surgeon, only expected to hear about in my patients. I took a hasty retirement, and went through surgery and other treatments, despite the raging Covid situation. During this time, much needed reflection on the very purpose of my existence happened. For once, I had the time to look beyond the wards and operating theatres. As I reviewed my life and career, I realised what an incredibly lucky man I had been. The instances of good fortune in my life were legion. But none came close to that stroke of luck, beginning with a simple phone call, which saw me on my way to Oman many years back.

This narration is about events that took place forty years ago. Yet, I am able to recollect every single detail, faces of people, locales, weather, etc., as if they happened but yesterday. The impressions on my twenty-something mind, experiencing a totally new way of life, must have been so deeply etched!

Thus, I have not had to add any *"masala"* to the story; there was enough of it already! During the writing of this book, I spoke to as many of the people featured in this book as possible. There was unanimous approval for my plans to put down my memories of those golden days. Naturally, as per my promise to them, I have altered the names of all people, and the names of some of the locations, for confidentiality purposes. The events themselves are fairly accurate—I have changed the outcome of some of them, for, like Alan J Lerner says in the introduction to his version of Bernard Shaw's *Pygmalion*, I believe these outcomes are more in keeping with life—or what life should be. I certainly liked the ending of *My Fair Lady* better than *Pygmalion*. I beg the indulgence of those in the know. And I fervently hope the reader approves.

The three years changed me forever—and not just in terms of my economic prospects. I think I grew up immensely in my understanding of people from all over the globe, their cultures and practices. It taught me to appreciate and understand, indeed celebrate, the differences and similarities amongst us.

My experiences were undeniable proof that deep down, all human beings are very similar in their attitude. I certainly heard the milk of human kindness (to borrow a phrase from PG Wodehouse) sloshing about in people from different countries and continents. It wasn't always loud and clear, but it was there. In some, it overflowed, and I was often the direct beneficiary of such unconditional goodness. In some, it needed an incident, a minor commonality, to start the sloshing. But it was there. It was very much there.

And it is with a great sense of joy and satisfaction that I see my own children show a high level of social tolerance, a desperate need of the times we live in. However, the credit for their bonhomie does not go to anything I may have passed on as a parent. It belongs securely in the ethos of the Indian Armed Forces. As children of an Army officer, they got tossed about all over India, changing schools rather frequently. The Army has the habit of throwing people of different faiths, cultural backgrounds, geography, and financial status together, repeatedly. Over time, the understanding and acceptance of one another becomes inevitable. To that extent, I believe the Indian Army is a great unifier of the incredibly diverse sects of people in India. I salute this collective conscience of the Armed Forces as a show of my respect and gratitude. I realise in retrospect that more than elevating my financial status, my army career, which paved the way for my deputation to Oman, made me a better human being. I could think of no better way to acknowledge that than through the medium of this book. *Jai Hind.*

1

Dream Come True

The phone rang. I cranked the handle of the phone, picked up the mouthpiece and said hello as loudly as I could. Electronics be damned, I knew from experience that shouting helped push the sound waves over the ether. 'HELLO.'

'Hi, Doc,' said the static-laden voice. My heart skipped a beat—it sounded like the Brigade Major (BM) and his phone calls were usually rather draining experiences. But his next words were anything but harsh: 'You've hit lottery, Captain!'

I was sure this was a ruse.

'MORNING, SIR!' I bellowed, sticking to my decibel choice, not wanting to be pulled up for being insolent. ('So, whatever happened to greeting a senior officer, eh?')

'LOTTERY, SIR?'

'No need to shout, Officer,' said the voice. This was closer to normal. 'Yes, lottery. *Tumhara foreign posting aaya hai.* (You have been selected for a foreign posting).' My heart tried to make up for the missed beat, throwing in a few hundred beats in rapid sequence.

The year was 1980. I was doing adjutant duty at an altitude of 14,000 feet in Ladakh. Usually, doctors (Regimental Medical Officer, or RMO) in infantry units in high altitudes have a cushy time. Few, if any sick soldiers to take care of, a heated bunker which automatically raises your popularity with other officers, and the

Commanding Officer (CO)'s company for Bridge and *pakodas* in the evening. True, the "doc" usually lands the Mess Secretary's duties, but that's a bonus as well. The Mess manager, or Mess *Havaldar* in Indian Army parlance ensures that your portion of the snacks and dessert are kept aside, safe from the other gluttons. Milk (powder milk, for sure, but still milk) and tea flow like free-issue rum, and dry fruits pass through your door even before the CO's. But fate usually catches up with most people, and fate has a special liking for me in such matters. The regular adjutant fell ill (damn it, *I* gave him SIQ for a week!), and the CO said, with a hint of sarcasm, 'Doc, you can do adjutant duty; the Brigade Headquarters wants us to start the field exercise forthwith.'

I remember mumbling a yes at a much lower decibel than I was using now. We were only six days into the exercise, and I was longing for the next eight days to somehow rush through by today's evening, so we could go back to the relative comfort of our Unit location, my warm bunker and bed (which, every once in a while, doubled up as my consultation chamber) and the luxury of four full hours of electricity every evening.

'You there?' said Mister Steel, aka BM, bringing me back to the present.

'Yes, Sir,' I said weakly, forgetting the golden rule of communicating in high decibels. 'How, Sir—I mean—where, Sir?'

'Muscat, boss, Muscat,' said the BM.

Muscat? *Muscat?* What the hell was that supposed to mean? M. U. S. C. A. T., short for something, may be? Was there a K instead of a C? I had no clue what this BM chap was talking about. Thankfully, the ever-dependable field telephone system came to my aid. It simply died!

The BM did not call again. I can imagine him, now after all these years, saying to himself, 'Bloody greenhorn. Gets a foreign posting within two years of service, while here I am, 14 years of selfless service, rotting in the cold. Bloody unfair.' Or some such.

Given the economic conditions of those days, a foreign posting was indeed a lottery. My monthly salary as a doctor, with five years of advance seniority on the day of joining, a qualification pay of Rs (rupees) 250, and the Rs 55 I was getting as a paratrooper was already probably higher than that of this 14-year-old veteran.

I cautiously asked around—not a single person in the Unit knew what Muscat meant, leave alone where it was. I was restless. I asked the head clerk if there was any message from Brigade HQ or Army HQ.

'No, Sir,' said the silly fellow, and went back to whatever research he was then doing with some yellowing registers. *Must be finding ways to stop someone's leave*, I thought, angrily.

It was the CO who shed light on the matter a full three days later. He was in a good mood, having won again at Bridge that evening.

'Great news, Doc,' he said. 'I always knew you were foreign posting material.'

I tried to imagine myself as a well-wrapped package with a London address or some such on the front. It didn't quite gel.

'So, when's the party? Should be special, I bet, knowing Bhim (our Mess Havaldar) is your personal property and all that!' he added.

I tried to look nonchalant. 'Sure, Sir,' I said, 'as soon as I find a map and locate this place I am supposed to go to.' I wasn't even sure of how to pronounce the name of the silly place. *Mush Cat? Moose Kaath?*

God, please let this not be in Siberia, I prayed silently.

The all-knowing CO cleared the matter. '*Arre yaar* (Come on, man), I thought you'd know, being so well read and all that. Muscat is in the Middle East. Go to Bombay, start swimming westwards, and the first piece of land you hit is Muscat. My cousin, Brigadier Sandhu, was sent on T/D (short for Temporary Duty) there once.' I lost him after that, having mentally started swimming already from Bombay's shores. Middle East? That's it? Some foreign posting; hell, why couldn't it be Sandhurst (in the UK, right?) or even Iraq or Egypt where I know Fauji teams have gone? At least I could have got to see the pyramids.

I complained to God, 'Pretty unfair, God; if you did want to give me a lottery, why this half-hearted one? And they say in the movies you sort of give *chhappad phhad ke* and all that?'

But at least I knew something about this goddamned place now. I could hardly wait for dinner to be over to get back to the privacy of my bunker and write a letter to my father, Appa, who would know all about this silly place; he always knew everything. I shot off a list of questions and told him to talk to anyone in the nearby army Units about the formalities involved in going abroad on posting. He was in Jalandhar those days, and there were at least three Units nearby and a big Military Hospital.

But even as I licked the free-issue Field Envelope closed, I realised with a sinking heart that it could be two weeks, maybe three, before I got any information. If the weather held, my little letter would hopefully travel to our location some 40 km behind us, and that would take all of tomorrow. With luck, and with weather holding there, it would travel the 120 km from our Unit headquarters to Leh the next day. With more luck, and with weather still holding (this was asking too much of the Gods, three continuous days of good weather in Ladakh!), it would go to Chandigarh the next day. Give one or two days to reach the GPO (the General Post Office manned by the Army) and another day to get into the civilian postal system, it would be, with a hell of a lot of luck, with my father a week from now. Appa would no doubt draft a reply within minutes of reading my letter. Knowing him, the matter would be extremely important— nothing short of his son getting the post of Ambassador to the USA!

As it happened, I got a lot of information—naturally, from Appa's letter, which came within two weeks: Muscat was the capital of Oman; an Islamic sultanate, bordering Yemen to the South, United Arab Emirates to the North, and Saudi Arabia to the West;

strategically important because of the Straits of Hormuz (whatever it was, Appa did not bother to explain); currency Riyal, worth close to 25 rupees to one riyal; direct flights from Bombay to the capital city, etc. Armed with this information, I was able to impress my colleagues in the Unit and at the nearby Field Hospital, where the surgeon first congratulated me for the windfall, and then promptly dampened my mood.

He advised me sombrely to give it up if I was serious about wanting to be a surgeon as I had been repeatedly telling him. But our 2-I-C (Second in Command) rubbished such advice. 'If you are serious about becoming a surgeon, you will—even after returning from your tenure in Muscat. But you let go of this chance to strengthen your finances forever, you will regret it all your life,' he said. He had a friend who had done a tenure abroad. When he returned, he had saved enough to buy a house, he said.

A house! Just like that? I couldn't believe it. I urged him to find out what pay I could expect in Muscat. He said his guess would be about 10,000 rupees a month. I couldn't believe my ears! Here I was, a relatively well-off Captain of the Army Medical Corps, getting nearly 2200 a month. And I was going to get nearly five times that much, every month! My heart raced. I started making a mental list of things I could buy Appa and Amma, and for our home (my brother's home really, since my parents were living with him). Luxuries like TV and washing machine started appearing before my eyes! Oh, my good God! This was so fantastic!

But even before I could thank the 2-I-C and leave, I had to make a note of the first of many requests that were to come my way from fellow officers in the course of the next few days. Here I was, barely aware of any details about the place I was going to, and I was being given a shopping list. The 2-I-C wanted a tennis racket for his 12-year-old daughter, who was showing a lot of promise in the game. The list grew steadily: a Littman stethoscope for the Medical Specialist at the Field Hospital, an "authentic" Parker pen for the surgeon (who grudgingly agreed that my entry to surgical training could wait), roller skates for another officer's son, and a "good quality" nail cutter for the head clerk *Saab* (Sir).

I woke up early the next day. The weather didn't seem too cold

after all. I wanted breakfast to be finished early; I had to see the *dak* (post) at the office—my posting order would be waiting for me! I went straight to the head clerk's desk. Even before I could ask, he doused my enthusiasm with '*Abhi tak kuch nahin aaya hai* (Nothing in the post so far), Captain Saab.' *These DRs*, I thought.

The Despatch Riders of the Armed Forces are the most cursed community of the Defence Services. They are blamed if they don't bring important letters from higher formations. They are also cursed every time they deliver news about one's posting—either because they bring you news that you are actually now posted to a far worse place than you thought ever existed, or because, like in my case, they did *not* bring the posting order pronto!

I cursed the chap, and went about my duties as adjutant, still buoyant at the thought of a possible fridge, maybe even one of those newly introduced cassette players for Appa to listen to his classical music collection. By that evening, the Officers' Mess had a festive look. There was much back slapping and 'Well done, bugger'-ing and '*Mess Havaldar, aaj sab drink Captain Saab ke naam pe*'-ing (all drinks to be charged to the captain, meaning me!). My bills were beginning to look like I was already working abroad!

The next day came and went, the next, and then the entire week. But there was no sign of the posting order. I began to seriously wonder if the BM, true to his reputation, had simply been playing a practical joke at my expense. I turned to the 2-I-C again: after all, his daughter's tennis racket was also at stake. He said, 'Relax, Hari. I spoke the very next day to the BM. It is true you are going abroad. *Dak* from AHQ takes its own sweet time; don't worry,' he said.

I wrote off a letter to Colonel Banerjee, who, as my first ever Commanding Officer (at the little Military Hospital in Bakloh, Himachal Pradesh), had strongly recommended me for a deputation abroad. I guess I was subconsciously hoping he would write back with some information about my posting order. He replied, of course, full of praise for me and wishing me well, but seemed no wiser than me about the posting order.

After another couple of weeks of impatient waiting, I decided to take matters into my hands. By now, my standing in the Unit was that of a minor superhero. Goaded as always by the 2-I-C (Oh! he so wanted that racket for the budding Wimbledon champ of the family!), I approached the CO for a few days' leave. The superhero effect was shining bright, and I was granted 5 days off in less than as many seconds. I collected my week's quota of Old Monk rum, the best currency in Leh Market, and the very next morning, I was on a Jonga (a biggish Jeep specially designed for the Indian Army by Nissan Corporation) to the Officers' Transit Camp in Leh.

The distance from our location to Leh was not much but usually needed about 6 hours to cover, thanks to the usual weather and road conditions. I made it uneventfully across the bleak, snow-clad mountains, stopping only at the regular outposts where one could have hot, sweet tea with pakoras or aloo puri, depending on the time of day.

There was an Air Force flight scheduled to Chandigarh the very next morning. I hurried to the small Leh market and bought two Wing Sung pens—about the finest fountain pens in those days—at one "dollar" (read one bottle of Old Monk) apiece. These were very useful as gift items. I hardly slept that night, so excited that I was. Leh to Chandigarh was a short flight of about an hour. From Chandigarh to Jalandhar used to be about three and a half to four hours by road in those days, but I didn't mind that—it gave me an opportunity to talk to at least 5 different chaps (not including the crew of the flight, the list of whose shopping requests nestled happily in my pocket) about my imminent departure to Muscat ('It is in the Middle East, you know, yes, close to Dubai'). At Jalandhar bus stand, I shocked a poor beggar with a five rupee note—after all, it was but a minute fraction of what I would be earning very soon!

Appa was thrilled to see me. So was Amma, but my father's reaction was as if I had won the Nobel Prize! I was already aware of the lottery I had got, for a foreign posting was nothing short of a lottery in continuum. Consider the facts: my present pay was around 2200 rupees all told, or under 300 US Dollars (the US Dollar was worth about 7.5 rupees then). Based on hearsay—and speculations varied wildly—I could expect anything between 1000 to 1200 dollars a month! A three-to-four times' increase in my monthly income. I did a bit of mental math: Okay, let us settle for 1100 a month, times 36 months. (The standard tenure of a foreign deputation was three years.) Oh, my good God, how will I ever handle so much money?

But the lottery was a stroke of unexpected luck in another way— I was from an extremely ordinary, lower middle-class background. The only Army "connection" I had was that my father had worked as a civilian clerk in the Army HQ at Delhi for a few years. And greenhorn as I was in the Army, I knew that the much-coveted foreign postings usually went to sons and sons-in-law of senior officers. All I had was my academic performance, which was by no means dismissive: a top ranker in my final MBBS from Delhi University, All India Second Rank in the Army Medical Corps entrance exam, Best All-Round Officer in the initial training course at Lucknow, and a paratrooper to boot. But merit was not known to figure prominently in the selection to go on a deputation abroad. Someone Up There had smiled especially on me... or maybe, even Up There, They made some mistakes! Despite going about boasting to people about my good fortune, I was aware that I could only count my blessings once I received the written orders from Army HQ. So, Appa going about comparing me with Sir C V Raman or such like luminaries was secretly embarrassing.

Every passing day added anxiety to the embarrassment. I had come on five days of leave. Although the clock started ticking on my leave only after I had touched down at Chandigarh (one of the benefits of being posted in hostile service conditions was that one's leave started and ended at the nearest railhead/airbase in a peace area), it was too short to try and make a run to the Army HQ in Delhi, nearly a day's travel by bus or train. I was also curiously more interested in spending time with my one-year-old niece than securing my own future. Malu, short for Malini, my brother's child, was the first female grandchild of the family, and was extremely special.

I therefore invoked every God I could, beseeching them to somehow get me that piece of paper which would read (or so I imagined): 'MR 03675L, Captain K M Harikrishnan, is hereby posted to Muscat. Officer to report for duty at the new station with immediate effect.' But my leave finished, and I had to tear myself away from Malu and the rest of the family and trudge my way back in a rickety bus back to Chandigarh and on to Leh. I do not recall talking to anyone en-route, leave alone mentioning my foreign posting.

All this was in January of 1980. I had recently turned 25. As the days, then weeks passed, my spirits sagged in inverse proportion to the length of the list of things I was being asked to bring back on my first leave back home. I remember worrying during moments of reckless enthusiasm about my imminent departure to Muscat: how would I ever bring 15 bottles of the "original" Old Spice aftershave lotion—and how would I explain if I could not? The list was rarely looked at by the time the snow started to thaw in early April. No letter from the Army HQ yet. Even the ever-positive 2-I-C confided to me that he had been similarly selected to go to Iraq once, but some big shot's son had displaced him at the last minute.

I could see this happening so easily with me—there were a whole lot of fellows of my seniority who were graduates of AFMC (Armed Forces Medical College, the Army's own medical school), and everyone knew that these AFMC fellows were all well connected, with at least an uncle or two in senior positions strewn all around the places that mattered. In my anxiety, I imagined harsh thoughts—how do I know my name won't suddenly be simply typed over with some Tom, Dick, or Harry? I went into self-induced despair. The back slapping and 'When's the party, mate?' banter slowly ebbed and died. I failed to enjoy the wonderful summer that was unfolding in front of me, the hills beginning to show hues of green, the coat-parkas no longer a must for survival.

And then, from Up There, They decided to smile! Just like that. Without any ado, my *dak* in the second week of September 1980— eight months after the initial excitement—carried the good news: 'The following officers to report to AHQ with immediate effect, but no later than 15 September 1980, for proceeding on secondment to Sultan's Armed Forces, Muscat, Oman. Officers may be advised to report with all necessary personal effects including all documents for Passport application to Section.' Oh my God! Passport! I didn't have one, of course, but even the thought of having to acquire one had not occurred to me all these months of waiting! I ran to the 2-I-C to share the good news and ask about the passport issue.

2

Muscat Ahoy!

C apt. Sunil Kumar and Capt. Deepak Sharma were valiantly trying to hide their discomfiture as the Muscat-bound Indian Airlines flight took off. That was a bit comforting as I had an equally queasy feeling in my belly. I had noted their names along with mine in the posting orders, and the last six hectic days at the Army HQ in Delhi had given us enough time to realise that all of us were struggling to come to terms with our good luck.

It was clear that none of us had any significant army connections, which made our selection that much more mysterious, yet precious. We had been running around like headless chicken—hordes of forms to be filled out each day, briefing by the Security Section, lectures on the Official Secrets Act, loads of advice about Omani Culture, healthcare system, their Army's organisation—we had been stuffed with enough information to write a book! Every day would start with our reporting in the morning to the Head Clerk at the Armed Forces Medical Services HQ, and each day, Subedar Major Bhagwan Singh would start off by treating us as crown princes, but as the day wore on, he would start to show his true character, treating us more like a bunch of undeservingly lucky upstarts.

On day six, though, we were crown princes all day through. As we wondered at our changed status, the reason became clear. He had a small list of his own, which he gave to *all* three of us, with promises galore of "good" postings when we returned in three years. He assured us that he would still be right there, adding rather diplomatically that two of the previous batches had been banished by him to the wilderness on their return for failing to get him the few "simple" things he had wanted from Muscat.

As I mulled over these thoughts, the plane was well on its short flight across the Arabian Sea. Not that we could see anything in the pitch dark of the night from the windows. We were going to a totally new place, and much of our briefing had made it sound like *Kala Pani* (Andaman & Nicobar Islands, as they were known to most in pre-Independence days), where the freedom fighters had been banished. I was acutely missing my parents, my darling niece and nephews, and the relatively carefree life up until now.

What if we didn't quite measure up to the expectations of the local fellows in Muscat? Would they send us back? Would that mean a court martial? I must have dozed off despite such frenzied imagination, because the next thing I knew, we were touching down on foreign soil. In the predawn light, the view outside was most depressing—drab, dry hills to the distance, not a tree, not even a blade of grass anywhere to be seen, not a single building, nothing! Coming from India, this was a big blow—not one soul had prepared us for the bleak topography we were going to land in, curse them!

The aircraft was parked in the middle of nowhere, or so it seemed to me. Lugging our duffel bags (wheeled suitcases hadn't yet made their appearance in the Indian market), we walked the short distance from the plane to the airport terminal. It was the size of a tennis court, not much more. Our "white" passports, declaring our diplomatic status, were of great help, and we were able to get through the immigration formalities with just our rudimentary knowledge of Arabic. We rather freely 'salaam alaikum'-ed and 'shukran'-ed, flashing our friendliest smiles at the immigration staff. There was a single luggage belt, where our luggage took a fair time to come out. Less than ten feet from the luggage collection area were the exit gates. We found ourselves outside the airport building, the sultry, hot weather outside doing nothing to soothe our nerves. This was September, for God's sake!

Luckily, we didn't have to wait too long. There was a tall chap in a funny kind of uniform—funny, because while he wore the standard olive-green coloured trousers and shirt, it looked like he was wearing fawn coloured suede shoes! Turn out in such fashion in any unit in the Indian Army, you would get stiff punishment for insulting the uniform. He strode directly towards us—our greenhorn faces must have been so easy to identify.

'Which of you is Capt. Sharma of AMC?' he said by way of hello. Sharma was the seniormost amongst the three of us (he was senior by two numbers to me—we were commissioned on the same day). 'Sir,' said Sharma, and I bet he regretted it later on. The chap who had come to receive us was Capt. Arun, a dental officer who turned out to be junior to us. But how could Sharma have known?

'Follow me,' said Capt. Arun, enjoying his moment of superiority, and we pushed our carts to where a gleaming green Toyota Corolla was parked, just a few metres away. The boot of the car was big enough for all our luggage to fit in; not that we had much. Sharma, using his "seniority", grabbed the front passenger seat—or so he thought, till he found out the passenger seat had the steering wheel! Our first shock—traffic flowed on the right side of the road! He was summarily despatched to the other side by Capt. Arun. Sunil and I piled in at the back. The car was hotter than the weather outside.

'Your bloody plane was half an hour late,' complained Arun, and we mumbled our apologies for someone else's incompetence. 'Bloody hot,' he muttered as he started the car. Within seconds, it became bloody cold.

'A/C, boss,' whispered Sunil in my ears. But I hardly noticed it all. I was totally unimpressed with Muscat and was muttering *Hanuman Chalisa*, pleading desperately to the powerful Anjaneya, 'Please, please, God, get me back to India—even the outpost in Ladakh would do—as soon as possible. I hate this place, I hate the airport, I hate this stupid, haughty Arun chap, I don't want this bloody foreign posting, I simply want to go back. I will *chadhao* a *108-vadai malai* as soon as I am back in India.'

Very soon, I would start hoping the great Hanuman had not heard my foolish requests; very soon, I would regret every wrong thought about Muscat, about Oman, and equally importantly, about Arun!

3

Landed and Grounded

The first few days after we landed in Muscat, it felt quite like back home. We had a similar round of briefing on a similar set of topics, and most of the people briefing us were Indians. Two things were different. There was no discussion about the Official Secrets Act, and there were classes every morning to acquaint us with essential Omani. Omani is different from the Arabic spoken elsewhere in the Middle East in some respects. We were given a book each, which taught us what to say when, especially when speaking to patients. Differences between Omani and classic Egyptian Arabic were highlighted. I ignored these bits. I had no intention of mastering Egyptian Arabic. I only needed to survive this silly place till my request reached the top of the pile with Hanuman Ji, and then, vroom! I'd be off back home. So, I didn't pay much attention to picking up the language beyond the *sabah al khair, kaif haal ak, kullu zen* bits.

My desperate desire to go back was due to the totally strange surroundings, pushing me well out of my comfort zone. I think I was rather impatient then, unwilling to give my new circumstances enough consideration. I could see that young Sharma was making rapid progress—and letting us know every now and then about some new sentence or phrase he had mastered—but I couldn't be bothered. *Let him stuff the entire book*, I thought. *Who cares?*

The one interesting thing in the first week was a visit to the Indian

Embassy in a ramshackle building at the other end of the town from our army camp. It was a long drive for the 8 of us (other chaps, mainly from dental corps, and two non-medics, had arrived in Muscat a day before us). We travelled in a minibus—oh, yes, a fully air-conditioned bus, with individual controls above each row of seats, much like an aircraft, which was cool in more ways than one. I fiddled with the controls to get some gentle breeze on my face, but even as I enjoyed the breeze, I reminded myself that it was only going to be short-lived, anyway.

The Ambassador was surprisingly young looking and spoke very well in measured tones. The embassy building may not have been great, but the Ambassador's room was impressive alright—a huge desk with a pile of files to his left, a bright, mini-Indian flag on a stand to his right, plush chairs such as those I certainly had never sat on before, a fine-tuned air conditioner silently doing its job, a large map of Oman on one wall, and the usual big shots' pictures on the wall behind him.

He said we were all ambassadors like him; we were not here just to help the local army with medical, dental, or military matters. He, indeed, all of India depended on us to strengthen the already good relationship enjoyed by Oman and India. *Good for you and good for anyone else interested*, I thought. I was waiting for him to finish and say, 'Any questions?' and then, I would ask him about the next available flight to India.

I got a jolt when he suddenly said, 'And you would be Capt. Harikrishnan, right?'

Boy, this man can read minds, I thought, as I mumbled a 'Yes, Your Excellency.'

'As you all know,' he said, 'every batch that comes here replaces an outgoing batch. The current batch due to leave for home is all set. Once they hand over charge to you new lot, they will be off by the end of the week, I guess.'

He continued, 'We have a designated officer—a liaison officer or

LO in short—and one of the medical officers in the outgoing batch is the current LO.' Looking me in the eye, he said, 'All of you are here because of very good reports from your superior officers. But you, Harikrishnan—is it okay if I just call you Hari? You come with a lot of praise for your communication skills. Let me read out something that may interest all of you.' He reached for the file on top and flipped a few pages: 'Two of your commanding officers have written almost identical sentences about you, Hari: "Given a chance, he would be able to charm the firearms off the worst enemy in under five minutes. Excellent command of Hindi and English besides his native tongue, this officer has a flair for languages. He might be better off if he had chosen to join the IFS cadre." Rather flattering, wouldn't you say?'

My head, expanding as it was with each word entering it, was beginning to hurt a bit. But the next sentence set it on a rapidly shrinking course.

'I am therefore recommending that you take over as the next LO. You are all going to be here for three years, and I want some good continuity—after all, that is what liaison is all about, right? I would like everyone to give Hari here a helping hand, gentlemen. And now, for a bit of tea and snacks before I shoo you all out, I have a meeting with the Omani Commerce Minister in thirty minutes.'

I never did get to ask him about the next flight to India. He did seem very busy.

On the way back, the one thing the others wanted to know was, how did I manage so much *povva* (fauji for influence or contacts)? I was preoccupied in my own misery. I had to have a serious chat with Hanuman Ji—obviously, someone had messed up with interpreting my request to him. And the same mischief maker had pushed my file to the top of the pile on the Ambassador's desk.

4

New Home Unlike Home

When you are not happy, the best things look and feel horrible. I was in that phase now. Not only was I not going home tomorrow (okay, even within a full week would have been alright), I was supposedly this liaison whatever, and I hated the idea. I hated everything. The rooms we were given, individual rooms, were fully air conditioned. But it looked like an isolation cell to me. I knew that normally, isolation cells did not come with an attached bathroom, plush ceiling-to-floor curtains, a six-inch mattress with spotless linen, telephone, and other furniture, but I was not much impressed. I wanted out, and now, I had to think of a way, first to wriggle out of the LO business, and then to find a watertight excuse for beating my way back home. But it looked hopeless.

The next day, the first of Hanuman Ji's long-term plans for me became evident when we reported for duty. As usual, a minibus picked us new guys up from the officers' mess at 7:30 a.m. We trooped into the office of Col. George, Deputy Director of the Force Medical Services (FMS), number two in the hierarchy. He had been working as Contract Officer with the FMS ever since it was started and had risen to the post of DDMS, which automatically entitled him to a full Colonel's rank. We were in Col. George's office for the usual morning briefing on what we would go through that day. It generally lasted just 2-3 minutes. I was hoping to ask for a few minutes alone with him after the meeting. The Director finished his remarks with,

'Run along, all of you. Hari, you stay.'

Although I was happy with this opportunity to be alone with him, I had a sinking feeling that things were going in a different direction. 'Get Capt. Ramesh, please,' the director said to his secretary, and the young Omani lady got busy. This Ramesh chap must have been forewarned—he was in the room before I could clear my throat and choose the appropriate words to lay my case.

'Sit,' he said to both of us, in his unspoilt Malayali accent. I knew I had a chance with him. I was, after all, a fellow Keralite, even if not a Malayali. Col. George was very frugal with his words. 'Ramesh, Hari will take over from you as LO,' he said and walked out of the room. I walked out, too, hardly hearing the 'Congrats, mate, well done,' or some such crap from Capt. Ramesh.

I hated this chap, too. The list of people I hated in this country was soon going to need a few additional sheets. I was introduced to a lot of other people who were jostling for space in that list, and I hardly paid any attention to their names and posts—or to Col. George's instructions on the LO's duties.

Just when I was subconsciously beginning to adjust to the creature comforts of my room, there was another twist in the plot. On the final day of the first week since our arrival, we were summoned to Col. George's office just as we were getting ready to leave for lunch. 'Which of you is keen on a career in surgery?' asked Col. George. My hand was up before he finished asking.

Ever since my third year at medical college in Delhi, I had wanted to be a surgeon. More accurately, I wanted to be like Dr Jalali, the Kashmiri surgeon who was head of one of the seven surgical units we had in our institute. I also happened to be assigned to his tutorial group—there were ten of us in each group, and from Day One, we were all his fans; the girls quite obviously were enslaved right away by his extreme good looks. *Keen Kumar* that I was, I had already read Ian Aird's book "The Making of a Surgeon", and I sincerely believed I had many of the characteristics he had listed as part of the surgical psyche. The clinching characteristic was that as per Aird's philosophy, most surgeons were poor at singing and other forms of art. Acutely aware of my deficiencies in the singing department, I was overjoyed to learn that this was actually a blessing. I was destined to become a surgeon! And Dr Jalali reinforced my desire and belief—he was an amazing surgeon and an even more amazing teacher. He had a sense of humour and was surprisingly tolerant with third year students with near zero knowledge of clinical surgery. Where was I now? Oh yes, in Col. George's room, with my hand up in the air.

I was happy for a fleeting moment to note that there were no other hands up. But then came the blow. 'Good, I will let the FST in Salalah know about your interest—be prepared to move by Monday.'

"FST" and "Salalah" were both as alien to me as Muscat had been a few months ago. FST turned out to be Field Surgical Team, and Salalah turned out be one thousand kilometres south of Muscat. I had committed hara-kiri! I downed my lunch without as much as noticing what I was eating and trudged back to the privacy of my room. Obviously, my file up there in Hanuman Ji's office had been removed, corrupted or simply misplaced. This couldn't be! I was hoping to go to India on Monday, not some silly blah-blah place. Grossly unfair.

But grossly unfair became hard reality, and I was on my way to Salalah by an Air Force flight in less than 3 days. I had no money—we had just landed in a foreign country with a few Indian rupees which were absolutely worthless, anyway. Col. George, a decent man, had ordered the office to loan me a hundred Omani riyals. In 1980, an Omani riyal was worth 26 rupees—but the money I had been given was worth much more than 2600 Indian rupees in terms of purchasing power. I reluctantly approached Arun, the dental chap who had picked us up at the airport, to take me to Ruwi market—which, like everything else, was at the other end of the city—some 40 km away.

Ian Aird was right in saying that I couldn't sing, but I bet he didn't object to surgeons in the making having an interest in listening to music. I had been dreaming of buying one of those fantastic new gadgets I had seen in the Officers' Mess—a Stereo two-in-one. The Akai machine in the Mess actually produced different sounds from the speakers at either end of the machine, and I had fallen in love with it on first sight. Having come to terms with my imprisonment in Oman, I intended to at least make it work—and I had the means now!

Arun turned out to be not so uppity after all. He said, '*Kab chalna hai?* (When do you want to go?)' almost as if it was our regular routine. Sunil and Deepak tagged along—we were already doing practically everything as a trio. The Ruwi market was an amazing place. We went first, straight, to the Akai Showroom, and in under 5 minutes, I had parted with 20 of my 100 riyals in exchange for a stereo two-in-one that was similar yet better than the one in the Officers' Mess. It came with a demonstration cassette: a plane could be heard revving up in the left side speaker, and then, speeding on its way, it *actually* took off from the right-side speaker. I was stunned.

At a nearby shop, a few more riyals got me a handful of cassettes— Hindi film songs, Malayalam film songs, and a couple of Jim Reeves cassettes. Arun recommended the recently released Boney M and Abba albums, but I was more than happy with what I had picked up—and I was already eyeing a few other things in close-by shops! The others, more impecunious than me, just watched, holding their drool back. That evening was the first time I very mildly, very secretively, regretted making that famous request to the Gods to send me back home.

Arun then took us for an unexpected treat—he said that it was almost a rule that if you went to Ruwi, you normally finished your dinner before heading back to the Army camp. As we walked into Annapoorna restaurant, we rookies could have been excused for thinking we had walked into some restaurant in Delhi or Chennai. It was chock-a-block with Indians. Oh, boy, did we tuck in, or what?

Arun was extremely friendly, giving us existential tips, money saving tricks, etc., while we chomped away at our *thalis*. *This chap isn't bad at all*, I thought. It changed to this chap is damn good, when, on our return to the camp, he handed over a large suitcase to me. 'Here, take this. With all the uniforms and shoes you have picked up from the quartermaster's stores, you will need this. You can return it to me as and when you come to Muscat next.' I wondered, as a small lump appeared in my throat, if I would have been so kind to some newly arrived bloke. Probably not.

And then it struck me—hey, I am off to the other end of the country, at least I will escape this LO crap.

But that was not to be. The LO bit stuck to me and stayed with me for my entire tenure in Oman. More on that later. Right now, I had to pack for Salalah.

Thanks to the suitcase given by Arun, packing was easy—I took less than 20 minutes to put all my worldly belongings neatly away and sat down to write a letter to Appa. I wrote to him excitedly about the two-in-one—I had bought it just for him. He was a great connoisseur of classical Carnatic music, and all my life in Delhi, I had seen him struggle to listen to music broadcasts from Chennai. We had an old Tesla radio—the one with a green "magic eye" that would indicate the signal strength. The stronger the green bar, the better the reception. Appa would struggle with it each evening, literally extracting Chennai station of All India Radio with his willpower and perseverance. Later, when my elder brother got a job, we managed to buy for Appa a cassette tape player—one of those narrow, monophonic things with large piano like buttons for start and stop etc. We would use cheap, duplicate tapes of the better-known brands to record music from the radio directly or from other people's tape players. One can imagine the quality of sound from such tapes! But Appa would enjoy listening to all the greats of Carnatic music, the horrible disturbance and background noise notwithstanding.

I was told that some shops in Ruwi, certainly some markets in

Dubai, actually sold high quality TDK and Sony and Maxell tapes with very good recordings of classical concerts. I made up my mind to explore the markets in Salalah for such tapes. All I wanted was for Appa to be able to enjoy some good music as he convalesced from last year's heart attack, when for a scary few days, we thought we would lose him. As I wrote about the two-in-one in detail, with a crude sketch of the front of the machine to help him appreciate what was in store for him, I could hardly wait to go on leave (even if I could not go back permanently) for the sheer pleasure of letting Appa enjoy some good music for once. As I licked the Inland letter closed, I hoped my earlier letter to him written after arrival in Muscat had reached him.

The day after we landed, Arun had taken a couple of us to "post" the letters. When we asked him, he had said dismissively, 'We will go to the airport after work.' We naturally assumed the main post office must be in the airport area—that's where we would go for telegrams and late-night post in Delhi. The Safdarjung Airport (by then supplanted by the brand new Palam Airport) had become the hub of all major postal activity in Delhi.

But we had a very different experience waiting for us that evening here in Muscat. A few others had given us letters to post as well. Arun hardly said anything, nor did we enquire, till we reached the airport. When he started hanging around the entrance to the airport, showing no signs of heading to the post office, Sunil and I were a bit irritated.

'Boss, shall we sort out these letters first, please?' we asked.

'What else do you think I am here for, guys?' he said, and in the same breath, added, 'Ha, there—a Sardar Ji! Come, come; we must catch him before someone else does.'

Not at all sure of what was going on, we ran behind him. We were going to get our first-hand experience of postal services in this blessed country. Arun, with obviously practised ease, made small talk with the Sardar Ji, and then came to the point.

'*Bhai Saab* (Dear brother),' he said in a pleading tone, 'can we please trouble you to take some letters to be posted in Delhi?' The Sardar was as genial as was expected of an average Sikh gentleman. '*Bilkul, Ji* (Definitely, Sir), no issues, no issues,' he said with a broad smile.

Accepting all the letters, he assured us he would drop them off in the airport post box in Delhi and disappeared through the entrance doors. That's it, we had "posted" our letters! Arun looked immensely satisfied. 'Two days before you guys arrived, I had to spend half an hour to find someone respectable. You guys are really lucky. Sardars are the most reliable chaps for sending post to Delhi,' he said. He exuded confidence which did not quite relieve our anxiety, but what choice did we have?

That was nearly a week ago, the day after our arrival, and I had no idea if my first letter had reached home. And here I was, ready for sending a second "post"! Actually, I wouldn't mind if the first one didn't reach home, I thought, since it was a bleak letter about everything that was wrong in Muscat. Appa would have been quite unhappy to read it, I thought—but this one, this would make him happy, and I was hoping a gentleman Sardar would put in an appearance at the airport when we went there. As it happened, there was not a single Sardar to be seen.

But Arun, our constant chauffeur, seemed quite content for us to hand over our letters to a suited and coated gent (*In this weather?* I shuddered privately) who seemed respectable enough. I put in a silent prayer as the man went through the double doors to the check-in area, and then we beat our way back home.

Before I knew, Monday turned up for duty, and I had to report in full uniform at the Air Force airport—an even smaller hall than the civil arrivals hall, just adjacent to it. The flight from Muscat to Salalah was just over an hour long, but I was impressed. I had expected to be bundled into a cargo plane. But the interior was every bit as good as the flight we had arrived in last week. Back in India, the flights from

Leh to Chandigarh—my only experience of flying up until then—
were usually cargo aircrafts with a long folding wooden bench along
the length of the aircraft, on both sides. You simply got in, grabbed
any place that was vacant, strapped yourself in, and hoped the cargo
jostling inside the netting in front of you didn't decide to try out your
lap for better comfort. Hardly had I time to congratulate myself on
this incredible luck—the ride was totally free by the way—and we
were beginning our descent. I guess it is a sign of human weakness
(or was it just mine?) that I was sort of disappointed there were no
air hostesses distributing food and drinks on the flight!

The driver from FST spotted me easily. I guess all he had to do
was look for a nervous Indian coot in uniform—I was perhaps the
only non-Omani on the flight. At Muscat, the ride from the airport
to our camp usually took about ten minutes. In Salalah, we were
home and dry in about four! The driver poured out his heart in that
short time, all in Arabic and I said 'Fi,' at appropriate intervals,
hoping the new word I had learnt was the right choice. He was
obviously not impressed—mumbling something, he dropped me off
in front of a large, single-storeyed building decorated in mysterious
Arabic lettering, took out my suitcase, saluted cursorily, and was off.
I had arrived for duty at FST, Salalah.

5

FST

There was not a soul in sight. Back home in India, I would have had a choice of a hundred people to ask where to go. I guessed the driver must have dropped me off near where I was supposed to stay, so I pushed the rather huge double doors, wondering why on earth they needed such huge doors for Officers' quarters. I found out why immediately.

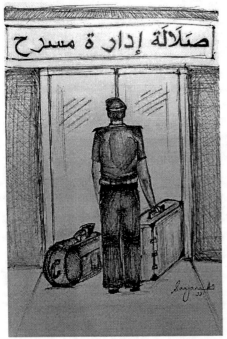

'And where do you think you are going, with all that luggage?' boomed a very heavily Scottish accented voice, followed by a big, burly *gora* (white man) in operation theatre fatigues. Of course, at that time, I didn't even quite understand what he said, leave alone guess the accent. Till then, I had only seen less than half a dozen *goras* since landing in Muscat.

I said, 'Pardon, please?' and the hulk repeated the question for me. From his tone, I guessed he wanted to know something about who or what I was, so I said, 'Good morning, Sir! I am Capt., sorry, Raees Harikrishnan (I still hadn't come to terms with the equivalent ranks in Omani army), reporting for duty. I just came from Muscat.'

Obviously, this was the local big boss—the few Brits I had seen in Muscat were all big bosses. But it turned out he was big alright, but not big boss.

'Oh, Hello, Sir!' he bellowed, the "Sir" in his sentence in no way diluting his big boss tone but continued, 'Sergeant (Something), Theatre in-charge.' Well, he didn't actually say his name was "something", but I could not decipher his name for the life of me. He put out a huge paw and shook my hand, up all the way to my shoulder joint. 'Welcome to FST. In fact, you are inside the FST, in the truest sense,' he laughed. 'That bloody Saif, he should have taken you to the Officers' quarters!'

I thought, *so that explains the double doors. This chap is not the big boss; a sergeant (Sgt. for short) is something like a havaldar back home; what am I supposed to do now?* All in a split second.

Sgt. Something or whoever was meantime bellowing towards another set of double doors behind him. 'Shyju, come here. On the double,' he said. This was a sergeant alright, I realised. A second later, the inside doors opened and a very obviously Malayali-looking young chap—probably Shyju—appeared. 'Sir?'

'Take Mr Harrykrishna to the Officers' quarters. I have spoken to Abdulla there. Make sure they know he will be in for lunch and dinner today.' He turned to me, 'Unless you have other plans?'

'Er, No,' I blurted. I was still reeling from the *"Mr Harrykrishna"* bit. *Mr? What the hell? It's Doctor*, I thought. The Mr really stung me. But a bigger dose was in store for me. As Shyju and I started towards the door, Sgt. Boom-Boom asked: 'What should we call you? Harry or Krishna or what?' *The audacity of the chap*, I thought. *He is a Sgt., I am a Captain, and a "doctor", by the way, and he wants to get rather personal?*

Instead of correcting his etiquette, I said, 'Um, anything, anything,' and walked through the open door to the hot welcome outside—the doors closed behind us, but there was plenty of time for the Sgt. to say, 'Harry, then. Sounds nice and English.'

Shyju set my things down in a room not very different from the one in the Muscat Officers' Mess and left. I sat down, feeling blue all over again.

6

Letter to Appa

I loved writing to my father. He would always reply promptly, and his mastery of English was a source of enjoyment and inspiration to me. A great P G Wodehouse fan, he could see the ridiculous side of things and make a person laugh. His play on words would have pleased Shakespeare, whose plays he knew inside out. He had mastered the imported language as a young man working in a British Army set up soon after his graduation from Victoria College, Palghat, in Kerala. Being a voracious reader, he had a far greater understanding of the nuances of English language than would be expected of a typical South Indian youngster.

So it was, that one day, he was hammering away at the typewriter during his lunch break, when apparently, his immediate boss, an English captain, walked in. Seeing the recently appointed clerk typing away, the captain asked him what he was so busy doing. My father replied that he was just putting down some thoughts that had occurred to him, lest he forget them later. Intrigued, the captain asked to read it, and asked where my father had copied all this from. As quick of temper as with his smile, my father retorted that he did not need to copy anything, he was quite capable of writing stuff like that, and more. Piqued by this insolent reply, the captain apparently gave him a topic to write on, right there, right then, in front of him. Needless to say, Appa came out with flying colours. The captain, obviously a gentleman, decided to do something about this dhoti-

29

clad Indian boy with such a brilliant command over a foreign language. He recommended that my father be given a commission.

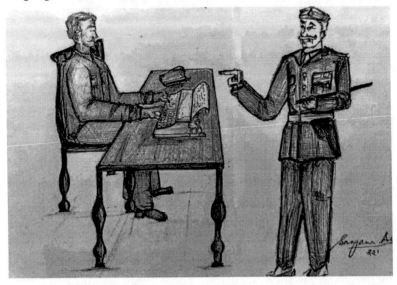

I remember my father wistfully recounting this story more than once, pointing out that it was around that same time, in 1936, that one of India's greatest military leaders, Gen. SHFJ Manekshaw, was commissioned as an officer. He would round it up by quoting, 'Of all the sad words in life, the saddest are these: "It might have been."'

I sat down to pour out my chest to Appa. He would understand. He certainly would tell me how to cleverly respond to this *Mr and Harry* bit, which was still stinging me. Not aware of the local customs from where Boom-Boom came (I had no idea about his name as of yet), I had assumed it was because he knew I was an Indian medical graduate. I knew my training was the best and was going to show him soon. Then I would ask, 'Hi, hey, am I still a Mr or a Dr?' That would teach him a lesson. Like with Arun, I had taken an instant dislike to this Sgt., and like with Arun, I would be proven totally off the mark, but as I wrote all about my Salalah experience to Appa, I did not have the foggiest clue about what the next few days and weeks held in store for me.

Armed with my letter, I was more than happy to consider a walk to the airport that evening—I knew all about spotting a decent person to act as my personal postman.

By the time I had licked the army issue inland letter, it was time for lunch. As soon as I walked into the Mess, a typically *fauji* voice greeted me.

'Ha! Here comes our new surgeon! Welcome, Harikrishnan. I am Major Kumar, surgeon in-charge of the FST. Hope you have been looked after? Sorry, we were operating, so couldn't say hello when you landed. Apparently, you came directly to the OT?' he smiled. (Americans called their operating theatres "OR", short for Operating Room. For the Brits, it was just "theatres". For us from India, it was always OT, short for Operating Theatre.)

'Thank you, Sir. I am alright. The room is comfortable, and I am all set to join you in the OT tomorrow,' I said, eager to please. A tall, extremely handsome Indian walked up. 'Meet Major Ravindranath,' said Major Kumar. 'Now you have met the whole bloody Dept. of Surgery,' he laughed.

'Col. George tells me you volunteered for surgery. Good. You will have a great time, we promise. Right, Ravi?'

Major Ravindranath agreed. 'If you are interested, in a month, you will end up doing enough general, ortho and a whole lot of other surgical work.'

They wanted to know why I volunteered for surgery, whether I had done any OT cases as an Intern or after joining the AMC. I had done precious little, and good guys that they were, they didn't pin me down when I mumbled some half-truths.

Lunch was just about okay, certainly not in my mother's class of cooking, but I downed it happily. As everyone got up to leave, I said I planned to walk to the airport in the evening to "post" a letter, and Major Kumar immediately said, 'Nonsense, boy, my room is just across from yours. Come knocking after the evening tea, and I will take you there. Do you know what the temperature outside is?' I had certainly not thought of that and was grateful for the lift.

I felt a lot better when, with Major Kumar's help, we found a decent looking Malayali chap at the airport to hand over a whole bunch of letters that evening. A good leader that he was, Major Kumar had collected letters from the OT and ward staff as well. Satisfied, and a bit relaxed at the attitude of the two surgeons, I slept well that night, dreaming of a happy conversation with Appa about the two-in-one that sat next to my bed, waiting to be united with the most loveable person in my life.

I realised the next morning that I had been less than two weeks in Oman, and a lot had happened. But I was disappointed that there were no surgical cases scheduled for the day, though that gave me the opportunity to get to know the team in FST. Mr Boom-Boom turned out to be Sgt. Mackenzie from Glasgow or some such place. There were two girls on duty in the ward, both Malayali nurses, and they seemed to be doing a fair job of looking after the ten-odd patients under their care. All except one were operated cases—appendix, a couple of fractures, and the rest all small lumps and bumps. One chap was waiting for a medical clearance (from the nearby government-run Umm Al Ghawarif or UAG Hospital—there were no medical specialists posted in FST) for a biopsy of a swelling in his thigh. I made a mental note to look up myofascial tumours when I got back to my room. Opportunity to impress the bosses!

I browsed through the various phone numbers—ward, OT, the Medical Inspection (MI) room and of course, the Mess. I didn't need to note them down anywhere—all the hospital numbers were six digits and started with 246. It took me less than a minute to commit the other three digits of the various places to memory. In fact, I wasn't aware of it then, but nearly a year afterwards, this ability of mine to recall numbers would bring in some much-needed excitement in my life. More about that later.

Right now, I had enough time on my hands, so I decided to have a look at the kind of cases they had been doing in the FST. Post lunch, I was quite free, so I decided to try out how Mr Jim Reeves sounded on my two-in-one.

Jim was asking Bimbo if his mummy knew, when there was knock at my door. I was surprised to see Sgt. Mac-Whatever.

'Hello,' I said, 'Case?'

His voice was surprisingly mellow. 'Good afternoon, Mr Harrykrishna,' he said. 'Mr Kumar and Mr Raavi would like to talk to you. Could you come with me to Mr Kumar's room, please?' *Oh, everyone is a Mr for you, is it?* I thought, pretty much offended that leave alone me, this bloke wasn't willing to accept even senior Majors as well enough qualified? Somewhat surprised that Major Kumar should send the Sergeant to call me over to his room about 5 metres away, I quickly put on my shoes and followed him.

'Come in,' said Major Kumar's voice. As we both entered, "Mr" Mackenzie very politely letting me in first, I found both the bosses standing up to receive me.

'Hello, Hari. Come in and take a seat,' said Major Kumar in a soft voice—maybe mellow was the day's voice menu. For some peculiar reason, the two majors standing and asking me to sit did not sound good.

I sat down, wondering what was up.

'Had lunch?' asked Major Ravi. Before I could answer, 'Some water, please, Mac,' said Major Kumar, gesturing to me. The uneasy feeling in my tummy was worsening. *Am I going to be sent back to Muscat?* I wondered.

But Major Kumar's next sentence sent a grenade exploding in my stomach.

'I'm afraid I have some bad news, Hari,' he said, tenderly, coming over and sitting down in the armchair beside me. In that instant, I knew it had to be Appa. *No, God, please no,* I prayed.

Appa had suffered his first heart attack a few years back, and one last year, but had done well under care of the cardiologist at the Military Hospital (MH) in Jalandhar. Things like angioplasty and coronary artery bypass graft were not yet common in most places in India those days. It was purely my mother's prayers that had brought him back from the brink of death. He had been keeping indifferent health since then but had insisted on moving into a house allotted to me when I went on posting to Ladakh. My mother and brother had had no say in the matter. He was determined to make the most of the first ever proper military accommodation bestowed on the family.

My prayers for his health were a bit too late—I could hardly fully comprehend what Major Kumar said next.

'I am terribly sorry, Hari, to have to inform you that your father passed away early morning today at MH Madras.' He put a hand on my shoulder, while Major Ravi and Mac looked on in commiseration.

The world came crashing down on me. My best efforts to bravely hold back the welling tears failed, and I sobbed. I was all of 26, had been Appa's favourite child from as far back as I could remember, and he was the rock on which I, and indeed all four siblings and my mother leaned on for everything.

I lowered my head, trying to hide my tears. The three of them, in true gentlemanly fashion, waited patiently for me to get a hold on myself.

'How, Sir?' I asked, between sobs. 'He was quite okay when I left just two weeks back,' I said, saddened by the unfairness of it all.

Two weeks! At the first round of briefing in Muscat, they had said no leave of any sort for the first six months. I had hardly any money, I didn't know how, if at all, I could even make a call to my mother, and the most unkindest cut of all was that I had just about started to feel proud of the great gift I had bought especially for him—oh, how he would have loved listening to the cassettes in the Akai two-in-one! I choked on this thought and my eyes welled up again.

'I know exactly how you feel, Hari,' said Major Kumar, 'I lost both my parents in a car accident the day I graduated—they were actually on their way to attend the ceremony. Life is pretty brutal at times,' he said, his hand still on my shoulder, comforting me. 'Please take your time. I know you need to digest this horrible news, but there are a few things we need to discuss. We will wait till you are ready,' he added.

Quickly regaining my composure, I said, 'No, Sir, that's alright. Please tell me, Sir.'

Major Ravi spoke for the first time: 'Kumar and I have spoken to Col. George. He wants to know what you would like to do.'

'But Sir, they said no leave of any kind, Sir,' I said, unable to prevent my voice from quavering.

'Oh, those are guidelines, Hari. Don't worry about that. We have told Col. George we are happy to manage without a junior for some more time. I guess you would want to go for about two weeks, given that the funeral ceremonies last till the 13th day. You can stay on for longer if you need to. But I would advise against staying away more than 30 days—Col. George will have to request a replacement as per rules if you do not return by 30 days.'

He continued, 'As for the rest of the arrangements, Mac here has done some homework already. Mac?' Mac came to smart attention and said, 'I have blocked a seat for Harry in the first flight tomorrow morning to Muscat.'

Looking at me, he said, 'This mud track here has no flights to India or any other place, so I'm afraid you have to go via Muscat, sorry. But,' he continued, 'No worries. There is a flight to Madras at 1030 hours, and one of the staff from FBH will meet you at the airport and oversee your formalities.' He reached into his pockets and pulled out a wad of notes, all Omani.

'I got 200 out from the Head Clerk, Sir,' he said, looking at Major Kumar.

The latter replied, 'Should do, I think, considering his ticket has already been bought by Col George's secretary. And here is about 2500 Indian rupees, Hari—that's all we had between us, but should be good enough for now, right? I believe your mother and family are all already in Madras or will be reaching well before you land there. I think you should go to your room, spend some time to get over your emotions, and pack. If you need anything at all, all three of us will be around, just knock,' he added. 'If you want food to be sent to your room, no problem. But I suggest you come over when you are up to it, have a drink, and eat with us all.'

'I will pick you up in the morning at 0515 hours, Harry,' said Mac. Thanking them all while still failing miserably to stifle my sobs, I trudged back to my empty room. Jim Reeves was asking the same question to Bimbo for the nth time on my auto reverse Akai Cassette deck.

I needed to be alone for some time. A million thoughts came flooding into my mind, those small things that make you so miserable when the reality of a loved one's passing hits you. I cried unashamedly in the privacy of my room and felt a bit better after that. But the sight of the Akai two-in-one, and the terrible feeling of Appa never enjoying music on it, made me break down again. As I packed, I wondered if Appa had even received my first letter written after landing in Muscat. A letter full of complaints. How stupid of me! I hoped he didn't get that letter—it would have hurt him so much.

7

Back Home

Mac was there, in full uniform, at 5 sharp the next morning. I had hardly slept, worrying about my mother, what the family was doing for all the expenses involved with my father's funeral, and so forth.

I hardly noticed anything on the way to the Salalah airport and during the short flight to Muscat. At the Air Force arrivals hall, the familiar face of Arun greeted me. With him was Major Kuriakose, Col. George's deputy. They handed over my ticket and money, and a signed leave certificate. (I had not even put in an application!)

After the usual commiserations, Major Kuriakose said, 'Your leave has been approved for 15 days. If you need to extend it, let us know by telegram—I know it will be next to impossible for you to call us—and I will do the needful. For now, the return flight is an open ticket.'

He cautioned me about the 30-day rule. At that moment, I had no intention of coming back, so I wasn't paying much attention. Major Kuriakose must have noticed, for he added, 'You must be understandably numb with grief, Hari. Please don't do anything rash. I know you have not had any time to settle down at all. The rest of your batch mates are all happily busy working in FBH. You have had the good fortune to get this deputation, young man. This is a good opportunity to hone your clinical skills, get practical experience in surgery under two of AMC's finest surgeons, and aim for getting an

FRCS while you are still here in Oman. You understand what I am trying to tell you?'

Alert now, because of that magic word *FRCS*, I said, 'Yes, Sir, I do. And thank you for all the help. I really appreciate it.'

Turning to Arun, I said, 'Thank you, too, Arun. Will you please give these letters to Sunil and Deepak?' I knew I would not be able to see them, and I had not spoken to them in the last few days. So, I had hurriedly written letters to them, to say "bye". I was sure I meant a permanent goodbye.

'No worries,' said Arun graciously. 'You just carry on and attend to the things back home and come back safe and sound. Make sure you let us know your flight details so I or someone else can be here to pick you up. Here, this is the contact number of my course mate in the Dental section in Army Headquarters, for any help you may need. You should be able to get through to him from any *fauji* set up in Madras through their signals network.' He handed over a parcel. 'Some parathas and *aloo-pyaz sabzi*, and mango juice—you have about two hours to board your flight. Don't waste money on food— you only get crap inside anyway.' And this was the Arun who was dismissed as arrogant by me two weeks back! I felt a bit ashamed as I gratefully accepted the paper bag. They left, but only after checking me in at the counter in the civil Departures Hall.

8

Another Journey

I landed in Madras, exhausted, late in the evening. All through the flight, I simply could not get over the unfairness of it all. My father was a simple man. He had cycled the ten kilometres to his office every single day, saving up money that would have been spent on his bus tickets—just so he could see his kids through good education. He never lusted after any luxuries. Surely, such a man deserved the simple pleasure of enjoying his favourite music on a good machine for some time. I knew that the Akai back in my room in Salalah would constantly remind me of his quote, *"It might have been."*

When I reached my uncle's house—for that's where I expected everyone would be, I was surprised to see just my uncle and his wife at home. My uncle, a very pious man, explained. 'I have sent them all to Benaras (now Varanasi), Hari. Your father was a very noble man. He deserves to have his last rites done in Benaras for his *moksha*.'

Devout Hindus believe that if the departed soul or spirit is sent off on its way with the right kind of rituals, it will attain *moksha*, or immortal bliss. The idea is that thus, one will merge with the Supreme Being, rather than fall into the trap of repeated cycles of birth and death. Benaras was the holiest of holy places for all Hindus to start their final journey. And my uncle was more devout than most. I learnt that he had arranged for sufficient cash for all the ceremonies there—the rituals would last for 13 days, counting from the day of death—and had given his friend's contact details to my brother. As the elder son, he would lead all the ceremonies. My brother had done the cremation the previous day, and they had left by the night train to Benaras with my father's ashes.

My heart sank. I wouldn't even be seeing my father's body then. What a shame!

Uncle had spoken to a friend at the Central Station in Madras about my ticket, he said.

'When do I travel?' I asked, to which he replied, 'Have a bath, eat a good meal, and get some sleep. We will go to the station first thing in the morning tomorrow and see which train you can get into.' Difference number one between Muscat and India, I realised. Travel in India was full of uncertainties. But I had not expected anything else, anyway.

The journey from Madras to Benaras was a harrowing one, over and above my emotional status. There were no direct trains to Benaras, so Uncle had told me I would need to change midway. Worse, the "contact details" of his friend were rather brief. 'Ask for Srinivasa Sastrigal at Benaras station,' he said grandly.

That was it? No address, no street, nothing. How in God's name was I supposed to trace my family in a city as crowded as any other in India? Benaras is up north, where the possibility of spotting a South Indian was not going to be easy, and even if I did, what guarantee they would know a priest by the name Srinivasa Sastrigal? I could only pray once again to all the Gods as I was thrust into the unreserved cabin of the Lucknow-bound train by Uncle's friend, who turned out to be a random porter at the platform.

In my life, I have realised time and again that when you need help desperately, help has a way of finding you. As we jostled one another in the compartment, an elderly gentleman who could have been Uncle's twin got into conversation with me. As I blurted out my problem, he asked me not to worry; he was going to Allahabad (now Prayagraj), just short of Benaras. We would need to change trains at Itarsi in Central India and hope for a train from there. He had an

Indian Railways Bradshaw, which told us we had a connecting train some 30 minutes after our scheduled arrival in Itarsi, and two more after a few hours' wait. Indian trains were notorious for running late. Despite our train being more than an hour and a half late, the connecting train was later still, and using the same *"jugaad"* (makeshift arrangement) as at Madras, we managed to get seats in the connecting train, and I arrived early morning next day at Benaras Station.

9

Benaras

The friendly gentleman had got down at Allahabad. He was not able to advise me about tracing Srinivasa Satrigal's address. He told me, much to my dismay, that there were at least 80 ghats in Benaras. Large numbers of priests waited in each ghat to try and get clients for the last rites of their beloved ones. That was even more depressing!

I got out of the train, baggage and all, and walked over a foot bridge to reach the exit hall. I had feared the place may be crowded. But I was nowhere enough ready to see the masses that thronged the hall, the ticketing area, the food stalls—every inch was covered with humans! I was totally at a loss. How in God's name was I ever going to find where to go?

Seeing a cycle rickshaw chap pulling up close to where I stood, I decided to risk asking him—I had nothing to lose! As soon as I made eye contact, he asked, *'Kaunsa Ghat jana hain?* (Which Ghat do you want to go to?)'

Many visitors came to Benaras for the last rites of their loved ones, while the elderly came there to spend the rest of their days in prayers and meditation, waiting for the final call.

'I am not sure,' I said, in Hindi. Feeling really sheepish, I blurted, 'Ek Srinivasa Sastriji,' and even before I finished saying the name, he said, 'Sit. Twenty rupees.'

I was not sure he had heard me. So, I hesitatingly tried again: 'Srinivas...' Again, he cut me short—a bit impatiently now. 'Yes, yes, Srinivasa Sastriji—Hanuman Ghati, sit, sit.'

I was fairly convinced he would just drop me at this Hanuman Ghati or wherever, take his money, and disappear. Within a minute of leaving the station, though, my fears were dispelled.

'Everyone knows Srinivasa Pandit Ji,' he said, in a somewhat reverential voice. 'He has been helping with the last rites of good Hindus for 40 years. He is a great man.'

I almost cried in relief! I had been so sure Uncle back in Madras was misinformed, and the very first rickshaw man I meet in this vast city says he knows exactly where to take me! And he did. I suddenly realised how desperately hungry I was and asked if he would stop for a cup of tea on the way. This he did, too, and gratefully accepted my offer of a cup of tea for him as well. That done, we rode for at least another 20 to 25 minutes (during which I readily poured out my heart to him) before he declared, 'This in front of you is Hanuman Ghati—Pandit Ji's house is up this flight of stairs. But he won't be at home; he will be at the Ghat doing the rites.'

He pointed to a flight of wide, concrete stairs just where he had stopped. I paid him thirty rupees, and he returned ten, thinking I had made a mistake. I said no, it was for him, and thanked him for all the help. But for him, I would never have been able to get here, I added.

He said, 'No, this is a big city alright, but everyone knows every Pandit Ji in these ghats by name.' Thanking him yet again, but still unsure of myself, I climbed up the stairs, hoping that someone here would surely know which one of the many small dwelling units Srinivasa Sastrigal lived in.

My feelings as I reached the summit of the stairs are difficult to describe even after so many years. I saw my entire family—my mother, two sisters, brother, brother-in-law, two nephews, and my darling niece climbing up from the other side—they must be coming back from the ghats!

'Amma!' I cried, dropping my bags down as a flood of relief gushed through my entire being. There was a chorus of 'Mama! (Uncle!)' from the three kids as they rushed to hug me. I knew then that my dad really wanted me to be around for his final journey.

We stayed there another eight days to complete all the ceremonies for my father's soul to reach his ancestors in *Vaikuntha* (heaven). The rest of the family had reached Benaras two days back, taking the same route I had. The Pandit Ji, in reverence to my uncle in Madras, had insisted that they all stay in his house. Five adults and three kids, and now, here was an additional adult to strain their accommodation! Sparse it may have been, but the Pandit Ji and his wife more than made up for all that with their generosity.

Having safely escorted my father's departed soul to his heavenly home, we had a feast to celebrate his attainment of *moksha* on the 13th day and bade farewell to the Pandit Ji and his wife. The total dues were a pittance of what I had feared. My brother had booked tickets meanwhile for all of us to go the short distance to Jalandhar (a mere 17 hours by direct train as compared to about 40 from Madras!).

10

Back to Salalah

At Benaras, the heaviness in our hearts was greatly lessened by the presence of the three kids. In spite of my grief, I had managed to pick up a few gifts for the kids while waiting for my flight from Muscat. We talked a lot amongst ourselves about Appa's last days—it seems he was admitted to the Military Hospital the day after I left for Muscat. I had had no idea whatsoever. He had complained of breathlessness, and his friend, who also lived in the same army enclosure where my parents were staying (in the house allotted to me), had insisted on seeing the doctor. But Appa had been discharged in under three days. My first letter obviously had not reached him yet. It never occurred to me to ask, anyway, knowing it took close to ten days to reach under the best of circumstances. Apparently, he took ill again a few days later, and was readmitted to the Military Hospital. He again improved, and was due to be discharged one morning, when, as was his wont, he had his early morning bath in the common shower of the male ward. As he walked out from the bathroom, he seems to have collapsed. Some other patients helped him, the ward sister rushed to start CPR, the duty doctor was sent for, but it was all over in the next few minutes. My mother was at home, getting his breakfast ready, waiting for his friend to come and take her to the hospital a few kilometres away, when they got the unexpected phone call. A few months back, I had received an unexpected phone call in the remote hills of Ladakh, changing my fortunes forever. This one had changed the fortunes too, mine and rest of my family's, forever.

I landed in Salalah after spending two days with my mother, stopping at Muscat just to get the connecting Air Force flight, arranged as usual with precision by Major Kuriakose. Salalah was hotter and more humid than when I had left less than two weeks ago. The sunglasses I had bought in Jalandhar were no match for the brightness of the Salalah Sun. I hated the place more than ever.

11

Unrelenting Grief

Abdulla was there with the car, as before. This time, he did not say a word—and this time, he dropped me at the Officers' Quarters. I was hungry, tired, and heavy of heart. But I chose to go to my room first—I was not ready to face anyone just as yet. I needed some time by myself. I could hear the whirring of the window A/C of my room as I approached. *The Mess in-charge must have turned it on*, I thought to myself as I opened the door.

The memory of what happened in the next few seconds will live with me till I die. As the door swung open, my eyes fell on something on the floor. It was an Indian inland letter. Despite having my sunglasses on, I could immediately recognise my father's handwriting, and for a moment, I lost all sense of time and orientation. My heart raced as I picked up the letter. Oh my God! Appa was alive! Here was a letter from him! Stupid me, thinking he was gone! The curtains were drawn closed, and so the room was dark—my glasses had misted due to the cool air inside the room.

Dropping my bag, I stumbled to the bed, sat on it, Appa's letter in hand, heart still racing, and tore it open. And then, one look at the date in the top right-hand corner, reality struck like a punch in the solar plexus. It was dated 11th October 1980 in Appa's familiar handwriting. His news had come on 12th, and I had left on 13th for India. As I read the first line, 'My dear Hari, I am writing this from Military Hospital Madras—BUT before you start worrying, good news! I am going home tomorrow…' I was totally shattered and broke down completely.

Those few seconds of false hope, cruelly engineered by Appa's unmistakable writing on the letter, the misting of my glasses as I entered the room, and my not having seen his body after he died, were too much for me to withstand. I cried, my whole body shaking in grief, my very being defeated, hopeless. Oh, how I missed him! As if in agreement, the Akai two-in-one sat in mute witness on the bedside table.

I heard approaching footsteps and rushed into the toilet to avoid eye contact. It was the Mess boy, with my breakfast—despite drowning in my grief, I realised I was among good, kind people. I pretended to be busy with the washstand and asked the boy to leave it on the coffee table and go, many thanks.

As I pushed the sandwich down my dry throat, I gathered courage and started to read the letter:

11th October 1980, M.H. Madras

My dear Hari, I am writing this from Military Hospital Madras— BUT before you start worrying, good news! I am going home tomorrow morning. I'm sure that by the time this letter reaches you, you would have made a mark for yourself in Muscat. My heart brims with pride as I think of my son, Captain K M Harikrishnan, a modern-day Captain Cook, going in search of fortunes for himself and his family in uncharted lands! Your mother and I would love to hear about your escapades, much like…

I could bear it no more. He obviously had not even received my first letter till the 11th! Oh, what a shame! What a terrible, cruel, shame! He didn't even know about the two-in-one then. That was too much for me to cope with. I just curled up in the bed and sobbed myself to sleep.

By lunch time, my tears had all but dried. I had to report to Majors Kumar and Ravi.

12

An Appendix and An Amputation... or two

I n the next few days, I started to get into a routine despite the dull feeling in the pit of my stomach. A million instances reminded me of Appa, but the rest of the FST team helped me distract myself. My two-in-one started coming alive regularly, though for reasons I could not admit to myself, I started listening almost exclusively to western classical, pop, metal, country, etc. Carnatic music was too painfully close to Appa for me to contemplate. I started getting interested in the OT life more and more. FST was exactly what its name said—a Field Surgical Team, with little or no general medicine practice. All that was managed at the UAG hospital (Umm Al Ghawaarif) a few km away. They referred all their surgical work to us—there was talk of a brand-new OT complex coming up there, and of the FST being merged with the UAG hospital by another few months. For the present, I wanted to learn some surgery. And I had all the opportunity. I was the only junior doctor in the surgical team, and the two surgeons were very happy to leave their paperwork to someone like me. I was hungry for work. When in the wards and especially when working with either of them in the OT, I was so engrossed that there was no time to brood over my misfortunes. The hard work I put in there was to prove very useful in later years, but I was of course merely concentrating on picking up basic surgical knowledge.

One day, we had just sat down for lunch when the Mess boy announced that Major Ravi was needed on the phone. He came back and announced: 'There is an appendix coming from UAG (what he meant was, of course, that a *patient* was coming from UAG with his appendix all inflamed!) in the next 15 minutes. Hari, gobble up your food, receive the patient, check him out clinically, check all his bloods—I doubt you will need to order any fresh tests—alert the OT (Mac wasn't yet in for lunch), and brush up your steps of surgery— your big time has come, boy!'

You can imagine my excitement! I had assisted in a few cases during my internship days—but that was three years ago. I hadn't seen a single patient with appendix in my days in Ladakh, and here I was, being told to get ready for *doing* a case! This was an unexpected bonus! Appa's blessings, surely!

I didn't know then that it was the turning point of my life and my attitude in many ways. Salalah—and Muscat, too—were never the same again, nor was my professional life. In the years since, I have done a whole lot of surgery, much of it at cutting edge level—and I owe a great deal of all that to two surgeons who encouraged me to believe in myself at a time when I was all ready to give up everything. As they say, when it rains good things, it pours!

I managed to get all things done and look up Bailey and Love's chapter on Vermiform Appendix with a few minutes to spare before the patient landed up from UAG. He was a 28-year-old soldier, otherwise fit. He ticked all the boxes for the diagnosis of acute appendicitis. We did not have ultrasound scan facilities in FST—but they had done a scan to confirm the diagnosis at UAG. Mac, the magician, knew all about the patient before I could begin to tell him anything. Shyju had alerted the rest of the OT team, and all was ready for the patient.

As I scrubbed, I mentally recited a *sloka* taught by my father the day I became a doctor. He had said: 'I am very proud of your achievement, son, and so should you be. But remember, with pride must come the type of responsibility that is unique to your profession. People's lives will be in your hands. Recite this *slokam* before you take any important step—you will not do any harm even if you do not end up doing a great deal of good.' He was merely putting in his own words what we were taught at medical college: "*Primum Non Nocere*", or above all, do not do any harm.

Major Ravi, surgeon on call for the day, was watching me without being obtrusive. I had no problems with that. A mild kind of show-off by nature, I was more than happy with this opportunity to impress him. I hoped to continue impressing him when I did the surgery, but there, I was sadly mistaken! I knew the theory of appendicectomy well enough. But the practice of it was proving to be very different! Major Ravi handed over the knife, and I gave the incision.

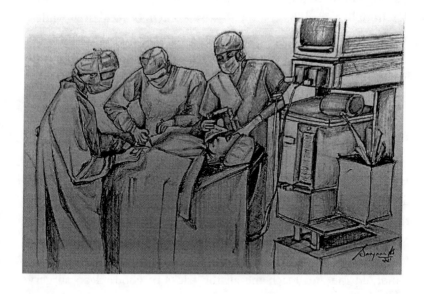

'The line joining the umbilicus with the right anterior superior iliac spine (ASIS for short) is divided into three equal parts; the line of incision should be perpendicular to the point $2/3^{rd}$ from the umbilicus and $1/3^{rd}$ from the ASIS. The incision should be about 2

inches long to begin with…' prescribed Sir Hamilton Bailey. All this
was okay. I drew the knife about two inches on the skin, waiting to
see some blood. But the patient did not bleed the slightest bit. I was
wondering why, when Major Ravi said, 'Hari, you have not even
disturbed the surface cells on the skin! Be bold, man, dig deeper.'
Practically every beginner in surgery has heard this admonition from
their seniors, in some form or other. I guess it is the Primum Non
Nocere bit running overtime! It took me a few more scratches to
make a dent in the skin. Well, eventually I got to the appendix, which
luckily did not play truant, but by the time I finished the skin stitches,
it was way past teatime. The anaesthetist had brought a thick book to
read, so he was alright. Major Ravi was this close to taking over many
times, but he persisted with indulging me. The rest of the OT team
must have been cursing their bloody luck, seeing this greenhorn
make a mountain out of a molehill! But no one said a word. For all
the fumbling and hesitation, I was excited beyond my wildest
imagination! My operation theatre notes and postoperative
instructions were long, but I bet my letter home to Appa—if only he
had been alive—would have been much longer, I had no doubt about
that. I hardly ate any dinner, I was so worried about my patient—*my*
patient, my first ever appendicectomy patient! Hey, Salalah was not
such a bad place after all!

   I must have seen the patient twenty times over the next few hours.
He made an incident-less recovery over the next few days and was
discharged within a week ('Sick leave for 4 weeks—review in FST
thereafter' I wrote in his discharge notes, duly countersigned by
Major Ravi). I have never, ever forgotten how incredibly lucky I was
to have had Major Ravi (and Major Kumar on various occasions) to
handhold me and teach me all the tricks of good, clean surgery.
Major Ravi, as much a gentleman as he was a talented surgeon,
insisted that I write my name as the first surgeon with his name
second, in the OT notes. He wouldn't have it otherwise. I made a
mental note to carry forward this goodness when my own time came

to play the senior colleague*. But right now, that was a long stretch of future road to travel!

The next morning brought more excitement, just as I was reporting to Major Ravi about my appendix patient's status. Mac rolled into the ward.

'Excuse me, Harry,' he said, and turning to Major Ravi, 'a traumatic AK amputation is coming from the regiment in Surfayt. He should be here in an hour—Major Kumar says he will take him.' He went off to make the necessary arrangements. *One hour, I thought, I need to finish the ward work and run to the room to look up the steps of amputation.* AK meant above knee—*bloody hell, we will need blood by the gallons,* I told myself.

The patient, another young soldier, came in a state of partial shock—he had lost a lot of blood before the unit medical assistant got to him and fashioned a temporary tourniquet using the soldier's belt (they had no doctor in the outpost). The details of the accident were sketchy: apparently, he was driving a Land Rover which overturned, and he somehow managed to get his right thigh between the chassis and the mud track road. The chassis had all but cut his leg off just above the knee, with the rest of his limb clinging to the thigh by a few strands of skin.

We rushed him in, while Major Kumar and Shyju spoke to the couple of carloads of relatives who had accompanied the ambulance. I will spare you the gory details of the amputation which we already knew was inevitable. Major Kumar was quick and clean with his surgery. In under 10 minutes after anaesthesia was administered, he was sewing up the skin, the amputation all done. One of the many

---

* Throughout my surgical career, whenever I have taught youngsters, I have won them over with such minor acts of goodness. I have had many of them come back to me in later years, as full-fledged surgeons, some internationally famous now, to convey their gratitude. I have always recounted the beginnings of my surgical career in FST to them, and it is my fervent hope that this habit of encouraging juniors is being carried forward by them as well. Both Major Kumar and Major Ravi, by the way, went on to achieve the highest rank in the Indian Army Medical Corps, something they both deserved in the fullest possible measure.

bottles of blood was on flow. The next few hours were going to be rather tricky. We would be counting heavily on the patient's youth providing a robust response to the physiological upset he was going through. We had no idea of the blood he had lost, but if his heart rate was anything to go by, it was a fair amount alright.

But that was the least of our problems right now: as I started writing the postoperative instructions, I heard some kind of uproar on the other side of the OT doors. *Not another emergency*, I hoped. It was indeed an emergency situation, but not in the form of another patient.

As part of his duty, Major Kumar had gone out—with Mac (as it luckily happened) to explain the patient's condition to the waiting crowd. The amputated limb was in a plastic tissue disposal bag in his hand—one look at that and the crowd had erupted violently. There was an angry protest by the elders, drowning out attempts by Major Kumar to explain what he had done and why. Many of the relatives had their traditional '*Khanjar*' (dagger) out in their hands. They demanded to know who permitted the *Tabeeb* (doctor) to remove a part of the body which was Allah's gift—and now they wanted a limb for a limb. All of them were talking at the same time, and the situation was getting out of hand by the second. I was truly frightened, having never seen such behaviour before.

Suddenly, Mac raised his voice above the din, and started speaking to the relatives in his accented Arabic. Mac was over six feet tall—but more importantly, he was a white man. I was witnessing the power of the white man over erstwhile colonials up close. He effectively told them all to shut up and listen. He said the boy was about to die, and would certainly have died, but for the timely amputation. He showed them the severed limb and said it was full of poison that would have spread to the rest of his body and killed him, but for the Indian *Tabeeb's* timely operation.

'Do you want a dead boy with his limb in place or an alive boy who could later get a false limb attached to his leg?' he demanded.

His voice continually rose, and his face was turning crimson with anger. 'Get lost, all of you,' he said, 'go pray for the boy to live, and God willing, he will walk out of the hospital soon enough.'

The crowd fell silent. I am sure they didn't like one bit of what they were being told, but they had no choice—this was an *"ingleezi"*—the dominant class of humans. Without the slightest show of gratitude towards Major Kumar or the rest of the team, they beat a retreat, mumbling their disapproval.

I was stunned by Mac's ability to handle the situation. He suddenly grew in stature in my eyes. As we came back inside, Mac said, 'They will be back with a fresh dose of shouting and shrieking, but we will be prepared for them.' This was a war-like situation!

Preparation was in the form of getting two senior Omani officers from the patient's unit to come over and be with us ASAP. For the moment, it was hard to see Major Kumar's reaction. He was shattered—he had done better than most—fast, clean surgery to minimise anaesthesia time and further blood loss, with all necessary pre- and post-operative instructions issued very clearly even before we started. Had he taken the time I did with the appendix, we would have been operating on a dead man on the table. And the crowd wanted his limb in return? Totally unfair!

The pity was that this was not the first ever Omani soldier to lose a part of his limb. Injuries leading to mutilation, gangrene, loss of limb and life, etc. were not unknown to the locals. But then again, don't we all react differently to different situations? When the same problem affects one of our own, we feel angry, let down, and cheated. Thinking about the events later that day, I realised one thing. I better learn to speak Arabic and speak it well, especially since I could not do much about my skin colour.

The amputation patient stayed on for close to two weeks with us. My moods, and attitudes about Salalah, my colleagues (especially Mac), and my newfound life improved along with his health. My own first successful appendicectomy patient went home much earlier, leaving me poorer by a fair bit—the result of a party in the Mess, where suddenly, quite a few doctors from UAG also landed up! We had what was called a Happy Hour—my first ever acquaintance with this term, at my cost! For the appointed hour, no one—simply no one—would be charged for ordering any drink at the bar in the Officers' Mess. All costs would be borne by the "host"! But here was the good thing. However senior or however insistent you were, you could not get a free drink a second after the sixty minutes were over. Yes, some clever chaps would go for a refill at 58 minutes, but that was rare. Come minute number 61, the barman would go back to "*jaise the*" as we say in the Indian Army—back to square one. I was a teetotaller, so alcohol bills were painful to accept. *Never mind, I thought, I will extract my pound of flesh by doing more cases in the OT.*

And I did. Almost every week, I would get to do one or two cases—both the surgeons were very happy with my diligence and indulged me with all the small cases like wound suturing, allowed me to close abdomens, and steadily built my confidence and surgical skills.

Surgery apart, something else changed my attitude towards things around me—I got my first pay slip! It was a ridiculously small sheet of paper, some 3 inches by 4. But it was heavy with goodness! My first month's pay (plus 5 days' worth from the previous month) was in excess of 600 Omani riyals. I knew already that one Omani riyal fetched 26 Indian rupees—so, I was richer by close to fifteen thousand rupees! It was close to some 7 months' pay back home—despite my getting special Field Duty allowances there! I shot off letters to my mother, sisters, brother, insisting they send me a list of things they wanted from here when I next came on leave. My Omani dream had started to come true.

I still did not have a driving licence, but that again did not matter. Majors Kumar and Ravi always made sure I got to go out with them whenever work permitted. We attended medical meetings at UAG, went to the marketplace (which wasn't much to talk about really, though), and occasionally went to the lone Indian restaurant where I managed to get vegetarian food, while they both tucked in all sorts of things.

I also got to see a bit of Salalah, but not through my senior colleagues. During the Happy Hour in the mess, I had met the Commanding Officer of UAG, a genial person by the name of Lt. Col. (Muqaddam in Omani parlance, Mqm for short) Ramachandran, and a dental officer called Capt. (Raees, like me) Suresh. The latter was a kind of Indian version of Mac—tall and hefty with a deep voice to boot. We hardly spoke during the Happy Hour, but two days after the event, I got a call from him, asking me to join him at his place for dinner. I accepted a bit hesitantly, not quite sure I wanted to switch one Mess food for another, but was pleasantly surprised when he picked me up from my quarters and said we were going to his home within the UAG campus. Apparently, his wife and two kids were visiting with him. I learnt that one could apply for visa for family members—and this made me wistful again for a few minutes, dreaming of my parents visiting me in Oman. Oh, how wonderful would that have been!

Suresh's wife, Usha, was a very friendly girl, and I felt very much at home. The two kids were charming, as most kids usually are. Better still, I had a true South Indian meal which was most unexpected. Suresh had also called his C.O., Mqm. Ramachandran. They got along very well, I could see. I was simply overjoyed when I learnt that Mqm. Ramachandran was a fan of classical music.

It was Suresh who showed me around Salalah whenever we both had free evenings. I was surprised to find that Salalah was lush green, full of palm trees—Suresh said it was called the Kerala of Oman. July–August were great months, he said, when the Khareef, or monsoon season happened. I had assumed Oman was a mere desert, and Muscat had given no indication of being anything else.

I was beginning to like Salalah—working with two seniors, each better than the other in terms of professional skills and bonhomie, getting lots of surgery to do, and now, a really good friend in Suresh. The icing on this Salalah cake was that all our outings ended in dinner at his place! I was keen on exchanging notes about music with Mqm. Ramachandran, but had not made bold as yet—he was, after all, rather senior.

13

Border Roads

Just when I was getting to like my life in Salalah, I had to move. Oman in those days had a sensitive border with North Yemen*. A lot of troops of the not-so-large Omani Army were stationed in the Dhofar region, of which Salalah was the main city. One of the outposts right on the border with North Yemen was called Surfayt, with a small Army Unit in position there to curb insurgency. They needed a doctor as leave replacement, and UAG refused to send anyone from their hospital. So, the axe fell on me! I spent nearly a month there—high up in the hills, with hardly any medical work.

The accommodation was in Porta Cabins. For an Indian like me, the biggest shock was that there was no bathroom or toilet! I was never particularly religious, but I liked to have a bath every morning and do some prayers. Some of the porta cabins had an attached toilet, while others did not. This was crazy. I discovered that they did have one toilet block—in common with the rest of the Unit, comprising of a motley crowd of about two hundred soldiers! And one had to climb down some 100 metres of the hillside to reach it. One visit

---

* North Yemen (Yemen Arab Republic) and South Yemen (people's Democratic Republic of Yemen) merged in 1990 to become one single country. Tensions still exist between the mainly Shi'ite South and the Saudi-supported Sunnis in the north. Recently, Indian Air Force and the national airline Air India won many laurels for safely evacuating thousands of civilians—not just Indians, but people from some 12 countries.

there, and I was back to invoking the Gods to send me back, this instant, to India; to hell with Salalah and my dreams of surgical training. Least ways, I was ready to seek an urgent interview with Col. George or the Indian Ambassador.

Luckily, my exalted status as a "doc" helped. The quarter master (QM) of the Unit, a severe-looking chap by the name of McKeown, agreed to let me use his toilet—under conditions that I would not reveal the location of the keys to the toilet door to anyone else. But for the QM's act of kindness, I would have certainly rebelled. The QM may have been helpful, but I still disliked him, because I discovered on day one that he had a large birdcage behind his cabin with a whole lot of small birds all cooped up, shrieking their protest most of the time. I hated the very idea of imprisoning some helpless birds in this fashion.

My porta cabin mate was an Indian—a clerk in the C. O.'s office. He was away the day I reported for duty but turned up the next day, returning from Salalah after some official duty or the other. This chap, Tripathi, a *Havaldar* from the Indian Army, was one of the few non-officers-class on deputation to Oman. He was pleasant enough to get along with, but I had to play dirty on him, allowing him to go down to the common toilet every day, while I secretly used the QM's toilet.

14

Freedom at Mid-Day

My gratitude to the QM notwithstanding, I did something I am vicariously proud of. During the weekends, a majority of officers, except the silly doctor, were allowed to go away to Salalah for R&R (Rest and Recreation). The whole place was deserted during these weekends. I had full control of the porta cabin which substituted for the Officers' Mess during this time, boring as it was. During the second weekend, I got a bright idea when I learned that the QM was also away. There was heavy wind blowing all day. The birds in the cage behind the QM's cabin were shrieking away, more frightened than ever. In a sudden flash of inspiration, I went to the cage to see what I could do to help them—by which, I mean, I went to see if I could let the birds free. No luck! The silly QM had locked up the cage door with a numbered lock.

I tried various combinations, totally in vain. My head scarf kept flying off in the heavy winds. That suddenly gave me an idea. The cage was mainly wire mesh with a wooden framework along the borders. It was sitting on a cement structure of sorts—*probably a site meant for another toilet,* I wondered. To my utter surprise, I was able to shake the cage a bit when I tried! I certainly could have done with a pair of hands to help me in my rescue mission, but I had no choice. This was me and my own secret. I heaved and I shoved, and I pushed with my hands and with my shoulders. Almost as if in reply to my prayers (and that of the birds, who were encouraging me by shrieking all the louder), the silly cage suddenly gave way, and rolled off its moorings (if there were any!).

It fell down the hillside, and even as I started to wonder if I had done a great blunder, I was treated to one of the happiest sights I can recall from my days in Oman. The door (or whatever part that was the weakest, I am not sure) broke open, and all the birds, every single one of them, flew happily away, crying a collective sound of thanks to me, their saviour. Of all the silly things I have done in my life, this was one of the silliest yet proudest!

Sunday morning, the R&R party came back, fully rejuvenated by their looks. I decided to break the news before someone asked me about it. Going straight up to the QM, I said I hoped he had a good weekend, because I had some not so good news to convey. I said his bird cage seemed to have fallen off in the heavy winds, lashing the hillsides all through the weekend, and when I ventured out the previous evening, I didn't hear the birds chirping, so I went to see why, and found the cage down by the hillside with all the birds gone.

I felt vindicated for my act of sabotage, when he brushed the news away, saying, 'Ah, never mind, they were a silly nuisance anyway.' *Silly nuisance? So, that's why you bought them, imprisoned them in a cage and deprived them of their freedom?* I promised myself that heavy winds or not, if he bought more birds, I would set more birds free.

But the Surfayt chapter ended without anything else exciting—except for a soft porn movie.

The Brits knew how to make themselves comfortable. In 1980, when India still had not seen colour television, the Officers' Mess in Surfayt, remote as it was from everywhere, still had a huge monster of a colour TV monitor, 72 inches in size. There was a Hitachi Video Cassette Recorder-cum-Player, a set of huge Bang & Olufsen speakers with amplifier—all this in a porta cabin, which I am sure was specially modified to meet the requirements of a gentlemen's place of relaxation.

A few days before I left for Salalah, the entire lot of officers—Brits and Omanis—sat down with great anticipation to watch a movie. I was told it had Peter O'Toole in it, so I expected something exciting. I had seen his *Lawrence of Arabia* and was mesmerised by his acting. It was exciting alright, but O'Toole had nothing to do with it—in fact, his role was all of ten minutes if I recollect well. The movie was the then recently released "historical" movie *Caligula*. It showcased the debauchery and decadence of one of the last emperors of Rome in technicolour on the screen that almost filled the room. All I remember of the "history" about this lowlife of a Caesar is that he slept with his sister (and with anyone else he chose to) and auctioned Rome to the highest bidder at the end of the movie. There was more nudity and sex than I had ever imagined movies would show. As for Peter O'Toole, he brushed himself off the high pedestal in my esteem.

15

More Surgery

I t felt good to be back in the FST. I still had no driving licence or a car, but that didn't bother me one bit. Both Majors Kumar and Ravi seemed happy to have me back, and I had my hands full of interesting bits to do. Major Kumar, an extremely well-read man, pointed me in the right direction for honing my basic surgical skills, both in the operating theatre as well by way of suggesting books to read. One such was a small handbook titled "The Art of Surgery", which explained basic things like how to hold a scalpel when making incisions, how to apply stitches so that they provide adequate approximation of tissues, how to tie a surgeon's knot, etc. I devoured every opportunity to learn from such books as well as by observing my senior colleagues.

For the next two months, I got deeper and deeper into surgical work and enjoyed every moment of it. My attitudes were showing a steady change. First, I stopped my prayers for deliverance from Oman back to India. I still very much wanted to go, but I wanted to hang in there till my authorised leave—which, unfortunately, would only come after 10 more months. We were authorised 28 days' leave for every six months of qualifying work. Both holiday trips were to be paid ones, including the tickets. Already, I had taken close to 20 days of leave when my father passed away. It was only fair that the Force Medical Services (FMS) HQ wanted to consider this as my first instalment of leave for the first year of my service. I was okay with this, anyway.

I had done some math in my free time. We were approaching the end of November. I had received some 650 Omani riyals as pay, of which I had close to 400 left in the bank. Suresh had very patiently explained to me the expected monthly expenses.

He said I could hope to save close to 500 riyals a month if I were careful not to fritter my money away partying and buying gadgets. I was never a party animal; my mess bill was never going to include alcohol expenses (except when I was forced to hold Happy Hours), but buying gadgets? That was going to be difficult, so I mentally sanctioned 50 riyals a month for that—a huge amount, actually—so, I could work with 450 savings per month. That was 5400 riyals in one year of stay in Oman. Or a whopping 1.5 lakhs in Indian rupees!

I had never even dared to dream of earning such sums, leave alone savings! *Boy, O boy,* I thought, *this is not bad. No, not bad at all.* I was willing to stay for one year—and I promptly informed all my Gods of the change in plan. I asked the Gods to allow me to stay till September 1981 (end of September, I hastened to add, please remember I landed in Oman on 26th of September). I would then wait for my annual leave, go home, and that's it. I would stay put there, thank you very much. The saved money would be enough to sort out all the family financial issues, even perhaps buy a plot of land for later use to build a house.

I would learn as much surgery in the meantime as possible, and no one would then be able to stop me from going up for my specialty training in Armed Forces Medical College at Pune. I already ticked the right boxes—top rank in MBBS in most subjects, but importantly, first in Delhi University in Surgery; best All-Round Officer in the Basic Medical Officers' Course after joining the Army; full Field tenure in a High-Altitude Area; Paratrooper; and hey, a foreign posting! I was practically King! I started dreaming of being a respected surgeon in the AMC, like Major Kumar or Major Ravindranath. It would then be my turn to be nice to youngsters, train them in basic surgical techniques, earn a name for myself—and start a family.

The weather had improved a good deal, with a promise of cooler weeks ahead as we marched towards December and January, the best months in Oman. My opinion of others around me was changing, too—Mac was proving to be a good chap—efficient as an assistant in the OT (often, he knew more about surgical steps than I did, and I picked up a lot of tricks from him). He wasn't much into reading, which I felt was the only weakness in him. My father would often talk of the sense of humour of the British officers he worked with—a bit sarcastic, he would say, but nonetheless funny. And Mac hadn't even heard of PG Wodehouse or Jerome K Jerome!

The rest of the OT team had always been nice. Young Shyju had recently bought a second-hand car, with a bit of a rattling sound from the engine, but he was more than willing to take me around when Suresh was not available. The palm tree-lined beaches of Salalah reminded me very much of Kerala. Indeed, just like Kerala, bananas were plenty in Salalah—I learnt that Salalah supplied bananas to all of Oman and some neighbouring countries. Funnily, the locals called them "mouz or mouza", although the word Banana itself is of Arabic origin, meaning a finger—after the shape of the banana. None of the Omanis I came across were anything but friendly—in fact, the sword-wielding elders had come back for review once with the amputated soldier (he was walking perfectly well with his artificial limb—arranged by Major Ravi from the world-famous Artificial Limb Centre of Indian Army, based in Pune), and left us with massive quantities of dates. I was picking up essential Omani words to impress my patients. I was rather free with "Fi", my first ever Omani word, but had added "Kaif haal ak", and "Sabah al khair" for greeting when first meeting someone. I knew "bathan" was tummy, and "waja" (or wagya by some tribes) was for pain. I knew I was "Tabeeb" or doctor, I could count from one to ten (and beyond) easily in Arabic, and even recognise the numbers in their script—

frankly, I was half Omani by now! Salalah was going to be okay—after all, just for 10 months or so.

Not so fast, said one of the Gods from above. There was a doctor waiting to go on leave from Thumrait, some 80 kilometres to the north, in a hilly terrain. There was an Air Force station there, and one Army unit, with a medical centre between them. They were authorised two doctors, and two they insisted on having at all times. Sure enough, Harikrishnan was chosen as the replacement doctor! I was once again disappointed—more than anything else, I was going to miss all the surgery I was doing.

I didn't go back to withdrawing my one year offer to the Gods, although it did occur to me for a fleeting moment. But I was going to miss working in FST. Once, in front of all the staff, Major Kumar had called me to look at the wounds of a young soldier. I had sewn his wounds up after an injury a few weeks back. Major Singh roundly complimented me on my handiwork. I was delighted, and proudly bought sweets for the entire staff the next day. (I got away without a Happy Hour, luckily!) We were using silk sutures for all our skin closure. Major Kumar had shown me some newly arrived suture materials made of nylon and had suggested I consider doing a comparative study of the two types of sutures for wound closure. (Three years later, I would work on four different types of sutures for my Master of Surgery thesis, thanks to this wonderful senior's encouragement). I was going to miss all these. It struck me that Thumrait may simply be one of many more such duties waiting for me. I was condemned to be nomadic; I knew it in my bones. Having no choice, I rang up Suresh to ask about Thumrait.

16

Thumrait in Waiting

I t is a small but very nice place,' declared Suresh. 'It is just an hour from here, and since you will be in a Medical Centre, you and Pradhan (the other doctor) can plan on coming down to Salalah alternate weekends,' he added.

It seemed he had gone there a few times—he said the best thing about the place was the food in the Officers' Mess.

'There are these immensely talented Pakistani cooks,' he said, 'who have been sent by the heavens for the specific purpose of getting people to overeat.'

But this news did not brighten me up much. He was most likely raving about mutton and chicken and so forth, and I was a pure vegetarian. The weekend trips—even if only once in two weeks— sounded great. I would have to find a way of getting a lift to come down to Salalah, of course. Suresh had said that his wife was leaving next week, so I was welcome to stay with him. Now, that was comforting, even a bit thrilling—I was aware of the large collection of Indian movies and Pakistani plays Suresh had in the form of video cassettes. These video players and cassettes were a novelty, especially to us, the most recent arrivals. I had not even heard about them in India. I remembered being awed when I first saw them the day after our arrival in Muscat.

Major Kumar was upset with the decision of the FMS (Force

Medical Services) to send me to Thumrait. In my presence, he had a fair argument with Col. George on the phone. He made Col. George promise that after the 1-month duty in Thumrait, I would be allowed to stay put in FST for at least six months without being shunted around. This suited me. Seven months down the line, I would need the support of someone like Major Kumar when I broached the topic of returning to India prematurely. He would surely understand my keenness to go back early and start a career in surgery.

I was reading a lot more these days: with Mac's help, I had got a book from London called Pastest-FRCS. It was a collection of multiple-choice questions for preparing for FRCS Part-I examination. One look at its pages and I knew I had a *lot* of reading to do. In the sample MCQ at the beginning of the book, I scored a high of 1 out of 20 questions. I was expecting to breeze through the questions—after all, I had been the topper in surgery from one of the best universities just a few years back. The trouble was not that I did not know the subject. The trouble was that I had never ever been exposed to MCQs. We used to have short answer and essay-type questions in our college. MCQs had not made their way into the teaching system yet. Many decades down the line, I still believe MCQs are a convenient and quick way for assessment of students— purely from the examiners' point of view. Indeed, with computerised marking, the examiner can have the results of all candidates within minutes of the test. But I doubt whether such tests really evaluate the understanding of the subject by a student. Many questions are hair splitting in nature—like *When would you NOT want to correct the serum potassium levels in a patient:*

a. 3.5 millimoles/Litre

b. 4.5

c. 5.1

d. 2.8

And so on. I hated the book, but I was hell bent on revising the book over and over again—the explanations at the Answers Section made for interesting reading and stimulated me to repeatedly look up my textbooks.

There was a small bit of good news before my Thumrait stint was supposed to begin. Major Kumar and I were selected to attend the Armed Forces Annual Dinner with the Sultan in his guest palace in Muscat… and I couldn't help but think Major Kumar must have had a fair bit to do with my being on the list.

17

A Majestic Dinner

E very year, His Majesty Sultan Qaboos bin Said Al Said, the ruler of Oman and the Supreme Commander of the Sultan of Oman's Armed Forces, held a dinner for the officers of his Forces on the 18th of November. It is his birthday, and the country celebrates it as the National Day. The year 1980 was the tenth National Day—the Sultan had ascended the throne on 23rd July 1970, a day celebrated as the Renaissance Day. I had already heard a lot about the benevolent Sultan from many of the Omani officers I had met. One of them had told me that His Majesty was educated in Pune, India, and in the UK. He had graduated from the Royal Military Academy at Sandhurst, South England.

Renaissance was perhaps the most appropriate word to use for the Sultan's ascension to the throne. Oman had emerged from economic and social darkness when the young Sultan took over the responsibilities of managing the country's affairs. In ten short years, Oman had made incredible progress in all fields. There were good roads in most parts of the country, even rural areas; good hospitals were being established in major cities; from just three schools when he became Sultan, now there were close to 400 schools, (for a population of about two million) with one in three students being a female.

When I arrived in Oman, there was already a full-fledged high school for expatriates, mainly Indian. This was understandable, as

71

one fourth of the population in 1980 was expat in nature, and a majority were Indian. The remarkable progress in economic terms was owed to the sensible use of the country's oil and gas reserves, thanks to the great foresight of its leader. No wonder he was happy to host a dinner for his armed forces officers—they were the true guardians of this fledgling country, galloping away to prosperity under the Sultan's able leadership.

Major Kumar and I landed in Muscat on 18th November morning. I had the chance to meet my friends Sunil and Deepak. We compared notes—I was the most travelled amongst the three! Salalah, Surfayt, and now all set for Thumrait. But the most exciting part of our discussion was what Sunil and Deepak had heard over the grapevine the last few days, leading up to today's dinner: there could be a pay rise! But our enthusiasm was dampened by the realisation that we had been there in Oman for less than two months! So, as we set out for the grand dinner in our uniformed finery, we had little by way of expectation.

The dinner was at a palace (one of many around the country) near the old port of Muscat. I was very proud to learn that the architect was an Indian. The beautifully manicured lawns behind the ornate gates, the muted lighting, and the overall ambience of the place was worthy of a great ruler. Our collective jaws dropped a foot when we saw the food laid out for the feast. I was sure none of us had ever seen so much food at one site before. The Indian Army is known for its fanfare and elaborate parties, but this was something else altogether. At a glance, I could see that there were at least some forty varieties of desserts alone! Even as we were drooling at the sight of all this, there was a hushed silence, followed by bugles to announce the arrival of the Sultan. He was a bit diminutive, I thought, but for all that, he had the unmistakable air of a King. There was much bowing and hand shaking, but sadly, he never came close enough to our group. He soon withdrew with his close aides, and the eating—gorging, more like—began. We ate, had our fill, and made our way back.

In the bus we had travelled from the HQ, the seniormost Omani officer, a commander of one of the two Brigades of the Army, made an incredible announcement.

'Thirty percent pay hike and a special Seiko wristwatch for all officers including those of the Royal Oman Police force,' he said. It seemed the Sultan's deputy had let him know. Even as people were gasping in delight, he added, 'From 1st of November.'

This was incredible. The November pay slip was promising to be rather heavy. Deepak, Sunil, and I were experiencing mixed feelings. We rather unfairly entertained hopes that the great Sultan would be magnanimous and include us, too, in this act of generosity. Hell, after all, we had joined the Force before 1st November. The chances, we knew, were rather slim, so we dared not ask anyone. Others were all too ecstatic to notice our lack of exuberance. Imagine our surprise then, when, after 12 days, we received our pay slips (I was back in Salalah, getting ready for going to Thumrait the next week). Thin as ever it was, but the bottom right corner said our pay was 770 Omani riyals! I couldn't believe my luck! I immediately dialled FBH and the three of us shared our collective delight—this was too much of a good luck bestowed on us.

I quickly did my math and found out that I could meet much more than my target of 5400 riyals in under 8 months. Then I looked at the figures again—wait a minute—let me set aside a full hundred riyals a month to splurge—I could still save 6700 riyals, or close to 1.75 lakhs in Indian rupees—if I stayed with the original plan of finishing the first full year before opting out. After all, I hadn't expected this pay rise, and was planning to stay on for ten months, anyway. Besides, I told myself, staying a full year would make things easier for me to get support from the senior lot—I didn't want anyone to think I was running away for any silly reasons. And then, curiosity got the better of me—some more mental math. If I stayed the full three years, even assuming I did not get any more pay rise (I told myself that it would be plain and simple greed even to dream of any significant pay rise year after year), and even if I spent more than a hundred riyals each month, I would still be taking—oh, my God, close to six and half lakh Indian rupees in savings when I returned home!

The plot of land I was dreaming of buying now looked like it could have a house built on it. A hundred other thoughts about what I could do for my mother, siblings, my nephews, and niece (*nieces* by then, who knows?), my close friends back home, all sorts of wonderful ideas were crowding my mind. Hey, I could perhaps even manage a trip to see London—even perhaps take the FRCS exam. And then, suddenly, I was squarely back on earth. Three years down the line, I would be way behind my contemporaries for surgical training. I would have to really do a rethink about money versus professional ambitions and then talk to the Gods with my revised request, yet again. There was something in the back of my mind clamouring for attention, but I couldn't quite put my finger to it then. I hardly slept that night, but for different reasons from the last time I had gone sleepless, when my father's news had hit me.

18

Thumrait Medical Centre

Suresh, as always, pointed out a lacuna in my readiness for Thumrait, and as usual, provided the answer.

'How are you going to come from Thumrait on weekends, young man?' he asked. It hit me—the public transport system in Oman was not much to boast of. Certainly, none existed between Salalah and Thumrait. I had been unrealistically counting on someone giving me a lift—of 80 km each way!

I was stumped, but not for long, thanks to this godsend of a big brother. 'Can you drive?' he asked.

I didn't have to really answer his question—my face said it all! My association with automobiles was limited to two or three trips in the back seat of our neighbour's car, back in India. We had no scooter, leave alone a car at home.

'Okay, let us see now,' continued Suresh, 'we have about a week before you leave for Thumrait. After work today, I will take you to a safe place to see what you can do behind a wheel. My car is a second-hand one—specifically purchased for training guys like you! If you are as intelligent as your reports claim, you may have a fair chance of learning enough over the week. Make friends in Thumrait and continue learning to drive with their help. I will drive up to Thumrait one day, bring you down for a driving test, and hopefully, you will be able to drive around by yourself after that. At TMC (Thumrait

Medical Centre, where I was going to be stationed for about one month) you will have a car to yourself.'

Oh, my God! A car all to myself? Oman was getting better and better, and surgery was being pushed to the back benches, one row at a time.

Even the affectionate Suresh was not ready for what happened over the next week—the first day, as expected, I just about managed to avoid crashing the car at every available lamp post, kerb, or tree. But by end of Day Two, I had got the hang of the steering wheel to avoid the car looking inebriated. I still had a major issue with coordinating the clutch, gear box, and accelerator. Full credit to Suresh for his ability to train a novice, and even more credit to his inexhaustible patience, by Day Three, I was changing gears properly and driving in a straight line. When I asked him about the driving test on Day Four, he told me to shut up. But the next day, he made me drive around for more than two hours—and I got used to driving with lights on as well. The next day, he came around during working hours, took Major Kumar's permission, and off we went—for my driving test! I returned around lunch time to the Mess, my face inscrutable. As I walked in, there was much sympathy from those at the dining table.

'Good to see you intact, bro! Hope the instructor is intact, too? Anyway, no one gets their licence quickly in this blessed country. Certainly not at the first attempt. Come, enjoy your lunch.'

And I dramatically pulled out a box of Baklavas from behind me, grinning from ear to ear, and said, 'Some do, it seems!'

There was a huge commotion for the next few minutes, which settled down only after Major Kumar made the gracious announcement that I would be hosting a Happy Hour that evening at the bar! I began calculating the cost of my driving licence, thrilled to bits nevertheless at this great achievement. A week ago, I was happy to sit in the passenger seat, a substantial promotion from my backseat trips in India. Now, I had qualified to move to the driver's seat! Wow! Oman, I love you! I love you loads!

I left for Thumrait on Sunday, two days after my momentous success with the driving test. Ali, the FST driver, seemed almost reverent towards me now that he knew I could also drive!

The TMC was a single-storeyed building, with consultation rooms, a 4-bedded detention room, a small laboratory, an X-ray room, and waiting areas for patients. Meant exclusively for the troops of Western Frontier Regiment (WFR) and the Air Force personnel of the flying unit based a few kilometres away, it was way better equipped than the MI Room (Medical Inspection Room) I had worked at before coming to Oman. The TMC and the WFR were on one side of the airport while the Air Force unit was on the other side. The other doctor there was from the Air Force—a junior doctor like me from the Indian Army Medical Corps, deputed to the Omani Air Force. Medical cover for the entire Omani Armed forces was provided largely by deputised doctors and other staff from India, with a smaller proportion made up of similar military personnel from Pakistani, Egyptian and Sri Lankan Armed Forces. In the two hospitals (Force Base Hospital at Muscat and Umm Al Ghawaarif Hospital in Salalah) there were non-military background doctors directly recruited into the Omani Armed Forces. They were called Contract Officers and could stay on in Oman as long as their contract was renewed every two years. Whereas we, drawn from the military of different countries, were labelled as Deputationists or Seconded Officers, with a fixed tenure of three years. But all of us wore Omani uniforms and ranks.

My stay in Thumrait was very pleasant. The Officers' Mess and our quarters were within walking distance of the Medical Centre, and the Pakistani cooks from WFR who worked there had only one goal in their life—to feed us silly! Suresh was spot on about their culinary skills. Even better, they were wizards with vegetarian dishes as well. I gained a couple of kilos in the month that I spent there. I drove my car every day all over the Thumrait Garrison, around the airport area, and wherever else my fancy took me. There was hardly any traffic to contend with, and in less than two weeks, I was a seasoned car driver. Or so I sincerely believed.

The car was a standard Army issue Toyota Corolla. It was as luxurious as it could get. It had air conditioning—something I had never heard of till we landed in Oman; it had a cassette player and speakers that filled the entire car with sound, bucket seats (another thing I never knew existed), and seat belts, which were compulsory. It was a bit cumbersome due to my lack of experience with such things, but the thing that tickled me the most was the little button in the back doors called the "child lock". I could not stop marvelling at the standards of the car. Imagine owning such a car in India! My equations with my Gods were rewritten just a bit more. In my prayers, I said to Him that I would be happy to stay on till I had just enough money to buy a car like this to take back to India, but in all fairness to myself, I remember repeatedly entreating Him to ensure this happened as fast as possible, so that I could go back to India soon enough to get into surgical training. Looking back, I am surprised I had not totally fallen for material comforts during my time in Oman. Sunil and Deepak, whenever I spoke to them—and we did this regularly because calling from one's own room to another's in far off Muscat was a mere job of dialling six digits—were already talking about how comfortable working in Oman was, and how they would like to explore converting to be Contract Officers, if possible, to stay on permanently! *Selfish chaps*, I thought, downright traitors if you ask me. All I wanted was the savings I had already worked out—plus money for a car, of course—and off I would go to India to do my surgery specialisation.

19

Astronaut on the Highway

I rang up Suresh almost every day to fill him in on my day's activities—especially the driving I was doing. He seemed fairly impressed, and why not? He suggested I drive over for the next weekend, when I told him I was free as per the rota. Even when I was on call, work was very light, with hardly any emergencies (I missed that bit from FST, for sure).

I learnt to play squash and an exciting new sport called Land Yachting. Both were taught to me by my new friend, Ashraf Khan, on deputation from Pakistani Army. We took to each other from the moment we met—especially as it turned out he was the first officer I met, being my next-door mate in the Officers' Mess quarters. He was known to have played squash at the highest levels in the Pakistani Army (the reigning world champion in squash was a Pakistani), and I was handling a squash racquet for the first time in my life! But he had immense patience, always giving me every opportunity to score a point, but of course, I regularly lost 0-9 to him, game after game. We spent most of our time together, watching movies in his room (he had a huge 27-inch TV and the latest VCR player), eating together (he refused to even look at vegetarian food, and I was a pure vegetarian). He would often accompany me on my driving trips and give me excellent tips ('Never look just beyond the bonnet, Hari Saab, the farther down the road you gaze, the better you will be prepared to react to hazards,' 'Always check your tyres before entering the car

and check the fuel and temperature gauges once you start the engine,'
and so on). As the weekend approached, I asked him if he would go
to Salalah with me. Confident as I was now with the car, I was still a
bit unsure of how I would cope with the curving, sloping roads on
the Dhofar hills between Thumrait and Salalah. Ashraf was totally
upset—he had already planned to fly to Muscat and on to Dubai for
a holiday with some friends.

He said, 'Doctor Saab, not to worry; you go. Your driving is as
good as mine (*of course, just like squash,* I thought), and anyway, you
will be going with a doctor in attendance!'

Call it overconfidence, young blood, or an acute desire for sambar
and rice, I decided to go by myself. Following protocol, I informed
the station duty officer about my trip, and set off immediately after
work for Salalah that Thursday. I had already called Suresh to fix up
a session of squash (but the real intention was to give him enough
time to lay out a good dinner), packed my toothbrush and other
essentials, and was on my way. The essentials included some of my
recently acquired cassettes. As I started off on the approximately 90-
minute drive to Suresh's place, I actually realised that Ashraf not
being with me meant I could listen to a full concert by MS
Gopalakrishnan (MSG for short), my favourite violinist, unhindered
by conversation—Ashraf and I tended to talk nonstop every time we
were together. I checked my tyres, mirrors, the fuel gauge and
temperature gauge. 'All check,' I happily told my reflection in the
rear-view mirror and set off. MSG started his concert with an
invocatory song to Lord Ganesha, the God who removes all
obstacles. 'Good, thank you, MSG,' I said as I changed gears, enjoying
the silken smooth sounds of the violin. It was just after 4 p.m., a nice
and bright afternoon, and traffic was light—most people left later in
the evening for their Salalah weekend. The roads were excellent, and
I soon gathered speed, enjoying the power of the car's 1.6 litre engine.

The road from Thumrait goes through the Dhofar hills, and that
segment of the way has winding, sloping roads. I was aware of that—

but not quite aware of what my car would do in those curves. MSG kept me happily entertained, and I hummed along as I drove. I must have been less than a kilometre into the hill roads when, all of a sudden, as I swerved left at a curve, my silly car decided to keep swerving more than I told it to; it climbed the kerb, tried to see if it could drive on just two wheels, decided no, it couldn't, and simply turned on itself to take a short rest! Before I could say what-ho, the car, having enjoyed the tyre-less skid on its roof for a few metres, came to a halt in the middle of the road!

It was all over in a few seconds. I found myself suspended in mid-air like an astronaut. I realised I had dutifully put on the seat belt and the car was upside down! It dawned on me much later that this automatic act had probably saved my life. I released the seat belt—and fell clumsily to the roof of the car. MSG continued with his beautiful elaboration of Kalyani, unaware of my predicament. I tried opening the doors, but no luck—it was fully jammed. So was the window on both my side and the passenger side. My heart started its belated marathon. Wondering what to do, I realised the windshield had happily shattered all over. I used my squash racquet to break it, and gently crawled out on all fours.

Again, it dawned on me much later that there was not a single vehicle all this while on either side of the road. I had seen enough movies to know about cars blowing up when they overturn, so I quickly put some distance between it and me. What was I to do? How was I to contact Suresh, who certainly would have a solution to this issue? I simply had to flag down some passing car and ask for help.

A pick-up van came along fairly soon enough, screeching to a halt not far from my car. A burly Omani got out, looked over the valley side of the hill, and not finding any dead bodies, came over to me and asked, '*Fi mauth* (anybody dead)?' I told him I was the driver, and that I was fully alive as far as I could make out. Totally disappointed, he marched off, and drove away to catch up with lost time, leaving me stranded. Two or three cars passed by, slowed down, and their curiosity quenched, sped away without as much as looking at me.

Finally, a car stopped.

'*Tabeeb* (Doctor)!' said one of the three chaps who got out.

He turned out to be a WFR soldier I had treated for some minor ailment just a few days back. They quickly took stock of the situation and offered to take me to Salalah. But I knew I had to wait till the police came, so I gave them Suresh's number and asked them to call him when they reached Salalah and tell him to come fetch me. I then braced myself for the wait till the police patrol arrived.

It was only now that the enormity of my accident got to me—I could have died, had the car continued its skid over the hillside. The engine could have blown up—it was still running when I was trying out my spacewalk inside the car. I had only switched off the engine almost as an afterthought, in the process of turning off the music system. I must have taken 3, may be 4 minutes to get out of the car. Anything could have happened in that time! My wish to go back to India was pretty close to being granted—except I would have gone in a box. I looked heavenward and conveyed a silent prayer of gratitude. I was 26, and I had a fair bit of things I wanted to do in my life. And I had been so stupidly proud of getting the driving licence in a week's time!

Reflecting on my life as I waited for the police patrol to arrive was one of the most telling lessons I learnt in my days in Oman. How casually we tend to take life's blessings! Especially in the ignorant arrogance of our youth, we all think death follows some kind of chronology! Even if I had not died but had been merely crippled, I would have been back in India, discharged from Army service, and, and... I could not even begin to think of the implications on my life, and that of my family members.

Suddenly, I wasn't all that thrilled about my getting the driving licence in record time. I was almost going to set up another record— that of holding on to the licence for the shortest time. What if I had hit another car, a pedestrian? What if I had killed someone in the process? A shudder went through my body as I realised what a champion idiot I had been. I resolved to look at my blessings and my limitations a bit more seriously. And I continued to wait by the roadside, some safe distance away from the car.

I had to go to Salalah Police Station first to file a report. Suresh, my saviour, suddenly appeared from nowhere. He took over—his Arabic was way better than mine—and I heard him pointing out frequently that I was a great *Tabeeb mal Jaysh* (doctor in the Army). He loosely described me as a surgeon, which no doubt improved my standing. All paperwork done, we left for Suresh's home. Luckily, I had not hit and damaged any other car or public property or killed anyone in the process of my circus act. Even as Suresh pointed out all these plus points, jokingly adding that beheading or hanging was thus totally out of the question, I maintained a stoic silence—the whole thing was just beginning to sink in.

I returned to Thumrait in a transport arranged by Suresh after a listless weekend. Even Tom & Jerry could not lift my moods all weekend. My reputation as "The Man Who Refused to Die" had already reached Thumrait, and there was a kind of minor celebration in the Mess—*at my cost, of course!* I stayed put in Thumrait for the rest of my duty days and returned to FST, my tail fairly well tucked between my legs. I plunged myself with a vengeance into the ward and OT work and spent every spare minute reading my textbooks. I was definitely going to be a surgeon. Even without being one, the label had saved my skin at the police station.

20

Back to FBH Muscat

The telephone rang, startling me a bit. It was just past 7 a.m. in mid-February of 1981. It was a call from Col. George from FMS, Muscat. I had just about done three months of work at FST with all the interruptions. Never one to waste time on meaningless formalities, Col. George came straight to the point.

'I want you back in FBH, Hari,' he said. 'I am told you are doing a very good job at FST, so I am attaching you to our Consultant Surgeon Mqm Sivanesan here in FBH. You are going to be his number two. I have told FST to relieve you in two weeks' time, so that you can complete all the follow-up work on your patients. When you come here, report to me at the FMS HQ before going to FBH. Take care.' That's it. He was done!

I didn't quite know what to think. Yes, for sure, FBH would have a much wider variety of surgical work, as they were open to military as well as civil patients, but... but I was just beginning to really enjoy my work here—I had made some really good friends, knew the staff well, knew my way around Salalah, and here we go gypsying around again!

One thing was for sure. Being next door to the FMS HQ would be a good way to ensure my exit as and when I decided on it (by now, the "the day I finish one year" bit had disappeared from my phraseology). Then, there were Sunil and Deepak, my friends. And then, one point on the flip side cropped up in my mind—what if Col.

George brought up the Liaison Officer bit again? Is that why he had asked me to report to him first? I didn't want the LO job. I had to study! Surely, I couldn't go around hobnobbing with the Embassy and the Ministry of Defence and Ministry of Health and so on? As usual, I decided to approach higher authority.

'Suresh,' I said, when I got through. He cut me short. 'Hey, I have a patient on the chair.' He lowered his voice, 'It is the Brigade Commander, Amid (Brigadier) Salim Said, and he is in pain. Come home in the evening, we will talk,' he said.

I went looking for Major Kumar or Ravi, but neither was free. They didn't even make it to lunch. Post my day's work, I drove down to Suresh's. (I had been issued a swank new car, the latest model of Toyota Corolla, a gleaming green colour, and oh, God, I would have to leave this behind, too.)

He welcomed me with his usual deep, warm voice. 'So, promotion, eh? Off to FBH?'

I was stunned. 'How did you know?'

'Listen,' he said. 'This is a small place, small army, and there is hardly anything exciting to do. Everybody knows everything,' he said. Apparently, he had a one-on-one with Col. George. Although Suresh was a Tamilian like me, he had grown up in Trivandrum, as had Col. George—so, they were country cousins of sort. His Malayalam was flawless. Suresh practically said he had been instrumental in ensuring my move, even if not in as many words.

'You are too good to be sitting here, Hari. Go to FBH, work hard, get the FRCS and then the whole world will be open to you. No son of a gun will stop you from becoming a surgical specialist when you get back home. Besides, you are the LO designate, and it never harms to keep up some good connections—you will see Col. George almost daily, and the DG too.' He winked before adding, 'Just in case you want to quit the AMC and stay put here permanently.'

I stood up. My blood was boiling. 'Like hell I want to stay in this horrible place. I want out—tomorrow, if I can manage that. And by the bloody way, how come you are sitting in this lowly Salalah if you are that close to Col. George? How come you aren't in FBH— meeting him *daily*? I tell you what, call him and tell him to make you LO, you go to FBH, and maybe he can leave me here in FST for the next few months. I am going back the day I finish my one year, anyway.'

It all came out in a rush. But Suresh was way better a chap to fall for such provocation. He handed me a cold beer and commanded me to sit down.

'Listen,' he said, 'Stop being a fool. Don't talk of going back in one year; that's downright silly. There are over 6000 doctors in the AMC. And less than one percent get an opportunity like this. The AMC sets a lot of credit by us who get selected for such foreign postings. And do you think you will be patted on the back and sent straight to AFMC for your surgery training if you go back? You probably will find yourself in some remote field area, mate! And you can then kiss your surgical ambitions goodbye!

'Your family background can't be very different from mine, so let me tell you this. This is a once-in-a-lifetime opportunity to straighten your finances for the rest of your life. Do your given job well, get a good name, and when you go back, your seat in surgery will be guaranteed. As to why I am in Salalah, I like it this way—I am already a postgraduate qualified dentist, and I will most likely retire with this qualification. I am my own boss here, with no one to breathe down my back. You better read like hell, stop wasting time on cartoons and other movies, get your FRCS before you finish in Muscat—you have less than two and half years for that, remember. Now drink up that beer.'

Only my dad could have talked like that to me. I wondered what Appa would have said if I were to go back halfway during my Muscat tenure and he was around. He would have been heartbroken for sure, I guess. I was nearly in tears when I remembered how he would wear clips on his trouser bottoms, mount his bicycle, and drive about ten kilometres each way to the Army HQ and back every day. Those days, he had to support his family of wife and four kids, a widowed mother, and a delinquent younger brother. Maybe he dreamed of a foreign posting as well? No, he must have only dreamed of a foreign posting for one of his kids—and that kid would most certainly have been me, his favourite. I was suddenly quite ashamed of myself.

21

Force Base Hospital 2.0

Maybe it should read 1.2. I had hardly spent any time in FBH when we first came here. I had left within a week of arrival for Salalah. Even so, I remember being impressed by the squeaky-clean floors and rooms, the well-planned layout of the hospital, the wards with curtained-off cubicles, immaculate consultation chambers with tiltable examination couches, individual blood pressure apparatus, etc., and an ultra-modern kitchen. I remember staring in awe at the way patients were served their food in covered trays, something I had never seen in the hospital where I trained. Now, I had the opportunity to study them up close, and I learnt a lot of things.

Sometimes, such things would make me a bit wistful when I compared the facilities available back home. Any number of ECG machines, defibrillators and emergency trolleys in all areas, plastic cannulas called Venflons for intravenous infusions (we often used reusable needles in our patients for this purpose in my hospital in India) ... I was beginning to fully comprehend the meaning of India's label as a "third world country". However, all that didn't prevent me from getting thrilled when, on my first night duty, the hospital chef walked into my room and asked what I would like to order for dinner!

But first, my briefing by Col. George. I went straight from the airport to FMS HQ. Col. George, meticulous as ever, had timed my arrival and kept aside some time for my briefing. As usual, he cut out small talk.

'Hello, Hari,' he said. 'Welcome back. Kumar and Ravi have had good things to say about you. Well done. You will be working with Dr Sivanesan from tomorrow morning. He is a tough taskmaster, but an excellent surgeon. Make the most of your time with him. He is very British when it comes to punctuality and discipline, so keep that in mind. We are hoping to get another surgical consultant, but you will continue as long as Sivanesan allows. We are a bit short on hands now, so you will have to join the general night duty rota as well. And this afternoon, I have asked for you to be taken to the Embassy and the Defence and Health ministries for formal introduction to concerned people as the LO.'

That was it! He dismissed me without another word. He was more military than most back in the AMC—and he had not worked one day in the Indian Army! The LO babel was sticking rather fast, I groaned inwardly.

I walked across to FBH to see if I could meet my friends. I poked my head into the first consultation room on the right, and was greeted by a short, stunningly beautiful English girl, who had one look at me and my uniform and said, extending a warm hand as she spoke: 'You must be Harry, right, from Salalah, the budding surgeon? Welcome! Been hearing a lot about you. Hope you get to cut a lot! Hope you remember to sew them all up after cutting!' and gave a cheery laugh.

There was something about the way she spoke, especially the way she said 'sa law law' that was very attractive. Her mannerism made me feel very much at ease. She had done her hair a funny way—it was as if she had a bun only for the front bit of her hair over a somewhat largish forehead, and a slightly crooked tooth on the left upper row gave a very likeable look when she laughed. I shook her hand rather hesitatingly. This kind of 'Hi, Harry'-ing and hand shaking would have been unthinkable back home. I was to learn a lot more about the differences between nurses back home and the British ones I had to work with in FBH—not the least being the disturbing realisation that Glynnis—that was her name—was paid more than I was, as a doctor! I learnt later that all the British girls were on a higher pay scale than basic doctors, and much higher than the Indian, Egyptian, Sri Lankan and even local Omani nurses. This was my first encounter with the lingering effects of colonialism.

I had hardly recovered from the handshake, when Glynnis said, 'Come, Jay (I assumed the doctor whose room it was) has gone for a tea break, so I have a few minutes, I will introduce you around.'

She marched off, and I, her lamb, followed, admiring her petite figure, the blue-grey uniform looking elegant on her as she walked with a springy step. I don't think I remembered the name of a single person she introduced me to; I was so busy admiring her looks and way of talking. She suddenly looked at her watch, dangling upside down from the top of her dress, and said 'Blimey, Jay will be back. I need to run, sorry,' and reached out to hold my wrist as she said this. Before I could even begin to register this yet another new aspect of work life, she was gone!

I must have definitely looked like a recently resurrected zombie, because I didn't register part of what was being said behind me, '... *aur atey hi ladki phasa liya?* (You barely just arrived, and already after the girls, are you?)'

I turned and was overjoyed to see both Sunil and Deepak, my batchmates. There was a fair bit of leg-pulling all the way to the wards where the two of them parted, promising to catch me at lunch. I realised I had not much time to go to my room—I had to first go to the Officers' Mess to find out which one had been allotted to me, unpack, and get ready for the post-lunch trip to the Embassy and wherever.

The next day started badly. Very badly. The previous afternoon had been very nice, meeting the First Officer at the Embassy, saying hello to dignitaries in the MOD (Ministry of Defence) and MOH

(Ministry of Health), visiting the huge medical library in the much huger MOH building and so on. The evening was very pleasant, too, with a lot of catching up on all sorts of gossip peculiar to bachelor friends. I had been allotted a lovely ground floor room with a balcony at the back, and, after a lengthy phone call to Suresh, I had gone to sleep, pretty pleased with myself.

I was a few minutes earlier than the expected 7.30 a.m. reporting time, although I still did not have a car to myself. Deepak had taken me with him to the hospital after an early breakfast. But as I entered the surgical ward, I heard a sharp 'I say! You, there! Come here,' from a balding gentleman in white coat. The tone was the sort one would use to summon an errand boy. It took me a moment or two to realise that this must be Dr Sivanesan. I had expected an Indian Army officer in uniform, but this person was in civvies with a white coat.

I had no time to confirm this, for I was unable to look at the name tag, as he continued in a rather rude voice that sounded Indian yet not quite Indian. 'You want to work here, you need to be here 15 minutes before I come, I say! And I come ten minutes before starting time. I hope your Indian brain will be able to work out the math. One minute late from tomorrow, and you can go tell George to send you back to wherever it was he picked you up from. No monkey business with me. Do the rounds with the Sister, prep the patient and I want you and the patient in under 15 minutes in the OT. Understood?'

Whether I did understand or not, he did not wait to find out. Good in a way, because my voice had got left behind somewhere. I wanted to say, 'Hello, Sister,' to the approaching nurse, but only a hoarse whisper issued forth. Till that moment, I had only come across nice people in Oman. Nice, did I say? I had come across some of the finest people ever. Even Ali, the driver at FST, was more friendly on Day One by comparison with this brute of a balding oldy. I was shell shocked from this totally unwarranted animosity—I had not even had time to do anything wrong! And this oldy baldy was teaching me, an AMC officer, about punctuality? And what did he mean by "your Indian mind" anyway? He was quite obviously not from AMC, but he looked every bit an Indian. I was to find out later that he was from Sri Lanka (Ceylon in the British days). I rued my failure to ask Sunil and Deepak about this "consultant surgeon" I was supposed to work with. Better do it today at lunch, I told myself. Little did I know about the routine that awaited me!

The Sister, also a Sri Lankan, was the exact opposite of Mr Oldy Baldy, thank God.

'Tamizha, Doctor?' she asked in a mellow voice, a great contrast from the recent one. I took a few seconds to regain my composure, looking away in the hope that she would not notice how close I was to crying.

'Yes,' I replied short.

'I am also Tamil,' she replied. Over the next ten minutes, she told me about the 4 or 5 patients she thought I needed to know, coming last to a lady who was already in an OT gown, and a cap covering her head and hair.

'Gallstones, Doctor,' she said, and added with the practised ease of a professional, 'LFT normal, no jaundice, Hb 12.5, only pain— nearly for 1 year. Anaesthetist seen this morning, consent done, patient only speaks Arabic.' Everything I needed to know for the moment. Together, we wheeled the patient to the theatre, where the staff, mostly Indian or Omani, received the patient. Thankfully, the anaesthetist was Indian, too, although I didn't like the way he hobnobbed with Oldy Baldy.

But my woes continued unabated. I was pulled up at every available opportunity—gowning was wrong, gloving was not good enough, I was too close to the table when he was prepping the patient—there was no end to this tirade. I kept quiet, mainly because I did not know what else to do. He asked me about where the incision should be, the blood supply of the gallbladder, and so on, and I didn't give him any room to catch me out. But assisting him was a terrible experience—I was either 'Too interfering, I say; who is the surgeon, me or you?' and the next minute, 'Here, this is not your bedroom, I say. Open your eyes and assist me where I need it.' On and on he went, and in that one single session, he all but snuffed out my interest in surgery altogether.

I came this close to taking my gloves off and boxing Oldy Baldy's face with my bare hands and walking out—to hell with surgery and to a bigger hell with my stay here. I think the occasional compassionate eye from the scrub nurse and the anaesthetist just about prevented me from doing that. After what seemed like a nightmare, the surgery got over. He closed the wound to the last stitch, not that I would have volunteered to put the skin stitches for this brute of a surgeon—he wasn't much of a surgeon compared to Major Kumar and Major Ravi, anyway, I happily told myself. He even applied the wound dressings himself, pulled off his glove, gave me rapid fire instructions about the medication and fluids in the postoperative period, thanked the nurse and anaesthetist, and walked off.

There was an uneasy silence after his exit, and after looking over his shoulders to ensure Dr Sivanesan was out, the anaesthetist—a Major Nath—said in a warm voice, 'Welcome to FBH, Hari. Kumar tells me you are brilliant, and I am sure we will find you so. I am sure Sivanesan will, too. Okay?'

Perhaps if I had been allowed to leave the OT without a word by anyone, I would have held on—but these kind words were too much to bear. Like an injured baby who waits to cry till the mother picks him up, I simply broke down—I was ashamed of myself, but I was also deeply hurt. The scrub nurse did something unexpected. Pulling off her gloves, she gave me a warm hug! She couldn't have been over 40, but she was being Mother, and I soaked her gown with a bucket full of tears.

My debacle—if that is what it was—was known to everyone before the day was out. If that was acutely embarrassing, it felt equally good to see that practically everybody's sympathy was with me. And why not? I had hardly started off at the hospital, and Dr Sivanesan's attitude towards me was totally, inexplicably hostile. I may have made a spectacle of myself by crying, but I was not beaten—not just yet.

I came back to the wards after a quick lunch and was luckily spared further assault by oldy baldy (by now, he had lost not only his name, he had also lost the right to capitalisation of his nickname). I finished all my post-op work, reviewed all the other patients, looked up the list for the next day, prepared the consent forms for the patients—they were not yet in—said my byes to the sister on duty, and left sharp at 4 p.m.

I wanted to go straight to my room—it would be a good 15 minutes' walk in the warm sun, but I couldn't care. As I cut across the parking lot of the hospital, I heard a familiar voice call my name. I turned to find Glynnis waving to me from inside a car—yes, the white nurses all had a car to themselves. I was beginning to get a fair idea of the importance of skin colour in this country which was still very much under control of the Brits. Not wanting to be rude to someone who had been so nice just the previous day, I walked up to her car and said a neutral sounding 'Hello.' She leaned across to open the passenger side door.

'Going home, right? Come on, get in.'

I was not quite sure how to react. A lift by car, short as it would be, was welcome, and could spare me unwelcome sweat. But I was hardly in the mood for a conversation with anyone. When I declined politely enough, Glynnis would have none of it.

'Oh, come on, Harry. My room is just two doors away from yours. And I know you are angry, but hop in—I need to tell you something.' I obeyed, more because of the persuasive magic in her voice than anything else.

As she drove, she said 'Look, Harry, I know all about the incident in the OT—Dr Seeva Neyson has trouble with all juniors—so don't take it personally. Not one doctor has worked with him long enough to know that even he has a good side to his nature. But you know what? If I were you, I would let him know what stuff you are made of—he is a typical school bully, expects complete control by being brash to start off, but I wonder how he would react if you faced up to him. Think about it, and if you feel like a chat, come over for a cup of tea anytime—the door number is G-11,' she said.

We had already reached the parking space in front of my room—and I hardly had any time to say thanks before she was off to park in front of her own room. I lingered a bit, and she waved oh-so cheerily as she strode towards her room. Her smile was like balm to my wounded ego.

22

The Bengal Tiger Waketh

As I switched on the A/C in my room and flopped into the bed, I was seething with anger. What a contrast between my last few weeks at FST and here! My first reaction was to think of calling Major Kumar or Suresh to complain—but I wasn't sure I could rely on my emotions not getting the better of me. I thought of calling Col. George—but my innate sense of Army discipline said no, I couldn't do that. That would be breach of protocol. And I knew what the correct protocol was and knew very well how to go about it. I had not topped the Basic Military Course in every subject including SD writing (Staff Duties, which teaches the proper way of writing letters in military parlance) for nothing. Soon, I was in my elements. I loved writing, and, like my father, I had a good command over the language the Brits had thrust upon us in 200 years of subjugation. I was suddenly full of energy.

Pulling a sheet of paper, I drafted a letter to Mqm (Lt. Col.) Salim, Commanding Officer of the Hospital, with Cc to Col. George, DDMS, HQ FMS, and on a sudden inspiration, a Cc to the Indian Ambassador as well. The latter had said he wanted us to be ambassadors between India and Oman, right? Then perhaps, he would also ensure we were treated respectfully, as ambassadors ought to be.

I got it right with the third draft. And remembering my father's advice not to ever send off a letter in a hurry, especially when one is angry, I put it aside and turned on some music. Father would say that one had to distract oneself for a while and go back to review what one had written; if possible, get a friend to read it, weigh their advice, and alter the wording if needed before posting it. I decided to do just that. An hour later, after re-reading my draft and making some minor changes, I knocked on Glynnis' door—why I went to her rather than to Sunil and Deepak, I do not know. But I did not regret it then, or over the rest of my time in Oman.

Glynnis opened the door. She looked bewitching in a skirt and top, as all nurses all over the world do when seen unexpectedly in non-hospital garb. Without thinking even for a second, I started my conversation with 'You look beautiful!'

As I stood there, picking up early roots under my feet, she said, 'Well, we beautiful girls don't like waiting at the door, so come on in and elaborate further! Tea?'

'Yes please,' I said, and for the first time, learnt that there are white teas, black teas, with-sugar and no-sugar teas and such like variations. Even as she put the kettle on, I was warming to the subject.

'Look, you said I should let him—Dr Sivanesan, I mean—know who I was, and I have decided to do so. I want you to read a draft letter of complaint I have written and tell me what you think. But first, I want you to promise not to talk about this to anyone else.'

As she stirred the tea bag in a huge mug of hot water, topping it up with about a gallon of cold milk from the fridge, she asked, 'One?'

Perplexed for a second, I recovered when I noticed the sugar container in her hand.

'Yes, please,' I said mentally adding one more piece of English dialogue to my vocabulary.

As we sat sipping the tea, Glynnis read the draft carefully. She reached out and touched my shoulder. For some reason, defying all anatomical rules, I felt tingling sensations being transmitted from the tip of my left shoulder to all other parts of my body.

Then she said, 'Two things, Harry. First, I really appreciate your courage, and more importantly, your honesty in recounting the events. Second, your English is way better than I can ever muster. Henceforth, I am going to take your help with every letter I write—except the ones to my boyfriend,' she said, with a mischievous smile. 'I think you have every right to send this to Mqm. Salim.'

I was already feeling victorious. I could see oldy baldy begging on bended knees for forgiveness. But in all this celebration, the "boyfriend" bit from Glynnis was bothering me, like an aphthous ulcer on the tongue.

Without any hesitation, I submitted my letter first thing next morning at Mqm. Salim's office, slightly relieved that he hadn't come in yet. I had asked Sunil to drop off the copy in Col. George's office. The copy for the Ambassador was just a ruse. I was wondering how my encounter with oldy baldy would go. I needn't have worried. He walked in with a clear war-like intent. My heart started racing, fearing the worst. But I was prepared. I was not going to stand any nonsense. He doesn't want me, I would be more than happy to go back to Out-Patient Department, FST, Thumrait or even Surfayt. Worst comes to worst, they decide to believe him and chuck me out of Oman, I would be most happy to go back to India—and I was prepared to face the consequences of being sent back within the year. But unpleasant as his tone was, it was clear he had not heard anything as of yet about my complaint.

'I say, are we waiting for an auspicious time to start working?' he barked. Before I could react, Sister Selvi, the Sri Lankan nurse in-charge said, 'Capt. Harikrishnan has already done the rounds, and given all instructions, Dr Siva,' she said. But oldy baldy was not impressed.

'So now, I have to simply correct all the mistakes he has made. Right, Selvi?' he said.

Selvi continued in my defence: 'I doubt it very much doctor,' she said. 'I have never worked with a more intelligent doctor,' and she gave me a 'Don't worry, I have this under control' kind of look. While my heart rate was inching closer to fibrillation levels, I was not going to depend on other people's defence of my actions, so I said, coolly, 'Let me assure you, Dr Sivanesan, that this is not the first time I am working in a surgical ward.' Not quite a hot knife into his flesh, but it still stunned him.

'Oh, at least they teach you guys how to be insolent in Indian Medical Schools,' he said, and roughly continued, 'Cut out the familiarity and learn to address me as Sir. Come let us see if they have taught you any surgical sense as well.'

In medicine, a senior can always trip you over things you never even can imagine, however much you read or practise. This is because no textbook can teach you everything that years of experience helps you to pick up. The rounds were trite and difficult, and I was getting hotter and hotter under the collar. Before I could reach boiling point, a surprising thing happened. In walked Glynnis. My heart was in for serious trouble today.

'Hi, *Seeva*,' she said. *Siva? No Dr, no Sir?* I was shocked and surprised. 'Sorry to interrupt, but I just happened to receive a call from Col. George, and he said he would like a word with you as soon as possible.'

'Hi, Harry!' she added, 'hope you are not taking over all surgery from Siva!' She winked at me.

Oldy baldy said, 'These admin fellows know nothing better than to hold meetings! Thank you, Glyn, so sorry they bothered you—the silly chaps could have called here or the OT!'

'No problem at all, Seeva,' said Glynnis, and, looking at me, said, 'I will see you at lunch, Harry! Bye, Selvi,' and off she went, busy as ever.

The rounds finally got over, and Dr Sivanesan left. I was expecting a major outburst from oldy baldy when he returned, as it was quite clear what Col. George would have called him about. But I never saw him throughout the rest of the day, and since there was no major surgery posted in the OT, he didn't come there either. I did a couple of dressings in the minor OT and spent the rest of the time hanging about here and there, till it was time to break for lunch.

In the Officers' Mess, I was delighted to see Major Kumar. Mqm. Ramachandran was there, too, and when I asked how come, they said they were in Muscat for a Unit Commanders' meeting called by Col. George on behalf of the DG–FMS. Apparently, this was held once a quarter. Major Kumar wanted to know if I was getting to do a lot of cutting. Without a moment's hesitation, I poured out my heart to him, not even bothering about Mqm. Ramachandran's presence. I pleaded with Major Kumar to take me back to FST. He said it was not going to be easy, but he would see what he could do. That was good enough for me. Hopeful, I went in for lunch with them, and when Mqm. Ramachandran changed the topic to Carnatic music, I had a very pleasant time, forgetting oldy baldy and his crappy behaviour for the time being.

As usual, I was very early for my breakfast the next morning, but I was surprised to run into the two of them again. They were grabbing a quick bite before going to the airport, having finished their meeting the previous afternoon. I was hoping I would be able to spend some more time with Major Kumar to convince him about taking me back, but as we finished our breakfast, he said, 'Hari, I haven't forgotten your request, but honestly, till some other surgically trained junior is found, I am afraid you are stuck here. But let me tell you this. You will not have any problems with Siva from now on, I assure you.'

'Bloody well he won't,' said Mqm. Ramachandran and they both laughed out aloud.

My disappointment must have been apparent, for Major Kumar said, 'Cheer up, partner, and call me for absolutely anything, okay?' And then the two of them were off to the airport, while I trudged my way to the ward.

The day was rather quiet. I heard from Sister Selvi that Dr Sivanesan had gone for an all-day conference at the MOH—quite obviously, he didn't think of letting me know. I did my day's work, and aware of the temporary freedom, spent the time looking up Sunil and Deepak for a few minutes, but truth be told, I was hoping to catch a glimpse of Glynnis. She was nowhere to be seen.

Suresh called that evening when I was in my room, writing a letter to my sister. He started off with the usual 'How are you, mate?' etc., but soon came to the point, talking mostly in Tamil.

'I believe this Dr Sivanesan has been bothering you a lot?' he asked but continued without waiting for a response. 'It seems Kumar and Mqm. Ram generally sorted him out yesterday after their meeting in FMS. They took him to his office and offered to arrange for free orthopaedic consultation for him just in case he ended up breaking all his bones by taking *panga* with any Seconded AMC officer.' He laughed out aloud. 'Ram and Sivanesan are actually very close—you see, Sivanesan comes to UAG regularly to help with difficult cases— but Ram made it clear to him, too, that the Embassy—both Indian and Sri Lankan—would be informed in writing if he troubles any of our team. Apparently, that fellow had a very bad time when he studied in Madras—and quit midway in his first year, it seems. Seems he later went to Malaysia to do his MBBS before going to the UK for his FRCS. He has apparently borne a life-long grudge against the medical education system in India. Just relax, and don't take any shit from him. Call me or Kumar if there is any problem, but make sure your work is thorough—don't give him any room there.'

I couldn't find the words to thank him—Suresh was continuing to be my big brother, my guardian angel from afar. And how I loved the "free orthopaedic consultation" bit!

Dr Sivanesan was rather cool with me after that day—he hardly spoke to me, addressing most instructions to Selvi. I was called in to assist only when he could not do without an additional pair of hands—most cases he managed with the scrub nurse alone as his assistant. My surgical training was the casualty of this ceasefire.

23

LO Duties to the Rescue

M eanwhile, despite my hopes and prayers, I started getting involved in LO duties. My responsibilities varied from sitting in on important meetings to discuss the number of doctors, dentists, nurses, and other staff likely to be needed in the coming years, to mundane things like leave applications of all seconded staff from the Army Medical Corps. I also had to meet the LO who was responsible for non-medical staff on deputation from the Indian Armed Forces. There were pilots, artillery, engineers and signals officers helping out with the needs of the SOAF (Sultan of Oman's Armed Forces). A myriad of lower-level staff from accountants to storekeepers were on deputation, too—all with a view to help the nascent Omani military to establish itself and become self-reliant. The real big shots everywhere were still the Brits, but they were very few in number. The biggest deputation force was from India.

That apart, I also had to sit in with LOs from other deputationist groups—there were military personnel from Sri Lanka, Pakistan, Iraq, and Egypt other than from India. Luckily, the meetings were few and far between, but it still involved a fair bit of paperwork— copies had to be sent to the FMS, Indian Embassy, Army HQ in India, and so on. Boring as they were, these meetings helped me get away occasionally from oldy baldy, and that was good. But as advised by Suresh, I made sure I did not give oldy baldy any chance to find faults with my work. I would put in extra hours in the wards before and after such meetings, since some of them required my driving to the MOH HQ or the Embassy, both more than 30 to 40 km away.

My hard work in the wards resulted in visible changes in the attitude of the rest of the staff towards me, even those I wasn't working directly with. The kitchen staff, always helpful, would bring me tea and biscuits, hot custard, and so on when I worked late evening hours—I don't remember asking them even once! The medical staff, the nurses, and the pharmacists were extra nice to me, though I must say, they, especially the Omani staff, were uniformly very friendly with everyone. Once, an Omani Sister brought me a special meal—home-made mutton and what have you. I was embarrassed—how do I say no to such affection—yet what do I do with such non-vegetarian food I never ate in my life? I had to pretend I was full, could I please enjoy it later in my room, and then pass it on to my friends who had an appetite for such things.

I was beginning to enjoy my life in Oman, despite the fact that I had not ventured out of the army campus in pursuit of civilian friends, about whom I heard from time to time. Most of the CEOs and CFOs in the corporate sector were of Indian origin, and I was told they had get-togethers once in a while. I wanted to be part of such groups, but right now, there was very little time for all that. The most important reason for my feeling good about everything, despite oldy baldy's cold war tactics, was, without doubt, Glynnis. She would turn up here and there when least expected—and conversation with her was, to say the least, exhilarating. I often wondered what she saw in me—a darky from India, not in her economic class, and a temporary visitor in Oman. I was not a Paul Newman or a Rod Taylor. Not that I was complaining—her company was always very relaxing, and I learnt something new from her every time we met. Once, I asked her where from in England she was.

'Harry!' she said, sounding upset. 'I am NOT English! I am Welsh. My name is one of the most typical, common Welsh names. I thought an intelligent chap like you would have made some effort to find out! And here is where I am from in Wales,' she said, picking up a piece of paper and writing down the name of her town. She had written "Llanyrafon"—which I, with my excellent command of the Queen's English, happily pronounced, '*Il-lan-i-rafon.*'

'I knew it,' she guffawed, flashing her bright teeth as she laughed, sending all sorts of sensations up my spine. 'You poor fish, two Ls together are pronounced 'Cl' in Welsh. I come from Clan-iravon,' she said, also pointing out that the "f" was pronounced "v". If my mistake could make her laugh like this, I thought, I must look for more such mistakes.

There were a few other British nurses in FBH, all very polite and friendly, but Glynnis was different. She seemed perfectly comfortable spending time with Indian doctors, and often, she would be the only girl sitting with four or five of us. She never bragged and was always ready with a smile. And she was super-efficient in the OPD. There was nothing she did not know: where the baby weighing scale was—ask Glynnis; when the consultant physician from the MOH was coming—ask Glynnis—ask her anything, you got an answer immediately. Rarely, she would say she didn't know, but return pretty soon with all needed information and more.

I could see that she certainly enjoyed my company. I dare say there was one area where I scored over Glynnis, but surprisingly, that quality endeared her to me even more! My penchant for remembering numbers surprised most people. Like in FST, it took me hardly any time to see the patterns in the way FBH phone numbers went. All numbers started with 471, and the last three digits were so easy for me to associate with various departments, wards etc., that I was practically a walking phone book. Glynnis would occasionally ask me for some random department number, and I would respond before she even completed her question. This would earn me one of her famous smiles, sometimes a thank-you squeeze of the hand or arm, and I would barely survive the bolts of lightning such physical contacts generated! I started wishing she wouldn't be so damn friendly with everyone, though. She was beginning to change the very way I looked at my surroundings and work.

The person that really did change everything was, most unexpectedly, none other than oldy baldy! He had been away at Salalah for a couple of days—probably operating there, I thought, without caring much more about it—and the day he returned, I was a good ten minutes earlier than usual, not wanting to be caught napping, if you like. After the usual freezing ward rounds, I was just about beginning to breathe easy, when, from the far end of the ward, he called out, 'I say, could you come to my office for a minute?'

I went, heart racing as usual, wondering what it was going to be— was he going to return the offer of an orthopaedic consultation to me in the privacy of his room? I was extremely fit, though not famous for any pugilistic talents. *I would definitely not allow him to abuse me in the privacy of his room, leave alone enter into a scuffle,* I thought, as I knocked on his door.

'Come in,' he said, 'Sit down,' pointing to a chair.

I nearly tripped over—first, there had been this unheard term *'Could you come,'* instead of a rough *'Come here, I say,'* and now, this offer of a seat.

'That's alright, thank you,' I said, taking care to avoid using Sir, which I had vowed never to.

'No, no, sit down. I want to ask you something, I say,' he said. I continued standing.

'Ramachandran tells me you are pretty good with Carnatic music. Why didn't you tell me?'

What? I thought—*where is this musical angle coming from?* Was this a trap?

I decided to take him on: 'Carnatic music does not seem to be part of surgical practice in FBH, Dr Sivanesan,' I said coldly, and added, 'Not that even surgical practice has been much discussed by you with me,' for good measure.

I wanted to stun him into silence, but funnily I found myself choking on the last few syllables. I was the one to be stunned, with his next words: 'I say, no need to be sarcastic, I say. I am sorry and all that, you know,' in a tone I never knew he was capable of. 'Ramachandran says you are some kind of authority on the subject. Have you had any formal training? Vocal or instrumental?' he wanted to know.

I was far from being an "authority", more of a keen enthusiast. Recovering from this unexpected turn of events, I said, 'I am not much of a singer, but I can play the violin. And the flute,' I quickly added, gaining in confidence. 'You also like music?'

'I probably have the largest collection of recordings of concerts by GNB, Chembai, Lalgudi ...' He ticked off the entire list of classical music giants, some of whom were no more alive, but revered greatly by the connoisseurs and lay public alike in south India. I was shocked—I never imagined someone fond of classical music being rude to others without any reason, such was my belief in the pacific influence of perhaps the only system of music totally confined to devotional music. Like Salieri complaining to Jesus about Mozart, I admonished the Carnatic Gods secretly: *you made this—this uncouth, horrible man take a liking to your music?* I couldn't believe Gods could be so erratic.

Before They could explain, Dr Sivanesan did. 'I say, when I was your age, every single holiday, especially during the Madras Music Season in December, I would travel by any means from Jaffna to Madras and listen to as many concerts by the greats as I could. I once sold the watch given to me by my father—a sort of a family heirloom—to get enough money for the two weeks of the Season in Madras. In fact, music was the only reason I chose to study medicine in Madras. You bet I love music!'

I found myself pulling the chair to sit down. The next half hour, consultant surgeon and neophyte surgical apprentice discussed— often interrupting each other to tell an interesting anecdote—only about music, music, and more music. When suddenly, he realised he had other work to do, he got up, and coming around his desk, said, sounding almost reluctant, 'I say, we better stop—I need to see a couple of referrals—some bigwigs from the MOD—but we will catch up soon over dinner at my place. You better scoot now.' And he put his hand on my shoulder!

I could have fainted, so light was I feeling! I sort of dreamily walked towards the ward, not quite sure of what I had just gone through! My first sane reaction was, *I need to find Glynnis!*

I got a call from Mqm. Ramachandran that evening. 'Ha-ha! All sorted, I believe? From sworn enemies to best friends and all that, I hear. You see, yesterday I had him over for dinner. We talked music, and I played that mega *Todi* raga elaboration by GNB. He wanted a copy, and I said, "Why don't you ask Hari? He was the one who made this copy for me and explained the nuances to me." You could have knocked him over with a feather! I knew this would totally change his attitude towards you, man, so sell your music knowledge to him bit by bit in exchange for surgery,' he said, laughing aloud. I was already drawing up a mental list of ragas and artistes in exchange for various surgical procedures.

Thus began the golden period of my stay in Muscat. I hurriedly went back to my Gods to let them know I was far from upset with my not going back as of yet to India.

24

A Surgeon in the Making... Finally!

T here was a dramatic change in the relationships from then on—
not just between Dr Sivanesan ('When we are alone, feel free to
call me Siva, I say!') and me, but my relations with almost everyone,
from Col. George to the hospital carpool in-charge. I found nothing
but oodles of goodness all round. I was practically swimming in the
ocean of milk of human kindness from then on! Dr Sivanesan (the
term Oldy Baldy was banished outright) gave me additional
responsibilities—one such being the selection of what music to play
in the background as we operated!*

One day, he asked me, 'Have you read The Making of a Surgeon?'

'Yes, Sir. I have,' I replied. If Dr Sivanesan was an avid book
reader, then between music and books, I was going to have a really
great time learning surgery from him!

My thoughts were cut short when he asked, 'Which one?'

Which one? How did he mean which one? By the great Professor

---

* Many years later, working as a surgeon in Vavunia camp in Sri Lanka, I connected with the
then retired Dr Sivanesan in Colombo, and we recalled those happy moments in the OT where
we took out gallbladders while Lalgudi Jayaraman regaled us with his silken violin and joined
segments of intestines as Mali elaborated a Kapi on his magical flute! We could not meet due
to the ongoing skirmishes all over Northern Sri Lanka—but he managed to send a set of four
precious concerts from his personal collections through a Sri Lankan army officer known to
him. They are among the few cassettes from the good old days I still refuse to part with, despite
making digital copies.

Ian Aird, of course! He was the surgeon involved in the first-ever surgery for separating conjoined twins in the world. He of the "Companion to Surgical Studies" book, one among the most borrowed books in our college library. But I didn't have to wait to answer.

Dr Sivanesan said, 'You are probably referring to the one by Ian Aird, right? That one reads like a textbook, I say! Rather dry. There is this fictional one, but based on real situations, by an American author called William Nolen. Heard of him?'

I certainly had not. I wanted that book this minute and asked him if he had it.

'Well, I had it, but I have given it to my daughter—she is training to be surgeon in Melbourne,' he said. That he had a daughter who was training in surgery came as a surprise. During my days of animosity with Dr Sivanesan, I always thought of him as a loner, no family ties or feelings, obviously.

'I bought a copy for my son, too, but he is not much of a book reader. He just about reads his surgical textbooks! He trained in Madras, you see!' The sarcasm was showing up again, I thought to myself, but answered evenly:

'I don't know about Madras, Sir, but in my college in Delhi, our library had a separate section on History of Medicine, and there were any number of books on medicine and related matters. We used to fight with each other for getting such books issued,' I lied freely but continued honestly, 'I have read "Brothers Mayo", Sir, by Helen-somebody; I forget her name *(I hadn't but was unsure of the pronunciation of the surname)*, and books by AJ Cronin and Frank G Slaughter as well. There is a famous book shop in a place called Chandni Chowk in Delhi where you can get any book. I am sorry I seem to have missed out on this other book you mentioned.'

'I get the point, young man; I get the point. Good, keep up your parallel reading—it will stand you in good stead,' he said, warmly. I made a note—I must write to my sister, a bookworm like no other, and ask her to buy a copy of this book that had escaped me.

As it happened, I had to wait nearly four years to get my hands on William Nolen's fantastic book, when I got it as a special gift from my beloved on our wedding day. To this day, that wonderful book travels everywhere with me, well-thumbed and savoured many times. This wonderful book, written in 1970 but timeless as far as its relevance is concerned, was my wife's wedding gift to me in 1985. It tells the story of a young surgeon in training in a busy hospital in Brooklyn, New York. Written straight from the heart, its message has always been my guiding light—surgical training is a lifelong process. It is a must read for every aspiring surgeon in the making, as much for its insights into surgical practice as for its lessons in humility.

In the present, though, Dr Sivanesan continued to intrigue me. A lover of music, avid book reader, good surgeon, but what was the reason for his uncalled-for aggression in the beginning? I never did quite find out, and there were many theories to his behaviour, but two things stood out. Despite being a Tamil from Sri Lanka—and they are essentially of Indian stock—he hated most things Indian, certainly its doctors (excepting those who were good in music!). As the days passed, this aspect of his character occupied less and less of my thoughts. The other was the way he took to me: I could as easily have been his son, his protégé, for the way he gave me hands-on training in the art and craft of surgery. Along with Major Kumar and Major Ravi, I owe a lot to Dr Sivanesan for inculcating an abiding interest in me for abdominal surgery, something that would define my lifelong pursuit. I was riding a high, and thoughts of rushing back to India had disappeared from my mind altogether.

25

The Girl Who Wanted Out

That day in the OPD started much the same way as any other day. Dr Sivanesan was away, and I was doing one of my non-surgical clinics. Sagar, one of the "contract" doctors, was in the next room. Almost at the fag end of the morning, Sagar rushed into my room, looking anxious.

'Hey, Hari, could you please come to my room for a sec?' he asked.

I did not have a patient just then, so I walked over. At Sagar's consultation table was an extremely pretty girl, quite obviously Indian, but wearing a proper hijab (the head scarf) and an abaya (the black loose gown worn by Muslim women in Oman). She must have been in her mid-twenties, at the most. Her eyes were extraordinarily bright and attractive. When Sagar introduced me, she spoke in excellent English.

'Hello! Dr Sagar tells me you are from Bangalore. I am from Bangalore too—Malleswaram,' she said.

'Well, yes and no,' I started to explain, but she was not interested. She had her own story to tell.

'Although I am from Bangalore, for the last four years, I have been more or less a prisoner here in Muscat.'

I had entered the room thinking my clinical acumen was going to be tested, and this was totally unexpected. The girl was obviously not given to beating around the bush. She continued with her story.

'You are both army officers, and I desperately need your help. I need to escape from here. I believe you, Dr Harikrishnan, are the Liaison Officer for all Indians with the Embassy. Please help me.' As she said this, she choked on her last words, eyes glistening with impending tears. I gave one look at Sagar which said, *'You bugger, wait till I get to see you separately,'* and, turning to the girl, I said, 'No, that is not quite correct. I am a Liaison Officer *only* for the doctors on deputation from the Indian Army, and that does not include even doctors like Dr Sagar who are on individual contracts with the Omani Army.'

She wasn't one to give up easily. 'How does it matter? I am an Indian citizen. You have contacts with the Indian Embassy. All I am asking is that you take me to the Embassy to meet the Ambassador, and I will manage the rest.'

Hey, I thought, *this is one girl with brains and beauty!* There were a million things that weren't quite right in all this. I needed to buy time—to think this through and break a few bones in Sagar's body.

So, I said, 'I wish I could discuss the matter more thoroughly, but I need to run; my patient is already on the table in the OT.' (I gave Sagar another look which said, *'Say anything contrary and you will be one head short.'*)

Sagar rallied around, 'Oh, that appendix patient?'

'Yes,' I said, 'I think it has perforated.' I decided to spare one bone from Sagar's body for this help, but just one.

'I tell you what, Dr Sagar, why don't you give this young lady…'

'My name is Priya,' the girl interrupted.

'Why don't you give Ms Priya…'

'Mrs Priya Al Zubaidi,' she interrupted again.

'Why don't you give Mrs Priya Zubaidi an appointment for some time next week and get all her details meantime? Nice meeting you,' I said and bolted from there before she could interrupt me again. I hid in the OT and sent an envoy from there—one of our OT assistants—to tell Dr Sagar to come over to help with the surgery. That I probably would help him escape from his room was only a small part of my plan. I needed to find out what kind of mess he had gotten himself—and me—into. When he came after a few minutes and started to thank me for bailing him out, I cut him short.

'Shut up now, and tell me what this is all about.'

Sagar practically broke down as he spilled the story. It seems this girl had walked in first time about two weeks back with complaints of tummy pain. Sagar had done the needed clinical evaluation but found nothing serious. He didn't say it, but I could make out that he had "gone beyond the call of duty" and asked her to come back a few times—how often does one get a beautiful, intelligent-sounding patient in one's clinic? Apparently, after a few visits, she had confessed that she actually had no health issues, she merely wanted to spend time away from home. Most Omani women could easily ask to go to see the "Tabeeb" (doctor) by themselves. Indeed, we all knew this and had seen a lot of women visiting the OPD with their assorted kids, with little to no serious complaints. It had never occurred to Sagar to find out why an obviously Indian-looking girl with a very non-Muslim name was coming to the hospital dressed in Arabic clothes. Talk of love being blind!

It seems that was the first time he found out she was "married and all". She had started to cry and wanted help, so our dear doctor immediately thought of involving the LO (for "all Indians"). When I asked him about the "all Indians" bit, he said he actually meant only all Indian doctors in the hospital but had been misunderstood. Anyway, he had got rid of her for the day, and given her an appointment a week later, the next Wednesday. And what did he plan to do next Wednesday? I asked. He said he was planning on taking leave! I cancelled my previous offer of sparing one of his bones and threatened to add a few more to the list if he dared to dump this girl on me and run. He surprised me with his answer.

'No, Boss, I have agreed to buy a ticket for her and will take her with me to India and leave her there. That's all she wants,' he said.

She had met this Omani chap in a cultural exchange programme some years back in Bangalore, while she was still in college. It was love at first sight, apparently, and she had been in touch with him for a few months, before informing her very orthodox parents that she wanted to marry him. Naturally, the parents had promptly put her on house arrest. She then decided to run away from home, aided and abetted by this Mr Zubaidi. Within minutes of landing in Oman, she got her first shock—Mr Zubaidi was already married—to *two* Omani ladies! Then she was instructed on wifely duties—no going anywhere by herself, follow the local dress code, etc. The other two wives had no objection to her—she was simply the third wife of their husband. Zubaidi also was very kind and generous—she simply had to ask for anything she wanted, and it was arranged immediately—anything except permission to run away, that is.

'She is really suffering, man; after all, it was a mistake, she didn't even know he was married, otherwise I am sure she would have never run away from home and country,' said Sir Lancelot Sagar, the self-appointed defence counsel. He was obviously besotted with this girl—I couldn't blame him—she was really quite beautiful with a figure to match, but I asked him if he was aware of the death penalty in Oman for attempted kidnapping. That brought him up quite short! He sat down and was about to cry.

'Please help me, man. My mom will kill me if I get arrested or something,' he said. I assured him that was unlikely, because he would probably be hanged from the nearest tree well before his mom could lay her hands on him. The reality hit him hard. Now, he wanted me to take *him* to the embassy, if possible, this very minute!

I thought long and hard that evening about the right thing to do. First, I needed more information. Would it be fair to let down a fellow Indian, however stupid her actions, when she was so desperately in need of help? Should I not discuss this with Col. George—or Suresh at least? Maybe I could find out from the

Embassy if any contingencies existed for such persons as this Priya? Full of contradictory thoughts, I decided to talk to Suresh first. But something or the other kept getting in the way, and I couldn't get through to him that evening. Anyway, I had time till next Wednesday, I thought. But no such luck.

The next morning, the first person I met as I crossed the OPD lobby on my way to the wards was Ms—sorry, Mrs Priya Al Zubaidi, of course. I pretended to be extra busy, and walked right past her, just about acknowledging her 'Hello, doctor,' and escaped to the wards. About an hour later, I was called to the OPD as a patient was waiting to see me. I came to the OPD reception desk—it wasn't even my clinic day—and learnt how gullible I was—the Omani girl at the desk pointed towards another Omani girl—a Mrs Priya Al Zubaidi. Before I could begin to protest, the receptionist said, 'Dr Sagar has called in sick, Sir, and the patient said she was happy to consult you.' Happy indeed! *Well, Sagar won't be happy,* I said to myself, especially since I just increased the number of bones I would break in his ugly body.

Unable to escape, I asked to see the patient in my room. She was rather talented, was this Mrs Priya Al Zubaidi. She profusely thanked me for seeing her and said that she knew she could count on a fellow Bangalorian to help her, and promptly started telling me the gory details of her life—which I already knew. Apparently, not all of it, though. She said that she was ready to go this very minute—without any bags, even any change of clothing, to the Embassy. Why, she was even willing to leave behind her three-year-old daughter, she added, sort of knocking me off my feet in the process! My face must have revealed all, for she said she had not had the "courage" to tell Dr Sagar about her daughter, for fear of his refusing to help her. She said she knew I was more mature and understanding. *Like hell,* I thought to myself, although I didn't quite mind the compliment about being mature. She had it all planned out, she added. Once she landed in Bangalore, she would fall at her parents' feet and beg to be forgiven. She was sure they would—she was, after all, their only child—and then, with her father's help, she would file a legal petition for getting her daughter away from the clutches of the crooked Mr Zubaidi, and then live happily ever after with her child, till she found someone mature and understanding to accept her. I suddenly didn't like my being mature at all.

Inspiration (or, in this instance, the ability to lie convincingly) comes to us when we least expect it, and most need it. This was such a moment for me. I kept a straight face and told her that Col. George, the big boss, had told me only yesterday evening when I went to discuss her case with him that a similar instance had happened three years back, and the officers involved had been severely reprimanded for breach of military code of conduct. He had wanted to have all her details to pass on to the military as well as civil police for further action. I was glad to be able to tell her all this, I added, so that she could avoid being arrested for attempting to escape and promised not even to reveal that I had seen her today. Not one to be easily put off, she tried pleading with me, appealing to the gentleman in me, the fellow Indian in me, the very human trait in me, and asked quite innocently if she would be sent to an Indian jail on being arrested. I assured her that it would be an Omani jail, and that I was aware the jails here were dark and dingy, and the food horrible. She then said she would have no other option left but to commit suicide, and her death would be entirely on me. Sagar was totally out of the picture now, I realised. It was just mature Harikrishnan who was in the line of fire. Hard as it sounded even to me, I told her that what she chose to do with her life had been her choice some years back in Bangalore, and it was again her choice now.

'I am sorry,' I said, 'I am first and foremost a soldier, and am duty bound to follow rules and regulations.'

There was a perceptible change in her language from then on, especially when she gave her opinion about cowardly Indian Army doctors. After impressing me a lot with her stock of expletives, she stormed out of my room, eyes all wet. I never saw her again. Nor, I think, did young Dr Sagar. Over the years, I have often wondered if she did manage to escape, or simply became an Omani matriarch with her own brood of kids and grandkids. I never did find out.

26

Friends in Civvy Street

A round this time, we had one other Sri Lankan consultant join us as a surgeon. Dr Sivanesan and he seemed to know each other from before—indeed, Col. George said the new surgeon—Dr Maharoof—was practically appointed because of Dr Sivanesan's recommendation. Work had started to increase—we were getting referrals from the entire north and west of the country—and not just soldiers, many civilian patients came to us, too. The FST in Salalah, one thousand kilometres to the south, was taking care of the lower one-third of the country. I was getting fairly overworked but didn't mind it, as I was also getting a lot more cutting to do. I got a fright, though, when one day, a new chap showed up at morning rounds—a Dr Wickramasingha—another Sri Lankan. He was a contract doctor, which explained how I, as LO, had not known about his arrival. I was worried, and with reason. Was another leave relief duty in the offing for me? When I spoke to Col. George the next day, he sensed my anxiety.

'Well, I have a lot of requests from all over for doctors, Hari,' he said. My heart sank. But he quickly added, 'Sivanesan is a terrible fellow. He has put down his foot and said you are not to be removed. I wonder how this total turnaround in your association came about.'

I was extremely relieved. I knew he must be aware of everything—after all, both Suresh and Mqm. Ramachandran chatted with him almost daily on the phone. But I was too thrilled to care about his sources.

A couple of weeks after Dr Maharoof joined us, Dr Sivanesan went on leave—I would have liked to go on leave then, too, but I realised that unlike most of my colleagues who had taken their leave as soon as they completed six months, I had to wait for my full year to be over before I could ask for leave. I didn't mind too much. All I worried about was how to continue to get surgery to do, now that young Dr Wickrama was there among the ranks.

Dr Sivanesan's absence and Wickrama's presence meant I had plenty of spare time. Most of my evenings were free. My social life started to blossom! Glynnis and I started to see a fair bit of each other. It was clear she liked my company, while on my part, I was constantly hungry for it. She had absolutely no airs about her, something most Indians automatically expect from the white races. She knew Muscat well, so we went off—sometimes with one or two other idiots, sadly, to see the beautiful palace near Old Muscat town where I had gone for the National day dinner last year, at other times to see some old forts and ruins in nearby towns. Luckily, one Friday morning, we managed to go, just the two of us, to one of the many beautiful beaches in Muscat, and had a beachside breakfast of sandwiches and fruits and some coffee. I was totally impressed by Glynnis' thoughtfulness—she had packed a beach mat, towels, and even a bin bag. She was used to swimming in the open sea (being from an island, I told myself). I was the exact opposite—scared stiff, I refused to be drawn by her, and stood around admiring her till, bored of being alone, she came back to join me.

'I will make you swim yet, dear Dr Harikrishnan, well before you finish with FMS,' she said. For the first time, it occurred to me that I would miss her company terribly when I would be done with my deputation in Muscat. I asked her what her own plans were. She wanted to stay on as long as the FMS would have her, since the money was good.

'What about marriage and settling down and all that sort of stuff?'

I asked.

'Settle down where?' she asked. 'India?' I was totally at a loss for words, but she was laughing. 'Don't worry, Harry, I wasn't making a pass at you,' she said. I should have said, 'You could if you want to,' or 'I wish you would,' or any number of such smart things, but the moment passed, and I said nothing. I was beginning to like this girl a lot and had started to occasionally imagine being with her for the rest of my life. The very idea was absurd, I knew, but I couldn't help thinking about it time and again. Surprisingly, Glynnis was also somewhat silent as we finished our breakfast and packed to leave before the sun became too strong to bear. We had already planned to stop at the Ruwi marketplace before the shops closed at noon for prayers, as both of us wanted to pick up a few things—including the first civilian friends in Oman for me, in a most unexpected fashion.

27

The Magic of M S

Glynnis and I were about to get into the car after our shopping in Ruwi when the magical voice of M S Subbulakshmi from the building nearby stopped me in my tracks. M S? Singing her inimitable version of *Hanuman Chalisa* here, in the middle of an Islamic country! M S Subbulakshmi, or simply M S, was undoubtedly the most renowned Indian singer, a household name in all of South India and most parts of the north as well. She was equally well known for her classical singing as for her devotional music. I simply had to know who was listening to this wonderful music. My hesitation, if any, disappeared as I heard the voice of a girl, may be eight or nine by the sound of her, talking to someone in the typical Tamil of Palghat—my father's native place. 'Are you coming or not now?' she was saying, obviously to a sibling. 'I am going up now—Mummy will get angry otherwise.' I simply had to know who these people were!

I said to Glynnis, 'Please, Glyn, could I just say hello to the people here?' It was a measure of Glynnis' understanding that she did not find anything wrong with a grown-up Indian male wanting to simply walk into a stranger's house for some ridiculous reason.

'Go ahead, Harry,' she said, I will be in the car.'

It was a block of apartments, some six storeys tall. A pretty little girl was standing at the threshold of the ground floor flat, looking a bit upset. The door was ajar, and a handsome young man appeared as I approached it.

'Yes?' he said, obviously wondering who I was.

I put on my most impressive smile. 'Hello, my name is Captain Harikrishnan,' I said. 'I work in the Army Hospital at Seeb. I am new here in Muscat and was delighted to hear M S Subbulaksmi's *Hanuman Chalisa* being played, and –'

'I know it by heart,' said the little girl. I was surprised and happy to hear her response.

'Oh, that's really good,' I said, sounding impressed. Not many children her age would know all 40 couplets of this great song in praise of Lord Hanuman. I extended my hand to the young man at the door, who gave it a warm, full handed shake.

'Hi, I am Siddhant, please come right in,' he said.

I hesitated. 'That's okay, so kind of you, but I am with a friend— I mean, a colleague, and I was just so surprised to hear the music, my curiosity got the better of me! I will come some other time. Look, as I said, I am an Army doctor, but I am also a terrific Carnatic music enthusiast, and when I saw this little girl…' but the little girl was not there! As I looked around, I saw that she was having a happy conversation with Glynnis! This was getting a bit out of hand, I thought. Meantime, a little boy, obviously the brother of the little girl, appeared behind Siddhant, a Lego toy in his hand, and came directly to the point:

'Who are you?' he wanted to know.

I came to attention. 'Captain Harikrishnan, Sir,' I said, 'And who may you be?'

A lady, quite obviously Siddhant's wife, joined the party now.

'Sid, aren't you going to call the gentleman in?' she admonished her husband.

Meanwhile, the matter was definitely getting out of hand. The little girl was leading Glynnis by her hand, announcing, 'Uncle Sid, look; there is an English girl here,' as if she were some rare object. I agreed with the rare bit, honestly, but was worried about Glynnis being called English—*not a great start if you want to be friends with her, little girl,* I said silently. Well, we all trooped in, and in the space of the next 30 minutes, we had tea, followed by freshly made Dosas and awesome coconut chutney, and I was amused yet impressed to see Glynnis eating the Dosas with her hand, like a seasoned Indian! We had meantime been joined by Indu's (that was the little girl's name) parents—they lived just two floors above the Siddhant's. The little boy turned out to be Arvind, and everyone was speaking at the same time—they were all great music enthusiasts, they had a sizeable group and often had singing sessions ('I always sing two songs,' Indu let me know just for the record), I was most welcome to attend, why don't we stay on for lunch (after the Dosas!) and so on. Acutely aware of the passing time, I asked to be excused, after exchanging phone numbers with Siddhant and Gopal (little Indu's father). Glynnis was deep in conversation with Indu and her brother about something very important, for sure.

As we got into the car, I was genuinely apologetic.

'I am so sorry, Glyn,' I began, but she cut me short.

'Don't be silly, Harry! For what? I have never had so much fun— more than what I had with a certain doctor who refuses to get into the water in a beach! Jokes apart, what loveable kids! And they speak such good English. And the *dussass!* Finger-licking tasty, oh God, but for you rushing me, I would have had at least two more. Shanti was most eager to feed me.' *My, my,* I thought, *Glyn even knows Sid's wife's name!* But then, such is the standard hospitality in any Indian home—where even today, we go by the philosophy of *"Atithi Devo Bhava"*. Guests are like Gods. *And white-skinned Gods are even better*, I thought!

Thus started my association with the large Indian community in Muscat. I was always welcome—for one, I was not shy of conversation, I was good with kids, using my small stock of Origami knowledge to full effect when needed. I was reasonably well informed in matters of Carnatic music, and, even if I say so myself, I wasn't too bad in terms of my landscape—there was a nice sharp nose, derived from my father, a smart, lush Army moustache derived from my upper lip, and at 5 feet 8, I wasn't a midget either. And the Army training had conditioned my body pretty well—I wasn't exactly a threat to Sean Connery or Paul Newman, but my tummy was flat, and biceps reasonable. But strength, goodness, or frailty is up to the observer.

I suspect the reason I was so welcome in many Indian homes in Muscat was another typical Indian trait—that of matchmaking, as soon as a reasonably eligible bachelor is seen on the horizon. And I was eligible in more ways than one. An Indian Army Captain was always a good catch—one on foreign soil, even better. It was common knowledge that Omani Army paid their officers a lot more than most private companies paid their CEOs (sans bonuses and things, I admit). And one who is good enough to impress a white girl and go about town in cars? Boy, this was certainly *the* Boy, for the younger sister or niece or cousin back home! During the rest of the two and a half years or so, I made the most of my status! Yes, I ended up spending my full term in Oman and some. But enough about me. Sunil and Deepak, my comrades in arms, are waiting to tell you about their adventures!

The Second Muscat Year

1

The Second Muscateer: Sunil

The rest of our first year in Oman whizzed past at terrific pace. I spent all of the remaining year—up to September 1981—in FBH, growing ever so fond of Glynnis and (hopefully) she of me. The good living and creature comforts were making me less and less of a challenge to Sean Connery in terms of my waistline. But as I promised, here is what Sunil was up to all this while:

Sunil was from Sitapur, a small town near Lucknow, Uttar Pradesh, in India. His was a large family—he was the eldest of five siblings. His father was a teacher in the local high school and had been a freedom fighter during India's Independence struggle. A true Gandhian, he had brought up his kids in his image—only khadi dresses and steeped in patriotism. Apparently, he was a strict man, too—prayers at home in the morning, mandatory temple visits in the evening on most days, and so forth. Sensing his eldest child's potential, he had decided Sunil would study medicine and steered his education appropriately. Luckily, the family finances were not stretched in any way by Sunil needing additional coaching for his medical entrance exam. He sailed through his school finals with flying colours and was given admission in King George's Medical College, Lucknow. It was one of the oldest and most reputed medical colleges of the country, from pre-Independence days.

By the year 1971, when Sunil joined the college, Lucknow had become a huge, modern city with expected changes in the attitude and attire of people. There were numerous English medium schools, many of them with European type uniforms for children. Sunil, on the other hand, had studied all through in a Hindi medium school, run by the Government along Gandhian lines—his father's choice. Sunil would recount how, on his first day of college, he was one of less than a handful of new students who came dressed in kurta pyjamas, the standard way of dress in most rural areas and small towns. He had no concept of the trouser-shirt way of dressing, and immediately stood out as a *dehati*—a village bum. That he was top of the admission list did not help in the least. He was labelled *"Babuji Sunil"* on Day One, a title that stayed with him till his graduation day. The seniors insisted he wear an Indian flag around his shoulders all through the first few months—those days, ragging was rampant, and this was a bright idea of one of the seniors. This led to his being also called "Babuji Sunil Jhandewale", but apparently, this disappeared from people's memories by the time he entered clinical medicine in Year Three—but the original label stayed with him. He never took any interest in extracurricular activities—he had never even thought about them in his school days, thanks to his father's idea of discipline. Having no other avenue to spend his energies, he channelled them all into his studies and picked up every medal that was on offer, leaving a big gap between him and the second rankers. He would say that this got him the grudging admiration of his class fellows.

Over the years in college, he picked up some good friends—mostly those who needed his help to get through exams. There was this one girl, from a background not very different to his, who seemed very fond of him. When he told us this bit, we were all excited—we wanted to know more. Sunil simply said that there wasn't any more. She was fond of him, showing it in various ways—a smile here, a look there, her vote for him in the college elections when they were in Year Four. Sunil stood for College Secretary, and with her vote, he managed to get to double figures, but the winner polled a few hundred votes more than him! Soon, the course came to an end, most graduated and scrambled for postgraduate admissions, while Sunil took only one exam—Army Medical Corps Direct Recruitment Examination for Permanent and Short Service Commission (which I also had taken) because that was the only thing his father would have him do. He sailed through that as well and joined the Army like I did. The girl in question got married promptly after (or during, he didn't quite know), the mandatory internship prior to graduation, and even more promptly got pregnant.

When he joined the AMC, she was already into her second pregnancy! They never talked or dated, taking their likes and emotions their way as they parted. This may sound very peculiar in today's time to most readers, including those brought up entirely in Indian conditions. We of the last generation were quite familiar with such things. I had no problem at all in accepting his decisions—in many ways, we were from very similar backgrounds, and running around with a girl during college days was unthinkable—it never occurred to most, and if such an aberration did come up, our impecunious status snuffed it out fairly quickly. Unlike me, Sunil had absolutely no interest in books or music. His command of English was fairly restricted to medical parlance—he wasn't the sort you wanted to go asking for a clue to your morning crossword puzzle.

So here was this fairly-rural Indian, a commissioned officer in the world's largest military medical force, now on deputation to Oman—entirely on his merits. Deepak and I were sure when we started our tenure in Oman that young Sunil Babuji would remain a *Babuji* physician despite all the riches we were now being exposed to. How hasty was our conclusion!

2

From Babuji to Gentalman!

Just as I had said I wanted to work in surgery, Sunil had requested to be given a chance to work in Medicine when Col. George had interviewed us all. He had been assigned to work with the only consultant physician in FBH, a very handsome English chap by the name Philips, whom we all found very peculiar. He was polite enough when anyone crossed him in the corridors of the hospital or in the Officers' Mess, but he never quite got on with anyone. He never smiled or indulged in chit-chat with even the seniors. Unlike Dr Sivanesan, though, he was prim and proper, always seen with a tie and a spotless white coat. He was never known to say a harsh word to anyone and was every bit the gentleman with his patients. I don't remember him ever going on leave. He would be always available in his room just outside the medical wards, and when there were any referrals of a surgical patient for his opinion, we could expect him to see our patient within a few minutes. When Sunil started off with him, Deepak and the others, who were in FBH, would wonder how long Sunil would last—given his typical English grammar and pronunciation.

But Dr Philips was able to see beyond Sunil's language issues. By the time I returned to FBH in March 1981, the story was that Sunil had become a kind of appendage of Dr Philips. They were always together, and soon, I discovered that every day, they had a morning meeting for about 10 to 15 minutes in Dr Philips' room before going to the wards for their rounds. Sunil told us these were called "Card Rounds", apparently a regular practice even amongst surgical teams in the UK. On the few occasions Dr Philips came to our wards to see surgical referral patients, Sunil would be there with him, too. They would talk in hushed tones, and I could notice that Dr Philips' attitude towards Sunil was that of an equal professional—not as if Sunil were his personal aide. In the early days when Dr Sivanesan and I were constantly sparring, this bonding between Dr Philips and Sunil used to stand out like a sore thumb. In the Outpatients, Dr Philips from very early on had insisted on Sunil sitting in a separate room and seeing his patients independently. This was creditable, and very soon, Sunil was treated on par with Dr Philips by all concerned.

However, as my own relations with Dr Sivanesan thawed and blossomed, I started to be invited to his house. All consultants were given huge villas with a dedicated gardener, cook, and driver. Dr Sivanesan and I would talk mostly of music, and with each such visit, I started learning a lot about the stalwarts in Carnatic music, thanks to Sivanesan's close association with many of them since his graduate days. Sunil, on the other hand, had a wonderful senior to work with in the hospital, but who never once asked him home or sat with him at the same table at lunch or dinner. Come 4 p.m., Dr Philips disappeared, available to come to hospital in case of any call-out from the Casualty, but he simply ceased to exist socially after working hours.

Sunil and he started sharing calls on alternate days and weekends—another sign of how highly Sunil was thought of from the very beginning. If Sunil was on call and he needed a second opinion, Dr Philips would be in the hospital within minutes—day or night— without any fuss whatsoever. But once the professional part was done, he would leave as quickly and quietly as he had come. It was obvious to us all that his refusal to mingle socially was not due to some drinking problem or some other unspeakable habit. He was not known to spend time chit chatting with any of the Brits, including the girls. Sunil suspected he spent all his time writing up papers. It seems that on one rare occasion, he had quizzed Sunil all about tuberculosis in India and had expressed a desire to be involved in the management of any tuberculosis patients Sunil got to see. It was not an uncommon disease in Oman (as in the UK), and Sunil knew everything there was to know about the condition, much more than any of us. Often, we would catch Sunil in his room poring over his copy of Harrison's Principles of Internal Medicine, the bible of all physicians. It was the most popular and most trusted book on General Medicine all over the world. No wonder the two of them got along! But as I said, the association started and ended at the gates of the hospital. Then, and later on, too, we never once saw Dr Philips ever go beyond professional relationship with anyone. For the rest of us, it was fine; we couldn't care. But we all felt Sunil was being cold shouldered by Dr Philips, despite all the status he granted to him as a near equal. *Peculiar indeed.*

Around this time—early part of 1981, the transformation of Babuji Sunil into *Gentalman* Sunil (this was one of the many areas Sunil's grip over the language got him into trouble—he could never say gentleman, even if we corrected him. It was always *Gen-Tal-Man* for him!). First thing to change about him was his glasses. He wore his glasses in very typical, round, reddish hued frames—something Bollywood movies had made a trademark ornament for teachers and professors. None of us noticed anything odd about it, though, for such frames were extremely common in those days in India. But oh, boy did we notice the change when it happened! One fine day at breakfast, in walked young Sunil wearing new glasses, with very thin, gold-rimmed frames. It actually lit up his face. He looked far more professorial with these than his standard Bollywood teacher's glasses.

Capt. Banerjee, a deputationist who had been in Muscat for about six months when we arrived, well known for his quick wit, remarked, 'Sunil, wow! You look *almost* intelligent, man!' making all of us burst out laughing.

'That's the idea, pardner,' said Sunil, smiling in his disarming way.

The glasses set in motion a series of other changes to our man from Sitapur. In the outpatient clinic that day, the Filipino nurse who ran his clinic for him was reportedly stunned by his appearance.

She apparently said something like 'You are looking beautiful in your new glasses, Doctor Sunil,' and, true or not, Sunil said he replied with 'Thank you, I bought this only to impress you.'

Thus started another new aspect of this *couldn't-hurt-a-fly* boy from rural India. His association with a *Filipino* girl shot Sunil to great fame amongst us all. At one point, he confessed in a sort of accusatory tone that I was responsible for the whole thing. He said that for all my *"occasional"* friendship with Glynnis, he had known from Day One that I had flipped for her at first sight, and he didn't want to be left behind! Glynnis herself, much to my chagrin, gave Sunil a big hug in the Mess that evening, congratulating his brand-new looks. *Why did she need to hug him?* I thought angrily. Later on, Sunil told me something that made me feel better. Apparently, the champion idiot had thanked Glynnis for noticing his good looks but wondered if she could help him improve his English.

She had told him, 'You don't need me, Sunil. Ask Harry—he is far better.'

I was relieved—not because she had approved of my command of the language—she had said that to me many times already—but because she had not agreed to spend time with Sunil. No doubt he would have tried to woo her, and it would be un-officer like for me to maim or murder him. I made it a point to actively encourage Sunil's affections for Kristine, his clinic nurse.

3

India Gets Colour Conscious

I n the first week of April that year (1982), the Indian Government declared that colour television sets could be imported for a small, fixed customs duty, and anyone living abroad could send such TV sets to family as well as friends. This was a very clever move with an eye on the Asiad Games that were to be held in Delhi around November. First held in New Delhi in 1951, the Asian Games or Asiad was a showcasing of the sovereignty of Asian countries post Second World War. India was hosting it for the second time now, and the changing social standards were an occasion for reaching the spectacle of the games to a larger population. With more and more people owning television sets—all black and white, due to the broadcasting facilities available then—the Indian Government had decided to go all colour for the occasion. The government was, therefore, encouraging people to invest in colour television sets. Although some rumours had been going around for a couple of weeks, I, the LO, was the proud bearer of the official news after a meeting called by the ambassador to explain what all this involved. Anyone could send a colour television set to a family member or a friend in India—but the flat 40% customs duty had to be paid by the sender at the airport customs checkpoint. TV sets were still heavy things, and the biggest screen going around at that time was about 24 inches. Most TVs in India were still in the 14-to-16-inch range, and of course black & white. Within days, we started getting letters asking for colour sets to be sent, please, cost no problem. Sure, cost would have to be borne by us, including the 40% extra for duty!

There was a flurry of activity in the evenings, with people racing off in their cars to Ruwi market for purchase of TV sets. I was excited, too, and immediately wrote letters to my sisters and brother—would they want one?

It had taken me one year of army service to buy the first ever black and white television for my parents—they were staying with my brother those days. The screen often would go blank but responded to a sharp slap on its sides. Often, in the middle of a programme, some alien creatures, snake-like things from outer space, would invade the sets. They waited for a dip in the voltage to take over our sets. We would have to switch off the sets, and hope and pray they would go away when the voltage picked up. They usually did. Not that their going away made the watching a better experience. There was usually some poor sod standing in front of the camera, reading from sheets of paper about the weather or detailing some insipid news. There was, of course, only one channel. When the programme changed, it moved to other absorbing topics like farming and the use of good quality manure for getting better crops. The only entertainment was the much-awaited Sunday evening movie—an occasion when one's social worth was clearly established. Since everyone did not have a TV, those who did clearly belonged to the upper strata of society. Invitations to neighbours were issued after much discussion about their worth, and plans were made in advance to keep out the street urchins who would try to sneak in. But more than all this, what I remembered was my father often going to the local TV repair shop with the heavy TV carefully balanced on a cycle rickshaw. I think the TV, like his mono tape recorder, saw as much of the repair shop as it did our drawing room!

TV sets were not cheap. Sunil and I, from rather similar financial backgrounds, were seriously keen on sending one, if possible two, sets home. With the duty added, a 14-inch TV set cost well over 200

Omani riyals or over 5200 Indian rupees. Luck was on our side. The SOAF (Sultan of Oman's Armed Forces) campus where we stayed had a Services Canteen where they sold all sorts of things—TV sets included. But despite discounts, it was still over 160 to 180 riyals for the basic set. Better, larger ones cost upwards of 250 riyals. I was willing to spend the money and was therefore surprised when I received a reply from my brother. *No TV,* he wrote, *we can manage without a colour TV for now, the Asiad games will be equally good in black & white. What we can do with is a new scooter. My Lambretta is 8 years old and keeps giving trouble. The Government has started a new scheme, under which a Bajaj Chetak scooter—export quality, will be issued on priority basis to those who can deposit 6000 rupees in foreign currency. If you have the money, you should book one for yourself, too—you will need one when you get back after your deputation.*

Reflecting on what he had written, I thought it made sense. When I put it to Sunil, he was able to see the financial sense in my brother's suggestion. He said he would offer his father the option, too. But strangely, it so happened that he did send a colour TV home, because his father felt the TV set was a better option! And I dished out 400 plus riyals from my savings—meant for various purchases including a car I was eyeing—so that we could book two scooters, one on my name and one on my brother's. I think this was one of the few good things I did for my family.

For the record, host India came fifth in the Asiad Games medals tally, and China and Japan tied in terms of total medals, but China had more gold medals and was hence right on top. Both had approximately 100 medals more than India! Pakistan did okayish, while Sri Lanka and Oman returned empty handed.

4

Orchestrating the Music Connection

T he day after Dr Sivanesan re-joined from leave, he invited me home for dinner. I hazarded a question: did he want me to bring young Wickramasingha, too? I thought this might be one of those surgical fraternity things; besides, Wicky was a Sri Lankan as well. But a bit of the old Dr Sivanesan surfaced.

'I say, if I want to call him or Reagan or anyone else, I will let you know well in advance, I say. Just come by yourself. Seven thirty.' When I landed a few minutes before the appointed time, Dr Sivanesan was at the door to receive me. At home, like on previous occasions, he was a genial man. He would talk about his daughter, son, his wife—who turned out to be a biochemistry professor back in Sri Lanka—and of course, plenty of music. He would reminisce about his trips to Madras, and his personal meetings with the greats of Carnatic music.

Today, it was all about his trip to the USA. Suddenly, he asked me, 'Have you heard Yesudas's *Bhagavad Gita*?' I knew all about the Bhagavad Gita, the great discourse between Lord Krishna and Arjuna just before the battle of Kurukshetra. I knew a fair bit about K. J. Yesudas. The fact that he was a devout Christian who also sang Carnatic music, coupled with his already huge popularity as a leading playback singer in many Indian languages, had made him one of the most admired singers in all of India. But I knew nothing about his connection to Bhagavad Gita. I confessed as much to Dr Sivanesan.

'Time for your education outside of surgery, I say,' he said jokingly. He went to his study and was back in a second. There was a sizeable, gift-wrapped packet in his hands.

He gave it to me and said, 'This is for you. Go on, Open it.'

When I did, my heart leaped with joy. There were two TDK cassettes, one titled "Bhagavad Gita—Chapter II by K J Yesudas, Music by R Parthasarathy". The other was similar, except it said, "Chapters XII and XV". But happy and intrigued as I was by these, my heart was already elsewhere. The packet also included two Long Play (LP) vinyl records—by my all-time favourite musician, the late G. N. Balasubramaniam, affectionately called GNB by all his fans.

'I know you like GNB a lot,' Dr Siva said. 'I believe you lectured Ram in Salalah about him for hours together! These two are special edition LPs released by my friend Parthasarathy—the one who has arranged music for the Bhagavad Gita as well.' He pointed to the Yesudas cassettes, 'And entirely at his own expense, mind you. Talk of devotion to music, man!'

I didn't know what to say to this doctor, old enough to be my father, who started off by treating me like dirt, and now was behaving exactly as my father would have—except my father could never have afforded to give me such expensive gifts. But even as I thought that, I realised my father had indeed given me a priceless gift—that of the ability to appreciate what was perhaps the greatest musical heritage of the world—and I knew that gift would stay and grow with me till my last breath. I hoped Dr Siva would not see the mixed reasons behind my eyes going wet all of a sudden. As we went in for dinner, I recovered from the mountain of emotions, and we hardly noticed the food we were eating, so busy we were; an elderly consultant and a wannabe surgeon, blissfully enjoying anecdotes about music and musicians. I drove back to my room and planned to visit my civilian friends on the morrow to show off my newfound treasures. I also needed urgent access to a turntable for playing the LPs.

5

Untying the Knot to Tie the Knot

One day, Sunil called me when I was just changing back into my uniform after a couple of minor cases in the operation theatre.

'I have an interesting patient for you,' he said. 'It's a *gora* and he has had a vasectomy.'

'So? What's so great about that? It is quite common all over the world. He has fathered a baby and is in trouble, is he?' I interrupted, not quite interested in failed vasectomies and things like that. During my internship days in Delhi, I had been involved in a lot of vasectomy camps. In the mid 70s, the Indian Government started a serious Family Planning campaign as a burgeoning population threatened to destroy its economic efforts. Most religions do not believe in curbing pregnancies, as childbirth is considered an act of God. Some sects, like Catholics and Muslims around the world, oppose family planning to this day. Hindus also bless newly marrieds to have plenty of children. But then, in the bygone era, it was important for the survival of the family line to produce as many children as possible—some would die of illnesses, many of them before reaching the age of one*, and it was hoped one or more will somehow survive to adulthood. But a galloping population would have the same negative effect on survival, as it would affect the per

---

* Infant mortality rate in pre-independence India was close to 200 per 1000 live births or one in every five babies born. The population, meanwhile, had jumped from 325 million just around Independence time to 638 million in less than 30 years.

capita income, which, in its turn, would have a direct effect on nutrition (and immunity) of the infants.

Unfortunately, the good intentions of the government were implemented very badly—even ruthlessly. We used to have "Vasectomy Camps" in makeshift operation theatres, doing up to 100 to 150 vasectomies in a day at a single centre. "Volunteers" were given a transistor (quite a recent gadget in the mid 70s, and a much sought-after novelty) and 50 rupees, but a lot many ineligible young men got vasectomised. A proper racket existed where middlemen lured such young men to come for the surgery without informing them of the consequences. Most candidates did not even get the promised money or transistor! Vasectomy became a dirty word, and I had lost all respect for the procedure.

But Sunil's patient was not asking for a vasectomy. He was a diabetic and was under regular follow up with Sunil, and today, he had asked for a favour—he wanted his vasectomy to be reversed!

'What?' I exclaimed, having never heard of such a situation before. 'Seriously? Why?'

The explanation was as simple as it was unusual—in the sense that this would have never happened in India. This young British soldier had wanted to marry his girlfriend, and she agreed, on one condition—she did not want any kids and had insisted that he get himself vasectomised—neutered, if you like, before they got married. Smitten with love, he had agreed, and everything went well. He got his vasectomy and a wife ("partner" in English parlance—in India, everyone around you was addressed a partner, without the benefits the British usage entailed). All was well for a year or two, and then, the association ended in divorce. Soon afterwards, he fell in love again, but this time the (new) girl of his life asked for a different promise from him—will he be able to give her children? She wanted the wedding, but also a family (Sunil, of course, was not sure if the girl wanted the two things in that sequence). He was most willing to oblige, smitten as he was (again), and wanted the mechanical blockage sorted!

I consulted Doctors Sivanesan and Maharoof. Dr Sivanesan had just returned from leave. They were as foxed by the request of Sunil's patient as I was. We had a chat about the pros and cons—neither of them had done a vasectomy reversal, such a procedure normally falling in the realm of plastic surgery. But we decided to have a chat with Rob, the patient. Dr Sivanesan led the discussions.

He was open and honest. He quizzed Rob about his commitment to the unusual request. It was explained to him that this would be a risky procedure, and that, if he wanted, Dr Sivanesan could give Rob a referral letter to see a plastic surgeon back home in the UK. Rob refused the offer flatly. Dr Sivanesan had pointed out the possibility of failure, infection, and other complications, especially given his diabetic background. Rob said he fully understood the risks involved and was willing to give a written undertaking.

Inwardly, I was excited at the opportunity to learn something new. I fell back on my copy of Farquharson's Operative Surgery and drew a blank—after all, this was only a textbook of general surgery, exhaustive as it was. The MOH library luckily had a good collection of books on all super specialties, and I wrote down the steps involved, the recommended suture material for the procedure, and all other details, including what complications to look out for and how to manage them. We operated on Rob, Dr Sivanesan and I, while Dr Maharoof, Wicky and Sunil (he was still the primary physician of Rob) looked on with interest. Rob was a lucky man. We got away without any problem whatsoever in the postoperative period, and when we did a semen analysis on Rob 4 weeks later, we were as overjoyed as he was to learn that the sperm count was as good as normal, all looking morphologically healthy and eager for action!*

---

* In August 1983, I received a handwritten letter from Rob, who was then stationed in a garrison in East of England. He wanted me to know that he had duly married the love of his life, and that she had been blessed with a baby a week before! To this day, it is one of my treasured souvenirs from my Muscat days.

6

Dr Sunil, MBBS, MRCP

Sunil kept Rob under follow up till he was posted out a few months later. After each such visit, Rob would drop by to say hello to Dr Sivanesan and me. Sunil continued to feed us surgical cases, patients found to have peptic ulcer or gallstones, and such like. He was getting better and better with his clinical acumen, and his theory was getting better, too, all the time. In August 1982, he declared he was going on holiday—to London, no less. Impressed, we wanted to know why. All he said, to very good effect, was that Kristine insisted on London! This chap Sunil was certainly going places, literally and figuratively. First, the glasses. Then, the visible change in his choice of dress. And now, this! He had trumped all of us, the senior lot included! Off to London with a girlfriend? There was more greenery to be seen in our collective faces than in entire Oman!

Sunil had bought a new Yashika camera for the occasion. We made him promise to bring as many photos as he could. But no one remembered to ask him for the photos when he came back after two weeks—because he informed us that he had cleared the first part of MRCP Examination of the Royal College of Physicians, and that, with some good luck and further preparation, he planned to go again next year to take the final exams. Dr Philip had agreed to give him the necessary recommendation. We were delighted for Sunil! What a fantastic achievement for the humble boy from Sitapur town!

We had a genuine scholar amongst us. We also had a fabulous Happy Hour amongst us all, at the expense of young Capt. Sunil MRCP! Personally, for me, this episode was a great instance of motivation. I decided to spend every available minute from now on for my own FRCS exams. Every available minute, that is, less the time I planned to spend wooing Glynnis!

By this time, it was well known who was going around with whom. Sunil and Kristine, Glynnis and I, and poor Deepak who was still unclaimed, went out together often on long drives and beach parties. Sometimes, Capt. Banerjee, he of the ready wit, would join us, too, and it was always fun to have him around. He was a willing apprentice under Sunil, learning clinical medicine one-on-one from him. But this did not prevent him from pulling his guru's leg when possible. Sunil was definitely getting anglicised, but his English was still quite Sitapurian. On one trip to the beautiful *Jebel Akhdar* (Jebel means hills and Akhdar means green), we had stopped at a typical Indian restaurant on the highway. One look at the menu card, Sunil declared he was going for the *"pineappel peeja"*. Banerjee seized his moment.

He burst out in Hindi, *'Arre buddhu, yeh Peeja nahi hai, yeh Khaja hai!* You want a Pid-Za, right?' Those of us who knew Hindi and English were rolling in laughter. I explained to Glynnis and Kristine that peeja, the distorted Indian—Sitapurian—pronunciation of Pizza, in Hindi meant 'to drink', while solid foods were usually eaten—*khana* (food), or *khaja* (to eat). While they both politely smiled, I knew much of the humour had been lost in translation.

At Jebel Akhdar, the highest point in Oman at nearly 3000 metres (about 10,000 feet), we were amazed to see the amount of greenery in a land we always thought of as a desert. There were pomegranate orchards and large rose gardens. We met with the curator of the orchards, an Indian from Kerala. Once he came to know I am from Palghat, he became very friendly! My Malayalam is fairly good, so I acted as interpreter for the others. He said he had been working at the orchards in Jebel Akhdar ever since the Sultan had taken over. But once, when he had done just about three years, he almost lost his job, and his neck with it! It seems a new ambassador had come from Spain. As was the custom, he presented his credentials to His Majesty the Sultan and gave a gift of Spanish saffron bulbs. These were despatched to our man at Jebel Akhdar with instructions to plant them and tend to them well. But he refused to plant them!

The concerned horticultural officer, or Minister, or whoever, felt very offended, and threatened to throw him into the dungeons for disobeying the Sultan's orders. Our man stood his ground, saying the bulbs were not saffron bulbs. This was even more unacceptable—he was all at once disobeying the Sultan's orders and casting aspersions on the Ambassador of Spain!

Apparently, he said he would rather die or be beheaded than endanger the Sultan, as he knew these were not Saffron bulbs but those of some poisonous variant. Somewhere, someone seems to have listened to him, and the bulbs were sent to England for testing. Prompt came the reply. The bulbs were of some Lily family, not saffron at all! It seems the Sultan personally sent for our man and thanked him, while the new Spanish ambassador was summoned to the Royal Palace and properly ticked off!

I was never able to check the veracity of this claim, but one thing was certain—the curator was alive when we saw him, so probably, he was telling the truth! Banerjee cautioned us all: if a wrong diagnosis of some silly bulbs could threaten a man's life, we had better watch out, he said.

'We better get our clinical diagnoses correct—who knows, this place may have something like a liver for a liver rule, or worse, a colon for an appendix or something,' he said, pointedly looking at me.

He wasn't very far off the mark, in a way. A couple of weeks later, Sunil and Dr Philip were called to examine a "suspect". A respectable-looking, middle-aged Indian man was brought by the military police to them for a medical check-up to make sure the man was not insane. Apparently, he hit an old Omani when the latter was crossing the highway (the speed limit was 100 kilometres/hour in those roads, but it was not uncommon to see locals crossing the road at leisure, especially at night). The police did not find the Indian gentleman under the influence of alcohol, so they wanted him certified as mentally stable, for purposes of the hearing in the court. The old man involved in the accident was the father of a serving soldier, so the matter came under military jurisdiction as per Omani law.

As things unfolded, it emerged the victim was more or less totally blind. This was more than likely—those days, trachoma, a condition that affects the cornea and turns it opaque, was extremely common in Oman. Especially in the dry, dusty, northern parts of Oman, up to 70-80% of the population suffered from various degrees of trachoma-induced blindness. In all probability, the old chap never saw the car coming, and decided to cross the road at the wrong moment. The Indian embassy appointed a counsel on behalf of the accused, and to be fair to the Omani courts of law, he was acquitted of homicide. But the court still ruled that the "blood money" (or Diyya in Omani) as per sharia law had to be paid by the gentleman. There was a proper gradation of blood money—the highest—about 4000 Omani riyals was for Omani Muslim males. The next in the hierarchy were non-Omani Muslim males, followed by Omani Muslim females, and at the bottom rung were all others—expatriates, males, females all included. The last category was probably valued at a couple of hundred riyals.

Four thousand Omani riyals was a huge amount of money. That was close to my personal estimate of savings I wanted before running away back to India! The Indian embassy asked the diaspora to help out, and all of us contributed various amounts, and I am told the gentleman involved was so upset by the experience that once the blood money was paid, he left the country for good. As usual, the witty Banerjee had some advice for all of us.

'Start a blood money account and regularly deposit money there,' he said, 'you never know when one would need it.'

We were fast approaching the end of our second year of deputation in this beautiful, bewildering country. For all these rules that sometimes frightened us, we were beginning to feel at home in this country of gentle, friendly people. We were never asked what faith we belonged to—at work or in our social interactions. Expatriate women did not have any kind of restrictions imposed on the way they dressed. They were free to drive cars and go anywhere they wanted without a male accompanying them. Indeed, many Omani women used to drive about and hold office in most professions. Our patients always preferred to be seen by *Tabeebeen* (plural for Tabeeb) *Al Hindi*—Doctors from Hind or India. The Omani courts had a reputation of treating citizens and expatriates by the same, if strict, yardstick. And nothing was clearer proof of the freedom of religious practice than the existence of a Shiva temple right in the middle of old Muscat town, rather intriguingly named Muttrah.

7

The Shiva Temple at Muttrah, Muscat

Oman and India had been enjoying bilateral trade for centuries. As was inevitable, some traders from both countries probably stayed on for various periods of time in the country where their business interests lay—and a small number must have decided to stay put.

People tend to take their culture with them when they emigrate to new lands, and the small Indian community of traders, mainly from Gujarat, seemed to have done the same when they chose to adopt Oman as their new country. As trade continued, the local immigrant population, received well by the native population, seemed to have grown in numbers. Unlike the European invaders everywhere who forced the local natives to accept their gods and religion, the Gujaratis seemed to have adapted themselves well to local conditions, retaining their own indigenous cultural practices while mingling happily with the locals. A sizeable number accepted the local customs and religion—Islam was already well established in Oman by the time the first of the Indians from Gujarat settled there in the early sixteenth century. The locals accepted them happily.

Many of them converted, but many also continued their Hindu practices, un-persecuted by the gentle local folk. Thus, to this day, there are pure vegetarian Hindus in old Muscat, who are many generations old in their newfound country. And there is a large line of Omani Muslims (the well-educated *Lawatis*, for example) who

147

derive from the original Indian stock of Gujarati settlers.

Temple worship is a part of Hindu belief. The settlers who decided to keep their religious beliefs consecrated a temple to Lord Shiva, the Adi Yogi, and a small temple came up within the congested confines of old Muttrah, close to the Muscat port. This temple, close to a hundred years old when Sunil, Deepak and I landed on our deputation to Oman, was the only Hindu temple in all of Middle East. I had heard a lot about this temple, but never managed to visit it.

When Sunil came back with his MRCP achievement, he said he wanted to visit the temple to show his gratitude. Most of us were game. I rang up Gopal, little Indu and Arvind's father, whom I had met a while ago with Glynnis. He was delighted to take us there. I was surprised to hear that typical South Indian rituals were conducted there regularly when Gopal asked if I wanted to do a *vadai malai* to Lord Hanuman's idol in the Shiva temple.

This was unbelievable. *Vadai Malai*, or a garland of soft savoury doughnuts made of lentils, is an age-old ritual in most South Indian temples. Usually, 108 small such doughnuts are made, strung together with a thread, and hung around the head and neck of Lord Hanuman, as part of offerings to Him. Once the *puja* or prayers are over, the garland of *vadais* is handed over to the devotee by the priest, with the blessings of the Lord. It is usual practice to sing the famous hymn *Hanuman Chalisa* which most Indians grow up learning by heart. Sunil, of course, readily agreed.

Our delegation reached Gopal's house, a few kilometres short of the temple, one Friday morning. Besides Sunil, Deepak and me, there were Banerjee, his batchmate Dasgupta, and Vijay—our dentist friend. There had been a fair bit of discussion, with Sunil and I pushing for Kristine and Glynnis to come with us, too, while the others vehemently vetoed our suggestion, saying this was a temple visit, not a party outing! Siddharth and his wife Shanti, Gopal, his wife Lalitha and little Indu and Arvind joined us. The kids suddenly decided they wanted to travel with Uncle Hari in his car! I was of course delighted. In the ensuing months, this would be a pattern with many other kids I got to know, something that always touched my heart.

When we reached the temple, we were totally surprised to see a typical Kopuram or temple tower, though not as ornate as in temples back in South Indian states. Even more surprising was the number of assembled devotees. *Friday being weekend day*, I thought to myself. Lalitha had taken on the responsibility of arranging the *vadais*—as she opened the large steel container and handed over the garland of *vadais* to the priest, the aroma of the deep fried *vadais* tested our spiritual strength to the extreme! Luckily, after first paying our obeisance to Lord Ganesha, the Lord who removes all obstacles, and the main deity, Lord Shiva, we quickly made our way to the adjacent part of the temple precincts where Lord Hanuman waited to receive our offering and bless us.

The priest asked us about our antecedents—another typically South Indian temple practice. Devotees are expected to say three identifying features about their ancestry—their *Gotra* or the primordial sage from whom the devotee is supposed to have descended, their full (usually sanskritised) name, and the star under which they were born. Lalitha suggested all of us tell the Pandit Ji our antecedents—but Sunil, Deepak, and Vijay had no clue even about the stars they were born under! The two Bengalis, Banerjee and Dasgupta knew theirs, and I of course knew mine—years of visiting temples with my parents had made me memorise all these details. The *puja* was over soon, and we collected the *vadais* and made our way to the part of the temple where the offerings—duly blessed by the Gods—were distributed. There was a motley crowd, many of them Tamils, and known to the Gopals. There was a round of introductions. Sunil, Deepak, and Vijay survived this round, as they could at least say their full names as per their passports! We wolfed down the *vadais*, and, after Lalitha had distributed *vadais* generously to others, the few remaining ones were packed away in her steel container.

The six of us were invited to the Gopals' residence for lunch. We found this incredible—but apparently, Lalitha had already catered for a dozen people! She dished out an incredibly tasty meal— typically South Indian— and we finished the remaining *vadais*. I had had time enough in all this to impress Indu and Arvind with my Origami skills—a bird and a frog—which simply blew them away. From then on, I was a regular, popular, uncle whenever I met with kids!

Before we took leave of our generous hosts, Lalitha asked me a question which seemed to have bothered her for some time.

She took me aside and asked quite directly, 'Are you going to marry that English girl?'

I was totally shocked. Much as I liked Lalitha and her family, I hardly knew them, and this seemed a rather bizarre question to put to a near stranger. She apologised profusely for being so intrusive, and added, 'Hope you don't mind, but I noticed at the temple that yours is *Kaundinya gothram*, which is different from my parents' *gothram*, you know. Both Gopal and I are totally impressed by you— I mean, Army officer, Doctor, and good in music as well! My little sister, the last in our family, is doing her bachelor's back in India …'

So, this was the reason for all of us being invited to give out our ancestry, despite the *vadais* being Sunil's offering at the temple! I was fairly happy with my perceived stock in the matrimony market, but Lalitha had also brought out in the open a thought that had been occurring to me of late—my own long-term feelings for Glynnis. I was quite confused. I managed to give an acceptably non-committal answer. Lalitha seemed very relieved! But on our drive back home, I thought, this offer of Lalitha's sister in marriage would give me a chance to test the waters with Glynnis. I decided to take the test at the earliest.

8

Vegetarian Food and a Question

I decided to do the "test" over a meal. I felt it would be safer to bring up the topic with Sunil around. Which meant having Sunil *and* Kristine around, but I didn't mind that. A new vegetarian restaurant had just opened up in Ruwi. I was aware of Glynnis' liking for Indian vegetarian food. I was equally aware of Kristine's dislike for any food other than hardcore non-vegetarian stuff. But I had already learnt about one weakness in her—she was very fond of softy ice creams. I had this inside information from none other than Sunil, who once confessed that his ice-cream intake had gone up considerably in recent times—every time he went out with Kristine, they had to have softies! One evening, I suggested we all go out for dinner—my treat. The four of us set off in my car, and I broke the good news first—about the softy ice cream post dinner. There was a roar of acceptance from the back seat where the two girls were sitting. Pausing for effect, I let slip the news of the vegetarian dinner. Kristine took it well. Actually, it turned out that she had become fond of Indian spices, even when they were wasted on simple foliage. So, we dashed off to Kamat Restaurant in Ruwi.

The food was excellent, though by Kristine's standards, it was probably not spicy enough. Over dinner, I gently brought up the topic of a distant cousin of mine (I didn't tell them he was created just a few minutes back) who was in America (and why not?) who was getting married to a local girl. A Christian, I added, and said I was waiting to hear the reaction from his parents and others in my family. What did the others at the table think? Sunil was all for it—he had *things* at stake, too, I guessed. Kristine was very practical. She said a girl should marry a chap who can keep her happy—lots of money for shopping—she added, qualifying her idea of happiness. I was hoping to get an encouraging reply from Glynnis, but her response startled me:

'I don't know, Kris,' she said, 'Money alone can't get a girl happiness, but it certainly will help! I think a girl should choose a fellow for marrying only after spending sufficient time going around with a few guys. I mean, how would you know what you are missing unless you move around, spend time, and feel comfortable in every way with a person? What if the chap is all nice and rich, but can't perform in bed? I mean, don't you think that's an important part of settling down with someone?'

I was quite speechless. Till now, we had not gone beyond an occasional kiss or a hug. Was she suggesting…? My heart sank a bit—I had never even dreamed of sleeping with a girl who was not already my wife—even this kissing and all that made me feel rather guilty. But her next words were pure music to me:

'Not everyone would be a darling like Harry whom you would want to spend the rest of your life with, for the sheer pleasure of his company.' She reached out and squeezed my hand.

She might as well have handed over a signed wedding contract. Sunil gave a *'Well done, you bugger,'* look. Kristine was laughing out aloud, whatever her understanding of all this was. The waiter had no clue why he was getting such a heavy tip. The strawberry flavour softy that came later on was the tastiest ice cream I had had in a long time! By Peter Pan's standards, I was so happy, I could have easily flown!

Sunil revealed a dark side to his personality that night when we returned to our rooms. He grabbed me when we were alone, and said,

'Pretty good progress, mate. What are you going to tell your mother?'

When I asked what he meant by "progress", I was shocked to hear that in his parlance, it went way beyond smooching! *This bloody Sitapur bumpkin*, I thought, part out of envy, part wonder. He continued with his dose of shocks for the evening.

'My *funda* (motto) is very clear, Boss,' he said. 'Have fun while you can. There is no way I can even think of any long-time arrangement with Kristine. When I go back home, my parents will line up some pretty girls, and I will end up selecting one, get happily married, and stay put. I have somehow managed to convince them that I cannot marry till I finish my three years here. Imagine if I got married while on leave and came back with a wife! One is trouble, Boss; two, can't even think of the problems!' He was laughing out aloud as if he were discussing the simultaneous management of two difficult patients in the ward. Sunil had not merely broken free of his *Sitapurian* shackles; he was galloping away! I wondered whether Deepak, Banerjee, and others had also broken free of their traditional Indian thinking.

Sunil's transformation from a village boy to an ultramodern gentleman (he had now got out of saying *Gental* man, but still had some distance to cover with his diction) was astonishing to say the least. But in defence of my friend, I need to add this: for all his running around, he did not lose sight of his professional goals. On the contrary, he was getting better at it by the day. When, finally, Dr Philip went on a month's leave (no one had a clue where he went) Sunil managed the entire medical department by himself, and I dare say Dr Philip wasn't terribly missed.

The MOH started inviting Sunil to local meetings and conferences. Local, only because there wasn't yet a proper university or medical college in Oman. We heard rumours of the government planning to start a university of higher education, with a full-fledged medical college in it, besides other institutions and departments. It would take a few years to come up, we were told. To the envy (and pride, too) of many of us, Col. George said in one of his rare appearances at the Officers' Mess that once the medical college was ready, if Sunil should be interested, a position for him would be a cake walk. Being a kind man, he said some of us others could hope to get a position, too, if we emulated Sunil's diligence and commitment to the profession. Banerjee wanted to know (in private, of course; he wouldn't dare risk his cheeky humour in the vicinity of Col. George the Serious!) if being like Sunil would also help us get appropriate Filipino connections.

Our second year in Oman was drawing to a close. All of us were already feeling the advantages of financial security. We were all buying electronic and household goods with a frenzy that would have surprised today's gadget-crazy kids. Sunil had already bought a car, a shiny red Toyota Cressida, the top of the Toyota range in Oman. I was keen on one—it would be a first in the family by a long shot. But I had to save money for a lot many things that kept cropping up, pushing all thoughts of premature return to India away from my mind. Many deputationists had sent television sets home during the Asiad rush, although the games themselves were a couple of months away—they were due in mid-November, and we were inching towards the end of September. The second year ended well enough for us. Our pay slips—thin as ever—reflected a 7.5% pay rise, which we learnt was standard practice. None of us complained, I assure you! Meanwhile, we were all learning to communicate in Arabic, some of us better than others. Well, at least that is what we thought, whenever we listened to Deepak speaking Arabic at dizzying speeds.

The Third Muscat Year

1

The Third Muscateer: Deepak

Deepak was born and brought up in Delhi. And he was every bit an urban rogue! Smart, handsome, very fair (which alone was sufficient as a qualification in the India of those days) with a shock of black hair that seemed so unruly, I often wondered how in hell he managed to keep his hairstyle in the Army.

He was the only child of his parents, both doctors—so, his profession was decided way before he was born! But he was a rebel of sorts, which explained how he ended up joining the Army, instead of happily pitching in with his parents' successful private practice. His father very much wanted him to become a cardiologist and take the family clinic to greater heights. Deepak had other ideas. He was extremely good in sports—he played all sorts of sports in school, excelling in all—from three-legged race to football and cricket. He didn't quite excel in scholastics—he was good, but nowhere near the top. When the results of the medical entrance examination came out, his father was shocked. His son would not be able to join either of the two medical colleges in Delhi—Maulana Azad Medical College (MAMC) where I had studied, or the All-India Institute of Medical Sciences (AIIMS). The latter had been set up by the Government as an institution of excellence on par with the best in the world. But they only took in 50 students each year. I had in my typically good-boy fashion, good-at-studies way secured admission to AIIMS as well, but my father couldn't afford the tuition fees and the compulsory

156

hostel stay for all students. At MAMC, on the other hand, I was
eligible for a monthly scholarship that was about four times the fee I
had to pay, so I simply joined MAMC. I haven't regretted it one bit
all these years, for it was (and continues to this day) one of the finest
places to go for medical education.

For the record, there was a third medical college in Delhi, the
Lady Hardinge Medical College. There were vacancies there, and
Deepak would have been absolutely delighted to join—but for the
small problem of that college being exclusively reserved for girls! So,
there was no medical seat for Deepak in Delhi. Deepak enjoyed a
fleeting period of hope when he thought that he could get away with
admission to some easy course in Delhi University and concentrate
instead on his ambition of playing for the Delhi cricket team. But his
father was not one to give up easily.

He scoured the area and found that a government-run medical
college in Rohtak, two hours north of Delhi, had a few seats reserved
for students with exceptional sports talent. Things moved quickly,
and young Deepak was packed off to Rohtak, where in addition to
finding his feet in the medical field (much to his own surprise), he
captained his college's cricket team (to no one's surprise). However,
his ideas about what he wanted to do with the rest of his life hadn't
changed—he was quite sure he didn't want to join the family
business. Without telling his parents, he appeared for the Army
Medical Corps entrance exam, got very good grades, and was
grudgingly allowed by his parents to join the AMC. In the north, as
opposed to the south of India, a great deal of prestige is associated
with a career in the army. The family's stock goes very high if they
can boast of a son in the army. Making an infantry soldier of your
son is the best you could do, but even a doctor who dons the uniform
was good enough. Deepak was delighted to join the army without
having to face any serious objection from his father. He was secretly
eyeing the Armed Forces cricket squad. It is a different thing that he
had given his father to understand he was taking a short service

commission of five years, after which he would be at his father's disposal. Luckily, his father hadn't bothered to find out—yet—that only permanently commissioned officers could ever make it on a foreign deputation!

Deepak was a roaring success with everyone. He knew how to say the right things at the right time. Yet, when needed, he could stop a person in his tracks when he chose to. When we were in the middle of the second year, we had a big get-together in the Mess with a whole lot of British officers from the nearby island of Masirah, which had a large air force setup. Many of them had never interacted enough with Indian doctors and lived on in their colonial bent of mind. During a casual conversation, things started to get a bit out of hand. One officer was hell bent on putting India down. During that time, a fair bit of insurgency was troubling the eastern parts of India, especially the oil and tea-rich state of Assam.

This officer manoeuvred the conversation to Assam and declared, 'There is a terrible situation in Assam, I believe? A lot of infighting between forces loyal to the government and those that like to have their own say in how they are governed. Terribly worrisome, what? You guys need to do something about winning people's hearts, you know.'

While many of us, offended by his supercilious attitude, were inwardly seething, Deepak rose to the occasion instantly.

'Well, what to do? We also have our own Ireland, you know,' he said. 'But where to go to learn about winning people's hearts? Surely not the UK? I understand all the guns and ammunition used so far against the IRA haven't quite won over any hearts?' He said this quite matter-of-factly, without raising his voice. There was a total silence all around. I thought, *this is going to explode; it took much less than this to start World War I!* But luckily, as if on cue, the barman announced the start of the Happy Hour, and the free flow of wine, whiskey, and beer drowned out all hard feelings.

Deepak's popularity was across the ranks. The Omani staff loved him. He was our go-to man for farm fresh dates, as the many Omani girls in the hospital would vie with each other to supply him tons of very tasty Omani dates. The nurses loved his inoffensive leg pulling:

'Sorry Linda,' he would say with a poker face to one of the girls in the OPD, 'can't let you see any patients today.'

And when Linda retorted with indignation, 'And why not, may I ask?' he would answer, without batting an eyelid, 'Because, my dear Linda, you are looking incredibly more beautiful than ever before, and most of my patients have a weak heart. Surely, we can't afford to have patients having uncontrollable arrhythmias with you around, can we?'

Everyone listening in would laugh, Linda perhaps the loudest, reaching out to pull his ears with a 'You naughty boy.' Linda's day was made, and so was, in a way, Deepak's.

And yet, while Sunil and I were trying to stake claim to "our own" girls, Deepak did not even seem to try. Once, when the three of us were alone, this issue came up. I mean, it looked like he could have hitched himself up with any of the girls. His reasoning was simple.

'Listen, we are short-term visitors here. Why get into any serious relationships? Me, I get along with all of them and am happy with some simple flirting. I will unleash the real Deepak charm when we get back home.'

Fair enough, I thought. I couldn't see myself parading young Glynnis in front of Mother and saying, 'And oh, by the way, Mom, meet your daughter-in-law,' much as I wanted to.

In all this, mind, neither Sunil nor I had even for a moment thought of what Kristine or Glynnis felt about our daydreams! So manifests the male ego!

2

Nizwa and the Deepak Factor

Like many of us, Deepak also got a temporary duty landed on him. He had to go as leave replacement to Nizwa, about two hours away from our location in Muscat. Nizwa was one of the oldest cities of Oman, and its capital at one time. It was a sort of link city between the north and south of the country. Set in the foothills of mountains, it was always popular for its shallow streams, date orchards, and big marketplaces. It even had a fort of its own, dating back to mid-17th century, partly damaged by the British shelling. They were helping the local ruler against the mountain-based rebels who wanted Oman to join the Saudi-UAE axis. The place was greener than Muscat in those days, with many orchards of fine Omani dates. Within days of going there, Deepak had made enough friends in the right places. We were sent a couple of boxes of fresh dates, with the promise of more, if we were to visit him. His was a one-man-show there in the Nizwa Military Medical Centre. Like in other places, the Army freely extended its services to local civilians. This kept Deepak busy, but not so busy that he couldn't take time off to explore local places of interest. He would extoll the virtues of the place when he talked to us on the phone.

So, it was then that we decided to visit him. *"We"* sadly did not include the girls. Both Kristine and Glynnis were on duty, so four of us—Sunil, Banerjee, Vijay, and I went one weekend to see young Deepak's domain. He was attending to a young Omani patient as we wandered into his medical centre. And oh, boy, were we impressed! Well, we were in the third year of our stay in Oman; we were involved in healthcare, catering to a population that almost exclusively spoke Arabic, so we better know a fair bit of conversational Arabic, right? Right. But we were impressed by Deepak's Arabic for two reasons. We all knew a fair bit of Arabic ourselves, so it was easy for us to know when someone was speaking a reasonably good bit of Arabic.

But the other reason for our getting impressed was based on our past experience with Deepak's fluency in Arabic. We—well, most of us, except Deepak, hardly knew any Arabic in our initial months in Oman. One day, the new lot of us, just a few months into our stay in Muscat, happened to witness a remarkable scene. In the OPD at FBH, Deepak was deep in conversation with a patient—in Arabic. I recollect we were all stunned by the fluency with which Deepak was engaged in conversation with the patient. It actually stopped the two or three of us passing by his OPD room in our tracks. There was awe and envy at this batchmate of ours speaking such rapid-fire Arabic in such short a time. Imagine our surprise then, when after a really long stretch of Arabic from Deepak, the Omani patient who had been nodding his head all the while, said in an apologetic voice: 'Maafi ingleezi! (Sorry, I don't know English!)' Deepak—the bluffer—had been called out! Oh, how we enjoyed referring to this great Arabic grammarian over the next many weeks! But today—in Nizwa—we were really impressed by Deepak's genuine sounding Arabic. When he was free, we reminded him of his "proficiency" in the early days. We all had a good laugh, but Deepak waved it off.

'Arre, nahi yaar (Oh, leave me alone),' he said. 'True, I can honestly speak a lot better than before, but I still get fooled, thinking I can understand Arabic in all its nuances. Just the other day, soon after I came to Nizwa, my driver knocked on my door at night. He came in, his brow all screwed up as if he was in discomfort and started talking nineteen to the dozen. He repeatedly touched his tummy and talked about waja (which we all knew by now, meant pain). As I started to ask for details, he said it was *wajid* (severe), *thalatha yom* (three days), *zua* (vomiting), *maa kadar akil* (no food intake at all) and so on.

'Somewhat irritated that he was disturbing me in the middle of the night when he had had the pain for three days, I decided that the best thing would be to quickly examine him and give a prescription. I made him lie down on my bed, examined him all over, but there was nothing seriously wrong with his tummy, although he said, "*Naam, naam* (Yes, yes)" when I pressed over the left side of his lower abdomen. Obviously, nothing more than indigestion or constipation, I thought, and wrote out an appropriate prescription, explaining how and when to take it, etc., and sent him off, with a "*shuf ante bukra sabah* (see you tomorrow morning)."

'That was three days back. He turns up today with a big box of dates and baklawa, looking very happy with himself. I was happy to see him looking good, and I said so. He said—and please believe me, he said it with total sincerity—that I was the best doctor he had ever met. He said he had never known a doctor to examine a person, and issue medicines for someone else. What's more, he said, his uncle had recovered fully after taking those medicines. He gave me a hug and a kiss on my cheek and has promised to seek my help if anyone else in the family falls ill. The family lives in Ibri, about hundred kilometres from here, so he would get himself examined and take the prescription!'

Poor Deepak! He was committing fraud earlier without knowing much Arabic, and he was committing fraud now despite his fluent Arabic!

3

A Fort and a Market

Deepak insisted we take away every single bit of the dates and Baklawa—he didn't want them to remind him of his discomfiture! We realised that there was a parallel to his experience. In one Bollywood movie, a young innocent Kashmiri girl—in love with the hero—goes to a doctor and asks for medicines to be prescribed for her to take. When asked why, she says she was too shy to talk to her loved one, but wanted him to get well, and that for his sake, she is more than happy to swallow any number of pills! We wanted to trace Deepak's ancestry to see if some doctor in the long line of physicians in his family had ever lived in Kashmir around the time the movie was made!

We visited the Nizwa fort, which turned out to be a smallish, mostly mud-and-brick affair. There weren't any unique architectural features, murals, or carvings. Yet it was impressive. Sunil pulled out his swank Yashika camera and we took a group photograph with the help of a total stranger. The Nizwa market was next on our list, where the variety of spices and dry fruits, not to speak of dates and sweets, was very impressive. Apparently, the market stands exactly where, centuries ago, tradesmen used to barter goods coming from India, Sumatra and beyond, with those coming from Greece and Rome. We bought some dry fruits which had probably originated in India, but who cared? We were well off and could happily afford the going rates. The heat in the market was oppressive, so we cut our trip short, got back to Deepak's room for some rest before an early dinner and the trip back home to Muscat. Short though the trip was, it was fun, and the conversation on the way back was entirely about Deepak's real mastery of Arabic!

4

Deepak Returns—and almost gets thrashed!

Soon after our visit to Nizwa, Deepak returned to base. The hospital staff were even more delighted to have their favourite *Tabeeb Al Hind* back in their midst. We were happy to see him back, too, because he always provided entertainment. He continued to do so, but one person was not amused, and actually was all out to thrash him. It took the combined effort of the rest of us to prevent Deepak from getting hospitalised for injuries. It happened like this:

One of the deputationists from the previous batch was a reserved, quiet kind of chap called Capt. Ghosh. Ghosh led his life strictly on the basis of save-every-penny-you-fools-you-are-not-going-to-get-another-Muscat-posting policy. Had Charles Dickens met him in time, he would have rewritten Mr Scrooge all over. Ghosh personified miserly behaviour. He cooked his own food (*The Mess is charging unnecessarily high rates every month; alcohol is a meaningless waste of money—except during Happy Hour; no point buying silly gadgets to take home—a black and white TV shows the same news as a coloured one, doesn't it?* And so on). He didn't mind freebies, though—since our army-issue car came with free petrol, he was in Muscat practically every alternate day, taking about an hour and a half to come from Rostoq, an outlying medical centre where he had volunteered to work. It was rumoured that in the rare occasion he called friends over to his room, he counted the number of peanuts he offered them. Knowing him, it was possible. Everything he did was with a view to enjoying *after* he went back to India. Every single thing he bought was carefully selected.

So, this master miser drew up his car one day right in front of Deepak's room, and walked in. Ghosh's mother obviously did not share her son's miserly attitude—she had fed her child well from childhood—he stood at 6 feet one, and his body was constructed as big as the external frame would permit. In Wodehousian terms, he had allowed his mother to fill him with food and she had forgotten to ask when. Indeed, everyone pitied the poor Corolla he was issued with—it was a tribute to Toyota's engineering skills that the car never tilted to one side when he drove. So, this incredible hulk walks in and demands attention. I happened to be sitting with Deepak then. Ghosh started by swearing both of us to secrecy.

'Promise me, you guys, and I will give you something to remember for the rest of your life,' he declared. After checking to make sure no unwanted chaps had breezed into the room behind his massive frame, he pulled out a video cassette from his humungous trouser pocket. 'Know what this is?'

Deepak said, 'Hi, Shorty. Of course, I know what this is—a bar of chocolate, right? Oh, come on, Ghosh, we have all been here for over two years, stop treating us like kindergarten babies.'

'Shut up,' said Ghosh. Turning to me, he said, 'Hari, I am tolerating all sorts of nonsense from this fellow here only because he is your friend. Shorty, am I? Wait till I show you my full height one of these days. Anyway, I am not here for an argument, instead I am here to ask you, young Deepak, for a favour. Remember my seniority,' he asserted. 'This here is a kind of chocolate alright. You will drool for sure. This here is "Ten", man. "Ten",' he said, and waited for us to gasp.

When it became clear that it would take a much larger number than ten to make us gasp, he explained.

'You poor cavemen, this is Bo Derek's Ten.' This time he got our attention, gasp included.

'What? Serious?' said both of us at once, trying to grab the cassette, which the big boy deftly avoided. Bo Derek was the ultimate news ever since her "reveal all" movie very deceptively titled "Ten" had been released sometime back. Ghosh came to the point.

'Listen, I have driven all the way from Rostoq because I know that Deepak here has two video recorders. So, here is the deal. This cassette belongs to one of the *goras* in our Unit. I have borrowed it just for the day, but I want to retain a copy. You make a copy of this,' he handed over a blank video tape, 'while you enjoy watching the movie. But I will be back in a couple of hours after doing some work in Ruwi. I will need to run immediately after that to Rostoq so no one knows I am making this copy. Better have it ready, okay? Remember, I am giving you free entertainment of the highest class.' He gave a wicked wink and was gone.

We sat down to the business of watching and copying the movie. As luck would have it, I was called away to attend to a young boy with suspected appendicitis even before Bo Derek appeared. Cursing my luck, I left Deepak to enjoy the movie and went off to the hospital. I was confident I could get Ghosh to loan his copy sometime soon. When I was done with the case, curiosity made me go back to Deepak's room before going back to my own quarters.

Deepak half opened the door and said, 'That thug Ghosh came and took away the original and his copy, man. So sad.'

Without Bo Derek, Deepak's company suddenly seemed less inviting than a good nap, so I declined his offer of a cup of tea. He didn't press too much either.

That weekend, all hell broke loose. The incredible hulk came, looking hulkier and angrier than ever, and barged into my room.

'Where is that swine hiding?' he demanded. Swine turned out to be Deepak's latest alias.

'He is not in his room, he is not at the hospital, so he must be hiding here or in Sunil's room. Sunil's room is locked, so you better produce that bugger now. I need to tear him from limb to limb, and then go back in time for night duty at Rostoq,' he raved, mumbling something about video cassettes.

It took me a while to convince him that there were no fugitives hidden in the premises. When I mentioned to him that I was aware of him having collected the original and the copy from Deepak, and that I was very much there when Deepak started the recording, Ghosh nearly blew his top.

'Oh, that's what the scoundrel did then, eh?' he said. 'Well, I am going around looking for him, but if he comes here, you can tell him there is one shop in Ruwi that is giving a huge discount on coffin boxes. He will need one when I am done with him. And don't you dare stitch him up together after I tear him up in shreds—unless you want to order another box for yourself.'

Threatening me thus, he stormed away, looking redder than at arrival. Ghosh was actually quite a mild chap at most times, despite his imposing frame. I was therefore really worried for Deepak's life— and a little bit for my own, to be honest. I set about looking for Deepak, in a bid to save him from extinction.

I never met Deepak that day. The next day was a total mess, with a series of cases to be attended to (no Deepak among them), and two boring meetings in the MOH that went late into the evening. It was thus only on the third day that I ran into Deepak, relieved to see all his limbs intact. I said, 'Hey, did Ghosh thrash you? Are you alright? What day is it today and what is your grandfather's name?' These are questions usually asked of people who may have had severe concussion. Deepak was totally unruffled.

'Cool down, buddy, no need for all that neuro stuff,' he said. 'If you are referring to shorty and his Bo Derek, all is well, all sorted. Everyone is happy, and if you want a bit of happiness, too, come to my room, and I will ask Bo Derek to perform again.'

He buzzed off, but I was not going to leave this till I learned the truth. So, I went straight to his room after work and found him whistling the bars of Ravel's Bolero, which later turned out to be the theme song of the movie. Bo Derek was good. Oh boy, she really was, but the story Deepak narrated was way better, and funnier!

It seems poor Ghosh rushed back with the original and the "copy" to Rostoq that fateful day and organised a small pre-dinner party in his room for a set of select friends—Indian friends of his from civvy street. He had hinted to them what was in store but had hurriedly added that he would provide the movie and peanuts to munch, but they had to get their own booze. Well, all eager beavers were in his room at the appointed hour. With bated breath, they watched him put the cassette into the player (borrowed from one of the civilian friends for the purpose), with some elaborate drama, and switched on the TV (borrowed from another of his civilian friends for the purpose).

There was expectant silence. Even the noise of various jaws munching away at the peanuts stopped. There was the initial disturbance on the TV screen when a re-recorded cassette started to play. People knew this, didn't mind, and waited. A few seconds passed, but the disturbance continued. Someone suggested fast forwarding to the action, and Ghosh duly did this. The disturbance on the screen persisted. Irritated (Ghosh was probably counting the peanuts that were disappearing down people's hatches), he pressed the fast forward button some more—no luck, the screen refused to show even the fully dressed version of Bo Derek. He did this repeatedly, till suddenly, the machine went on its own into auto rewind mode! He had reached the end of the tape! Imagine the collective disappointment of the select audience! All his friends (now ex-friends) left, and despite shaking the tape, tossing it up and doing many other diagnostic manoeuvres, Ghosh could not extract even a little Bo, leave alone Derek. When he realised what had happened, he had apparently let out a blood-curdling howl that had made the local camels take refuge in their masters' tents. He had to grit his teeth and wait for the next day to drink Deepak's blood.

'Well, it was like this,' Deepak said. 'I made the copy, but on balance thought that there were many more deserving souls here who needed education on Bo Derek's methods of seduction, than just young shorty at Rostoq. So, I gave him a blank tape, you see, because he would have never agreed to wait another two hours for an additional copy. I only forgot to tell him his copy was blank. Actually, he never asked me either,' he said, shifting the blame. 'But when he came the next day, we made an agreement. I gave him the second copy I had made overnight and bought him a big bag of peanuts, and now we are the best of friends—in fact, he may be here any minute with another sky-coloured movie. He will be staying overnight so we can make two copies.'

Deepak showed no signs of a man who had survived a body bag, but then, there he was, and there Bo Derek was. We picked up our drinks and settled down—me to get educated on Bo Derekism, and he to revise his knowledge of the technique. Since that day, every time I hear Bolero, a secret smile of recollection crosses my face and contorts it, as I give free reign to my thoughts if no one else is around!

5

Where the Hell is Dubai?

Deepak had a streak of a gypsy in him. Something to do with his origins from nomadic hunter gatherers, I guess. He couldn't sit still. While I constantly complained about getting thrown about on temporary duties, he relished them. I used to argue with him about this often. But I didn't disagree one bit when one day, he suggested we drive to Dubai. He had it all worked out.

'Simple, guys,' he said, 'we apply for two days' leave before the weekend, start early morning after coffee and make our first stop at the Nizwa Medical Centre for breakfast. The Centre's cook makes excellent omelettes. Eat, take some sandwiches for the way, and we drive nonstop to Buraimi. There is an FF unit there (Frontier Force, another regiment of Omani Army). My friend Nqb. Suleiman will host us for lunch in the Officers' Mess. We refill our kahwa flasks, cross the border into UAE, and after another two hours of driving, we are in Dubai. We shack up in some hotel, and do nonstop, insane shopping for two days. We retrace our route the next day.'

Sounded very doable, but we had to get border crossing permits from HQ SOAF. That would allow us, with our white passports and our Omani Army uniforms, to cross into and out of Dubai without having to go through visa applications. We were all pretty excited.

Since I was practically a blue-eyed boy now with Dr Sivanesan, I had no problems getting leave. Deepak, the diplomat, sweet-talked the FBH Commanding Officer into letting him off as well. Sunil wasn't interested.

'Dubai? Waste of time, man! Plan on London, guys, London. What a bloody city! There is Soho in central London where the most beautiful and talented....' He launched yet again into recounting his escapades—till today, I haven't found out what he did with Kristine when he went gallivanting on his own. But we lost interest in his advice when we realised he wasn't coming. Banerjee had been told he may have to move to one of the smaller medical centres within Muscat on short notice, so he was out. Some of the others were not quite ready for a road trip. I insisted that we should take someone senior and sensible like Suresh with us—he had been to Dubai more than once and would know where to stay, where to do shopping, etc. Deepak agreed, so I spoke to Suresh.

He said no problems at all; he would be able to join us. That was a great relief. If we got into any trouble with Omani or Dubai *shurta* (the police) on the way or with the Military Police at the Buraimi border, he would be the go-to man. I was fairly proficient by now with Arabic, so I could handle any language-related issues. Deepak was there, too. So, we decided the three of us would go and set the date. On the day before our departure to Dubai, Suresh flew down from Salalah by the Air Force Flight. I went to pick him up and came back with one more—Suresh had taken the liberty of inviting Rakesh, of the camel-crossing fame*, to join our trip. It was going to be okay, four of us in a car, although Deepak was disappointed inwardly—the crook was planning to leave all the driving to Suresh and me and stretch himself out on the back seat.

Suresh said that things were much costlier in Salalah than even Muscat. Anyone who had ever been to Dubai said things were at least 25 to 30% cheaper than in Muscat markets. I was eyeing a good national Panasonic Video Cassette Recorder (VCR)—the latest model had all sorts of new functions, and I was in love with it. I could

---

* The famous crossing takes place in Chapter 7, page 183

buy a few VCR cassettes as well and look for some TDK or Maxell audio cassettes for my use in India.

I was also secretly madly in love with the recently introduced Sony Walkman. It was a wonder. Not bigger than one's palm and light weight, it could produce unbelievably clear stereo music when heard with specially designed headphones that came with it. Someone had said there was even a model with recording facility—now that would be ideal for me. You see, I was an extremely law-abiding chap in everything—speed limits, parking, licences, you name it. But when it came to Carnatic music, I was a villain nonpareil. My love for classical music bordered on the obsessive. I would not hesitate to secretly record concerts if half a chance presented itself. But I had so far been condemned to live within the law. My father's mono tape recorder was small, but too big to be hidden in a pocket. If taken in a bag, it attracted attention at the entrance to concert halls. In all fairness, I never intended to misuse a secretly recorded concert commercially. No, never. But there was immense pleasure to be had in reliving the special moments from a concert in the privacy of one's own home.

In those days, concerts were not yet being officially recorded and sold. So you went to a concert, enjoyed it, and thereafter it was just you and your memory. I wasn't happy to merely recollect the concerts—I wanted to listen to them again and again. A Sony Walkman had been invented specially for me—I knew it. I was equally sure it would be a few years before it was freely available in India, and by then, I would have returned home, and with a bit of luck, recorded a few grand concerts in Delhi and Chennai. Oh, was I excited!

But even before we left, our excitement was turning into anxiety. Those who were not coming started giving us their shopping lists. Suresh and Rakesh had brought elbow-length lists from their Salalah mates. We were definitely going to run short of space in the car! Suresh, always the man to come up with solutions, picked up the phone and talked to the FBH 2-I-C, Major Kuriakose, the one who had so kindly arranged for my urgent flight to India when my father had passed away.

'All done,' he said, after a couple of minutes. 'Kuriakose will give us his Toyota Crown—it has a massive boot. Hari, hand over your car keys to him when we meet him at dinner tonight in the Mess. We will exchange cars there.'

Boy, this Suresh was truly a magician—did he have an answer to every problem or what? Sure, he did. Except for the ones he himself created, as I was to learn very shortly!

We set off one fine day, loaded with chips and juice cartons and plenty of music. The latest of Boney M, Abba, Baccara, Osibisa and the like filled the car with music as we drove, often at 120 kmph. When I drove, I insisted on playing Jim Reeves, James Last, Paul Mauriet, Neil Diamond, Bob Dylan, and such like soft music. After protesting initially, the other three decided that such music agreed with their plans of taking a nap, so everyone was happy, I most of all. We made excellent time to Nizwa, and post breakfast, we set out for the four-hour journey to Buraimi. There was a fair bit of traffic on the way, mostly comprising of pick-up vans driven by Omanis, many of whom would have failed a vision test had they submitted themselves to one.

Buraimi came around in due course, and as promised by Deepak, we were well looked after by Nqb. Suleiman, who had put out a special spread for his friend's visit—mostly non-vegetarian, which meant I had to settle for Khubs, Hummus, and leaves of some plants. Buraimi is the border town between Oman and UAE, but there is hardly any way of telling where one ends and the other begins. I say this in terms of any distinct border posts—we had reported to a Military Police check-post a fair bit within Omani territory and had been flagged on without much ado. We had to make a cursory stop at the Omani Civil Police post on the UAE side of the border to show our papers—proof that we were travelling in an authorised military issue car and were Omani SOAF officers travelling to Dubai.

The difference between Oman and UAE was suddenly more than obvious as we crossed a board which welcomed us (surprisingly, both in Arabic and English) to Alain. Suddenly, there were six-lane roads—we had been amazed with the four-lane roads of Oman, having not seen such roads back in most places in India, and here we were, driving perilously in six-lane frenzy.

Rakesh had offered to drive from Buraimi but quite hurriedly handed over the car to Suresh—who drove as though he had been born and brought up on these very roads. The landscape had hardly changed from Oman—there was desert land to our left and to our right, with nothing other than scruffy, dust-covered bushes along the way. When we were beginning to feel rather let down, the first of the tall buildings came into view. And then a few more—each tall building more impressive than the previous one. We keenly looked out for a board welcoming us to Dubai, but saw none, definitely not in English.

Suddenly, there was a patch of very few buildings. We had been driving for close to two hours now, and as per our calculations, we should have been in Dubai. Suresh said there were far too many new buildings as compared to his last visit about a year ago. He wasn't so sure of his bearings now. We decided to stop and enquire. At one point, we saw a few people who looked like non-locals, as they were walking in the hot sun on foot. We asked them the way to Dubai.

'Arre bhai (Hey, brother),' said one of them in Hindi, 'you people are coming from Dubai! Make a U-turn, go back some 15-20 kilometres, and you will be in Dubai. This is Sharjah!'

We had crossed one country and entered another without being aware of it! For us Indians used to distinctive towns and villages, this was an interesting, even shocking, revelation. We turned back as quickly as we could, and finally caught Dubai before we ended up being back in Buraimi!

6

Shop Till You Drop Dead or Go Broke

Dubai is a linear city, disposed more or less in a north-south direction. We had hit one end of it, coming from a roughly easterly direction, and had headed north, towards Sharjah. Retracing our route back to Dubai, Suresh suddenly recognised some buildings he remembered from his previous visit. We managed to find a seedy-looking hotel to stay the next two days. The place reeked of *shisha* (hookah) smoke, admixed with invigorating kahwa smell. We had arrived in the shopping paradise of the Middle East, at last! Not wanting to lose a minute, we checked in, changed into civilian clothes (we had travelled all along in our uniforms, as it gave a distinct advantage wherever we stopped), had some tea and biscuits, and set off to the markets.

Oh, boy, did we indulge ourselves! I got my Sony Walkman easily. Choosing the VCR player was more of a problem, so spoilt for choice we were. Taking all factors (like cost, mainly!) into account, I finally settled for a Hitachi with a wired remote control. In the same shop, there were offers on VCR tapes, so we looked up our various request lists and ordered—400—yes, four hundred—of them! I was tempted to buy a lot more items. In particular, a Philips spool deck and an Olympus SLR camera with detachable lenses—wide angle and telescopic, were terribly tempting. But I had to tear myself away from the shop for fear of overdoing my shopping. *God willing*, I thought, *I will make another trip to Dubai in a few months, but right now, I must save up for my top priority—a car.*

The others, Deepak especially, were going berserk, and in the first evening of shopping, we had accumulated enough electronic gadgets to open a shop in Muscat! We had a hurried dinner and came back to the hotel, each one absorbed in his own thoughts and monetary calculations! We were so preoccupied with our shopping, we hardly paid any attention to the other attractions of Dubai—but honestly, at that time, we didn't care; we simply saw Dubai as a large market full of enticing items.

The next day, we had a relaxed breakfast at the hotel and set out again with the intention of clearing the shops of their goods. We did a fairly good job, I must admit, though I didn't buy any costly items. I hung about the shops as the others did their frenzied shopping. Suddenly, a small shop next door caught my attention: "Thomson Electronics", the signboard proclaimed.

It was evidently selling all varieties of cassettes—recorded and blank. Interested in getting a box or two of blank cassettes, I sauntered in. My attention was immediately drawn to a shelf that said "Malayalam classicals", and in that shelf, one title sprang out at me: "Maharajapuram Gopalakrishnan—Vocal", it said. I was intrigued: I knew enough about Carnatic music to know the names of the greats in the field. There was a famous singer called Maharajapuram Santhanam. But I had never heard of a Gopalakrishnan vocalist. I knew one eminent violinist by that name and a flautist, and a mridangist, but never a vocalist.

I asked if I may see the cassette for details. Turns out it was an authorised copy of a concert by the great Maharajapuram Santhanam, accompanied by M S Gopalakrishnan, my greatest idol, whose violin had so transfixed me as I drove that fateful day in the hills outside Thumrait. Recollecting once again that I could have quite possibly died that day, I thanked my guardian angels for letting me live to see this day and this cassette.

I bought it without blinking an eyelid—but I need not have blinked at all—it was being sold for just Omani 250 baizas or, as the young Malayalee shopkeeper said, four for a riyal. Dubai shops happily accept Omani riyals in place of their own currency, the Dirham. It was interesting to note that most shopkeepers used the Indian term Rupia or Rupayya when referring to Dirham—*evidence of the Indian influence over millennia of trade with the Middle East*, I thought. I picked up a whole lot of classical cassettes from the shop, almost forgetting to pick up blank cassettes in my excitement! Absolutely delighted with my find, I returned to the shop where the rest were— they had managed to collect a lot more stuff in the process.

When we returned to the hotel, reality stared us in the face. We had half a dozen two-in-one players, 400 VCR tapes in cardboard cartons, audio cassettes, sarees (mainly Suresh's purchase), shoes, you name it, we had a few! And we were four thugs also waiting to be transported back to Oman along with all this junk! How in heaven's name were we going to do that? We debated the issue, and finally decided on two things: absolutely, strictly, totally, no more shopping. And we needed to use every inch of available space in the car—the boot, large as it was, was not going to suffice. We got rid of as many of the cardboard boxes as we could—they were bulky. The VCR cassettes were evenly distributed on the floor of the car—passenger seat and back seats were packed four cassettes thick—which meant that the guys at the back would have to sit with their knees close to their chins! Suddenly, there was a great deal of enthusiasm from Deepak and Rakesh to drive—but Suresh and I firmly put down the uprising.

That evening was therefore spent eating and roaming around. I hardly have any recollection of the places we went to. Despite our desperate situation, all four of us ended up buying some more things—remote-controlled toys (Suresh for his kids, me for my niece and nephews), modern telephones for use back in India (Deepak and Rakesh—this despite neither of them having a connection in their homes. In those days, one had to wait for up to a year or more to get an allotment of telephone connection). Cursing each other for such ridiculous extravagances, we downed some softy ice creams and returned to our rooms. One good outcome was that we were all practically down to our last baizas, so a unanimous decision was taken to drive back to Muscat the next morning, a day in advance!

We had a fair bit of excitement on the way back as well. On the way up, we had been waved along by the military check-post within Oman and the Omani Police check-post just on the other side of the Buraimi-Alain border. The UAE border forces couldn't care less. People from the Omani side were more than welcome—most came to do shopping, and the more the merrier. On the way back as well, we discussed all this in the car. We would merely have to contend with the Omani Civil Police check-post, as they would be interested in ensuring contraband goods were not being brought in by returnees. The military check-post, seeing an Army vehicle being driven by people in uniform, would simply wave us through. As we discussed this, all of us stopped in mid-sentence at the mention of the word uniform—Suresh wasn't in uniform! The other three of us were, but Suresh was sporting a nice new T-shirt he had bought the day before.

'Oh, hell!' he groaned. 'You know what, I think my bloody uniform shirt is hanging in the cupboard in the hotel, along with my rank badges! I thought I would change in the last minute.'

'Not to worry,' said Deepak, 'take mine.'

'And what will you say to the *shurta*, Sir?' asked Suresh. 'How will you explain not being in uniform? Besides, none of you skinny fellows is my size.' Deepak had assumed only the person driving had to be in uniform—but no, we were claiming to be army officers visiting Dubai, as per our manifest, so we all had to be in uniform. As always, having created the problem for once, Suresh still managed to rise to the occasion, as magically as ever.

'Well, we will have to make a short detour,' he said after a couple of minutes. 'My friend Ali's family lives in Alain. We have to stop somewhere where we can make a phone call, I will talk to Ali, and get his home address—I will ask him to call his wife and hopefully, if he has a spare uniform at home, we can borrow it, and I will have it dry cleaned and give him back with a big round of thanks when I get back to Salalah. I will bill all of you 25% each for the expenses involved in the thanksgiving,' he said cheekily.

'Oh, yeah,' retorted Deepak, 'You forget the shirt, and we pay for saying thanks, eh? No problem. I am totally broke after the shopping, Hari or Rakesh can pay on my behalf.'

This started a line of loud and heated debate, but Suresh shut us all up as we passed by a petrol station and decided to see if we could make a call from there. Surprisingly, all went really well. Ali on the other end of the phone was most willing as soon as he had recovered from a fit of laughter. He said he was quite sure he had a spare dress at home, gave us his address and directions, and promised to call his father at home. It took us the better part of an hour to finally locate his house.

Ali's wife had the uniform ready. Suresh alone went in, picked up the package and came back to the car. We were on our way immediately and heaved a sigh of relief—and immediately changed it to one of continuing despair. Ali was a Captain (Naqeeb or Nqb. for short), but the uniform had the epaulets of a Lieutenant! And to add to our misery, Lieutenant Ali seems to have been a far thinner version of his Captain model. Try as he might, Suresh could not get the last three buttons on—his tummy was far more prosperous. The other problem of the third star to make Suresh get the captain look was easily solved, thanks to some ingenuity on the part of Rakesh.

A fairly talented artiste, he drew the shape of a star next to the other two on the epaulet, using a black ball pen. A careful examination may have revealed that the last star was flat on the surface, and a tad bit too crowded next to the middle one—but we were counting on my Arabic, my *Tabeeb-al-Amelia* (doctor-of-operations) status, and the general lack of interest of Omani *Shurta* in Army personnel. But what if they wanted us all to get out of the car? Suresh's uncovered tummy would be a dead giveaway! Well, we had no option but to push our luck and hope for the best. Deepak provided the soothing information that he had heard from one of his soldier patients that the food in Omani jails was pretty good.

We devised a plan. The two at the back would pretend to be fast asleep—one way of explaining why their knees were practically touching their chins. Suresh was to stay put at the wheel, with his best possible smile and free usage of "Fi" or whatever else was appropriate. I would have to deal with the *Shurta* and let slip my *Tabeeb-mal-Amelia* status ASAP. And pray like hell.

In the end, it was a bit of an anti-climax. I got out of the car, walked up to the waiting police officer, and handed him our papers. I was waiting for him to finish whatever it was he was discussing with his friend on the other side of the booth window, so that I could impress him with my "me-big-surgeon" routine. He continued talking to his mate, took one cursory look at me and the papers, put a long tick on the front of the paper, and said, 'Roh! (Go!)'

That was it. He didn't ask how many people, what was in the car, nothing. I had to control my impulse to avoid running back to the car.

I walked as sedately as a secretary bird, got in, and told Suresh in a whisper in Tamil, 'Start moving and let's get the hell out of here.'

The back benchers wanted to know what and how, but I shut them up. Once we were out of sight of the booth and well into Buraimi limits, we let out a collective yell that must have frightened a few stray camels in a five-mile radius! The two at the back and I joined in berating Suresh, trying to figure out how much of the total shopping expense should be passed on to him as punishment! Loud music and plenty of coffee and snacks saw us home by late that evening. Rakesh was surprisingly very forgiving of Suresh. When we dug deep, we found out why.

7

Rakesh Disagrees with a Camel

Once, Capt. Rakesh almost made it to the obituary columns because of a misunderstanding with a camel, which is best explained in Wodehousian terms: Rakesh thought the camel was not dead, but the camel felt it was dead. Sadly, it was right. The camel owner, though, had a different set of emotions—anger, laced with a liberal dose of greed. Camels are good money in the Middle East.

Rakesh was from the batch that came to Oman one year after us. Soon after joining duty, Rakesh had been posted to one of the infantry regiments in the outskirts of Salalah. And there he remained, till the incident with the camel about a year later.

Rakesh was driving down one of the major arterial roads of Salalah towards the town centre, on his way to a weekend party with some friends. These outlying roads did not have any street-lights—the volume of traffic was very low, especially in the evenings and nights. The road itself wound its way through many date and coconut groves. The row of trees often started very close to the edge of the road. Like everywhere else in Oman in the ten years since His Majesty Sultan Qaboos bin Said had taken over, there were excellent road surfaces in this part of the countryside as well. Rakesh was running a bit late, so he was going at about 100 kmph, the legal speed limit. As he negotiated a curve, his headlights reflected off something very red. Rakesh realised a split second later that he was staring at a pair of camel eyes!

He started to slow down, but to his horror, the camel started running towards his car. Maybe, it mistook his headlights for an attractive female camel! Whatever its thought processes, the camel was determined to settle the matter—and would not stop even when it was pretty close to the car. Luckily, Rakesh had slowed down a fair bit, and he hoped that up close, the camel would get frightened by the headlights and go away into the fields. No such luck. The camel decided to get to the bottom of the approaching object, or rather, to its top. It came straight on, climbed the bonnet, up the windscreen and on to the roof, where, finding nothing of interest, it suddenly decided to turn left, and jumped off the car. Camels are ungainly creatures, and its fall broke one or maybe two legs, and the poor thing simple lay there, disappointed with its adventure.

Meanwhile, Rakesh, taken totally by surprise at the camel's aggressive interest, was in a fair bit of trouble himself. The camel's hoof had shattered the windscreen as it took the upward route, and shards of glass came flying in. Rakesh had his glasses on, but the flying shards broke his glasses as well. Result—Rakesh found something wet around his right eye and got scared when he found it was blood. He was already scared—hitting a camel is serious business in Oman (and other parts of the Middle East) and Rakesh was aware of this. We all were.

Holding a handkerchief to his right eye, he stopped the car, and got out to see the fate of the camel. To his surprise, he saw, with his partly hazy vision, that the camel had managed to get up. It ever so slowly crossed over into the coconut groves and disappeared from sight. Relieved, unable to believe his incredible luck at not having killed the camel, he got back into the car. All this while, not a single vehicle had passed by in either direction.

But Rakesh was now worried about himself. His glasses were shattered, so his vision was bad, and blood was still trickling from his right eye. Holding a hanky to the right eye with one hand, he drove as reasonably fast as he could, and went straight to the Casualty at

UAG hospital, a fair distance away. Once he told the casualty team who he was, they moved real fast.

One of the nursing assistants very kindly called Suresh on Rakesh's request. Suresh, living in the doctors' quarters close by, was there within minutes. Luckily, Rakesh was only bleeding from cuts in the conjunctiva and the upper eye lid. His cornea was intact, with no injuries to its surface. While he was being attended to, he narrated his camel encounter to Suresh. He had not sustained any other injuries, so he was allowed to go after dressings and medication.

Recovering from the shock of the episode, Rakesh insisted that he and Suresh should go to look for the camel, just in case. They drove back to the spot which Rakesh was able to identify fairly accurately— he must have driven on that stretch of road hundreds of times in the past year—but there was no sign of the camel. Thanking his good luck once again, they returned home to Suresh's place for a quiet dinner. It was too late to go to the party, anyway.

Feeling much better in the morning, Rakesh reported back to his Unit, and informed the Commanding Officer of the incident. Everyone was relieved that their doctor was alright, *al hamdulillah*. But the matter was not quite over, as yet. Some three days later, the owner of the camel turned up at Rakesh's Unit. How he found out who had hit his camel was not clear. But here he was, claiming his camel had been found dead in the coconut grove not far from the accident site. He insisted his poor camel had been deliberately run over by one of the Unit officers and demanded the camel's blood money—about 7000 Omani riyals! With that kind of money, he could buy four new camels, or even contemplate a fresh new wife! Apparently, he was very insistent.

Help came in the form of the Unit Second-in-Command, a Brit officer. He, like Mac in FST, had a good command of Arabic, laced with an impressive British accent. He summarily told the camel owner that far from getting any compensation, he should quietly leave before the Unit decided to call the police: as per law, camels were not to be left unattended even during daytime, what to talk of wandering about alone at night, especially near the highways.

The law decreed that any loss of public or private property as a result of wandering camels was punishable by a fine and prison sentence to the owner. The officer congratulated the camel owner on his incredible luck that the doctor had not died on the spot, nor was he pressing any charges against the owner for letting his camel run about loose. The matter was amicably closed over some fresh dates and Arabic kahwa, the traditional cardamom coffee.

8

Amma Conquers Oman

I remember my sister's first advice to me when I visited her in September 1980. I was stopping by at her place in Dehradun for a quick visit before going on to Delhi to report to the Army HQ prior to my departure for Oman.

'Hari, please do not squander away your earnings in Oman. I don't care if you can't get me or the kids a single thing, but you must save enough to arrange a trip for Appa and Amma to visit London,' she said. Our father was the most well-informed person about all of Europe, especially England. He knew most of the "classic" English literature by heart. He could tell you where Piccadilly Circus was and how to get there, where to go for fine vegetarian cuisine, or why a Savile Row suit was worth its colossal cost. He could quote from Churchill's speeches as easily as he could describe Mr Micawber. Yet, he was a true Indian, a true Gandhian.

With equal pride, he would tell of how his idol, the Rt. Hon'ble Srinivasa Sastri, the "Silver Tongued Orator" of the then British Empire, once stumped the entire House of Lords (could be House of Commons, but it hardly matters), when he was challenged by some arrogant dignitary:

'Mr Sastri, they say you can speak on any topic. Is that true?'

'I endeavour to live up to that reputation, Sir.'

'Alright. Speak on *Nothing*, then.' As the challenger sat down, feeling imperious at having put this pretentious Indian in place, Sastri started with these famous opening words: 'Nothing is England without India,' and apparently went on to speak for ten minutes or more, silencing the entire crowd. The way my father used to describe the scene, you would have thought he was there inside the British Parliament building, listening.

My sister felt that if anyone deserved to see London, it was our father. But my father, in his hurry to meet with his maker, didn't give me any time.

When I lamented about this after he passed away, my sister said, 'No problem, take Amma in his place—he will feel equally happy, watching from his place in heaven.'

Not quite sure about taking Amma to London, I felt I should at least bring her to Muscat. This I now set out to do, in my third year of stay. I had not yet bought my dream purchase—the car, but that could wait.

With great difficulty, I managed to get her a visit visa. In mid-1983, just a few months short of our repatriation on completion of deputation, I went on a short leave and brought her back with me to Muscat. Her arrival was eagerly awaited by the rest of the deputationists in FBH. Whenever we missed home food, each of us would extol our own mother's culinary skills. But mine was the one coming over, quite literally armed with necessary spices and herbs.

A small delegation of my colleagues came to receive us at the airport—but we were whisked away by Gopal and his wife Lalitha— they wouldn't hear of her staying cooped up in a small room with me and had threatened she would stay with them all three months of her expected stay unless I arranged some proper accommodation. And that's how Deepak had his first beer with an orthodox Hindu lady of sixty.

9

The Old Lady and the Can of Beer

I continued to be busy in the surgical wards, as always. The second day after my mother and I had landed in Muscat, Major Kuriakose called me to his office. Without much ado, he handed me his house key, and asked for mine in return. 'Hari, I am a bachelor. You have your aged mother here, so make her stay comfortable. When she goes, we can change rooms again.'

As simple as that. This man's goodness was beyond my understanding. He had given me money and bought my ticket when I had to rush home within three weeks of landing in Oman. Not once did he ask me about the money. I went to give him the money once I got my first pay, and all he had said then was that there was no hurry, I could pay him whenever I was comfortable. And now he comes offering his house without my even asking for it.

I guess some people are simply born good natured, I thought. I had no words to thank him. I had already started to feel awkward about mother—she was staying somewhere, about 40 km away, and I had not seen her for two days. I expected only to meet her on the weekends. I was happy that I could at last be with her, thanks to Major Kuriakose. But then again, I realised it was still mid-week. I could only go on Friday morning after rounds to bring her. When I mentioned this to Sunil and Deepak, both offered to go and fetch her. Deepak was going the same afternoon to the MOH library to return some books, so he said he would be more than happy to bring mother back.

I rang her up at Gopals' place. Lalitha said she wasn't happy at all with letting her go. The kids—Indu and Arvind—had found a wonderful grandma to have fun with. But she agreed when I pleaded with her. She would be doing the school rounds in the afternoon, but she would explain to Amma how to manage the door, etc., just in case Deepak dropped by when she was not there.

When I finished work that day, I suddenly realised I had not even checked with Deepak if he brought Amma over, and where she was— Major Kuriakose's key was with me. I rang up Deepak in his room. He answered at the first ring.

'*Arre*, I knew you might call. She is resting, man, why did you have to call? If you are done, come to my room.'

When I went there, Amma was awake and fresh, and she and her latest son were having tea and Danish butter cookies, the craze with all of us. Deepak accosted me:

'*Yaar,* Hari, you said your mom is quite forward thinking and all that, despite her orthodox background?' Amma was listening in. I was a bit upset. What did he mean?

'You never told me she is ultramodern boss!' He was smiling. So was Amma.

Deepak went on. 'I went and rang the bell at your friend's place. Amma was alone at home, but she said that since I had come in the hot sun, I should have something to drink before we started. She said she would get me something cold. In a minute, your modern mom comes back with two cans of Budweiser, places one in front of me, and says, "Take this, *beta,* and open this other one for me. I tried some time back but couldn't open it!" I was simply blown away.

'When I asked, "*Mataji,* do you know what this is?" she said, "Lalitha said there are cold drinks in the fridge. Why, is this not good?"'

I looked at Amma. She was smiling but looking rather uncomfortable! Poor thing, having never seen a can of beer before, she assumed it must be some cold drink like Coca-Cola in a green can! Trust Deepak to let everyone know about this incident! Till her last day in Muscat, everyone would offer her beer first—and when she refused, they would feign disappointment, 'Ah, you only have this with Deepak, eh?'

Mother more than made up for all that. The very first weekend, she single-handedly made a hundred Idlis (bachelor boy Major Kuriakose's kitchen had everything needed for a large family). When I came home from work and saw a large amount of sambar and chutney to go with hundred Idlis, I asked her if she had gone out of her mind. But, as they say, mothers always know. She just smiled and said nothing.

Her assessment of the gang's appetite was accurate—there was not a single Idli or a drop of sambar left when the fellows finished. The true mother that she was, she hadn't kept any away for herself. I could only watch her with a lump in my throat when she settled for rice and curd after everyone left. The only redeeming feature was that every single plate and utensil had been washed and laid out to dry by the guys—a practice we all learnt soon after going to Muscat, where there were no house-maids.

Amma was nothing short of a magic wand when it came to making friends. I would unleash her in a large store, and within minutes, someone would spot this old lady in the unmistakable garb of a traditional South Indian Brahmin lady.

'Hello, Mami (Aunt), are you new here?' would be the opening conversation, which invariably ended with us going over to the house of these strangers till that moment—for an impromptu dinner! Sunil, Deepak, and others, knowing the food value of Amma, would often offer to take her to show the city—and never failed to come back without a proper dinner in yet another new friend's house! My stock was already high as a bachelor, as I have explained before. Amma's presence confirmed my "good" antecedents and offers of sisters and nieces and cousins in marriage for me started piling up. And all this while, I had been agonising about introducing Glynnis to Amma.

I managed to do this cunningly one evening. I took her to "see" the hospital after ensuring Glynnis was on duty. I had asked young Deepak also to be with me, but he disappeared at the last minute. As we entered the reception area of the hospital, Glynnis was walking in her attractive, brisk fashion from one consultation room towards another. She saw us and came straight to us. I had mentally practised the correct way of introducing her to mother, but with Glynnis, usually her way would go.

She gave a cheery hello and said, 'Where have you been, Harry? Haven't seen you for so many days! What's up?' And then, seeing mother, 'Oh, this must be Mom!' She gave Mother a hug as if she had known her all her life, and said, 'Hello, Mummy, welcome to Oman!'

Mummy? I was thinking when she continued the conversation, 'Your little Harry is a very naughty boy! Hasn't even said hello to me in the past three days! So, when did you come? Safe flight? Where have you put her up, Harry?' I was quite speechless at the barrage of questions. But Amma seemed quite at ease.

'Yes, Hari's mother,' she said in her limited English. 'What is your name?'

'Oh, how silly of me. My name is Glynnis,' and she gave Amma a happy handshake. Thankfully, Sunil appeared from somewhere, and happily hugged mother with a 'How are you, *Mataji*?'

Amma acknowledged him, but her eyes were still on Glynnis. I gently steered Mother away from there in the pretext of showing her the rest of the hospital, giving Glynnis a wave and saying, 'I will see you soon, Miss.' Her look at being addressed "Miss" was priceless!

Mother was a hit with the hospital staff as well. For some of the Omanis, her typical South Indian saree was a great attraction. The Sri Lankan and Malayalee nurses were all over her—Amma was fluent in Tamil as well as Malayalam. In the Dental Centre situated in between the OPD section and the wards, our Sri Lankan Army dentist—a Capt. Senanayake—was overjoyed to see her. He immediately offered to make a full denture for her in return for a session of Dosas and Idlis. Amma graciously invited him over the very next day for lunch, and for the rest of her stay in Muscat, young Capt. Sena was her slave!

He offered his house and car in Sri Lanka for us to go and stay—irrespective of whether or not he himself was there—so that I could take Amma to visit the grand Murugan Temple in Kadirkamam, one of the holiest shrines for Tamils all over the world. The Sri Lankan girls wanted her to come to their quarters for a meal, which again Amma happily accepted—except that when we went there one evening, we found that every single dish had onions, which in her typically orthodox fashion, Amma had never touched all her life.

She would happily make onion-based dishes for us kids but would herself never eat any food containing onions—or garlic for that matter. Yet, not wanting to disappoint the girls, she took a little of this and a little of that, feigning fullness in the tummy, and won all the girls over totally. Even Dr Sivanesan couldn't resist her. The man literally knocked me off my feet when, meeting her near the wards, he spoke in chaste Sri Lankan Tamil to her, much to her delight! He had never once—even during my visit to his house, said a single word to me in Tamil.

While everyone liked Amma, she evoked strong emotions in some friends. I remember an incident involving Mr and Mrs Prasad. Prasad was a high-ranking official in Datsun, the rival company of Toyota in those days in Oman. He kept on telling me to bring Mother over to stay at least for a day or two in his house. One weekend, I took Amma to town, and we ran into the Gopals, who insisted we go over to their place in Ruwi for dinner. Post-dinner, they would hear nothing of my driving back to the Army camp. We were forced to stay over, and Amma, always partial to small kids, couldn't resist Indu and Arvind's entreaties.

The next afternoon, after a heavy lunch, Amma and I set off home. On our way back, I remembered that the Prasads stayed en-route in a place called Shatti-al Qurm. When I asked her, Amma was game, as always, to drop by to say hello. We were heartily welcomed, but when I told them we were actually coming after an overnight stay in Gopal's house, Prasad was visibly upset.

He looked at me accusingly and said, 'Doctor, I told you so many times to bring her to our place for a stay. She reminds me so much of my mother who is no more. I wanted to look after Amma, as I had never been able to look after my own mother in her last days. You should have given me that privilege, instead of going elsewhere.' And he actually broke down. I was astonished by this open show of affection to Amma, and ashamed of not having thought of the Prasads earlier. Such was Amma's abiding charisma. Months after she left Muscat, the first bit of conversation in all my friends' houses would always be about Amma and how they missed her.

Glynnis got to meet Amma a few times, once even in our (Major Kuriakose's) home. I was happy that the conversation was general, with no embarrassing questions or comments from any of the parties involved. I would bring up the necessary conversation at an appropriate time, I thought to myself. I had to first make sure my thoughts coincided with Glynnis's feelings. I was therefore a bit relieved when Suresh landed up in Muscat one day, fell promptly in love with Amma like everyone else, and without any room for protest, insisted she had to go with him for a few days to Salalah. To my utter surprise, Amma readily agreed!

She spent the better part of a week in Salalah, adding a lot more names to her ever-growing list of lifelong fans. Suresh even took her to Thumrait, where this spring chicken of a lady, not many weeks from her sixty-third birthday, actually went land yachting in the Thumrait airstrip! Suresh confessed later that he was not sure if he was doing the right thing, but apparently, after hurtling past the entire runway once, she asked him if he was short on time and if not, she would like the breeze on her face one more time!

A couple of weeks before she was to leave, Amma hesitatingly asked me details of my pay and allowances. It took her some time to comprehend the enormity of her son's financial status. I use the term in all honesty and humility. As a young woman—girl, actually, as she was only 15 when she got married, she had started her life with her husband earning 45 rupees a month. For someone who had to manage a family of four kids, a mother-in-law (and a widowed sister-in-law for most of the time) with her husband's salary which never ever approached four figures in her entire married life, her youngest child starting his career as a commissioned officer in the army on a pay of Rs 1800 a month was in itself a massive leap of financial status. Then, to fly by plane for the first time in her life to a foreign country, there to find her son driving around in an air-conditioned car, living in air-conditioned, carpeted, furnished comfort was almost like living in a dream. And now, to be told that the son was earning the unheard-of sum of close to 20,000 rupees a month was an enormous piece of news, difficult to comprehend. After an entire life of self-sacrifice—never more than two sarees in her possession, always given to extracting the most out of every grain of pulse or rice, forever making do with leftovers after feeding her family—this sudden change was understandably difficult to cope with.

One day, I had taken her to a shop which was selling China Silk sarees—a craze which sent all Indian women into a frenzy of shopping—and she selected one single saree! I had to practically fight with her to take a dozen more—for her, my sisters, sister-in-law and other relatives. The ease with which I paid for these and other items we bought that day must have prompted her to ask me about how much I was earning. She was in total silence for a while, contemplating, assimilating the great good fortune bestowed on her son by the Gods. Ever the practical woman, she recovered soon enough, with a clear plan of action.

'Son,' she said affectionately, 'I want you to promise me one thing. Soon, it will be time for you to get married. I want you to buy every single item needed for your married life—fridge (always on top of the wish list for most middle-class people), television, cooking utensils, dinner set (she had admired the quality crockery and cutlery in my friends' houses with a visible longing), bedsheets, towels, everything. You should not have to ask the girl you marry to spend a penny on any wedding related expenses. Promise me that. Will you have enough money for all that?'

I assured her I would, and more. On an impulse, I promised her that we would do all the shopping before she left for India. I would be following in about three months, anyway, so I might as well buy all the things on my list well in time.

The shopping I did with my mother over the next few days brings back some of the happiest memories I have of Amma's visit, indeed of my entire Muscat years. Every day, she would write to my sisters about the purchases we did, in her neat Tamil, and would insist I "post" it at the airport.

She even wanted me to buy sarees for her future daughter-in-law. I would try and dodge this—what if Glynnis actually wanted to cement our relationship by wanting to marry me? I certainly could see that possibility but could not see her in a saree! *No harm*, I thought, and bought a few just to please mother. As she gained in confidence about my purchasing power, her list expanded to include relatives and friends. *In due course, I would have to buy boxes and crates to pack all these items for transportation to India,* I thought. *Hope I get a good posting on my return to India.*

My passion for surgery was strong as ever, but I was under no illusion that I would go straight from Muscat to Pune (where the Armed Forces Medical College is located) for the surgery course. I pushed those worries away to see what else I could do to please mother. When I asked her, she said something that is so typical of most Indian women. She wanted me to organise a prayer in the Shiva temple as thanksgiving for all the blessings He had given me. That was easily arranged, and we had a temple *"prasadam"* lunch after the puja the very next weekend. It was attended by most of the people who knew Amma, including, of course, my colleagues, or, more accurately, Mother's Idli fans!

Finally, the day came when Amma left for India. She was being escorted by one of my civilian friends who was going on holiday to India. Many of the hospital staff had turned up at our (Major Kuriakose's) residence when we were to leave for the airport. Glynnis dropped by at our place to say bye to Amma. She gave Amma a big hug. After she left, Amma said quite matter-of-factly: 'Such a beautiful girl. I hope she gets married to someone nice.'

A typical Indian wish, but something that I tried to read deep into. I didn't get very far with my Freudian analysis, though! The crowd that came to see her off at the airport would have made a minor dignitary turn green with envy! A host of our—her—civilian friends were there, including the Gopals, Prasads, and her other fans. Deepak, Sunil, Banerjee, Vijay, Senanayake, were all there at the airport as well, fussing over Amma's bags and things.

After seeing her off at the airport, I exchanged keys with Major Kuriakose and returned to my room, feeling rather empty. I had always been my father's pet, but that did not prevent my mother from truly loving me with all her heart. This was the first time I had really got to spend quality time with her—what little I got away from the hospital—and I realised how terribly I missed her. But in all that emotional upheaval, I was happy at the thought that I could now write a long mail to my sister about having fulfilled her wish.

Even as I exchanged letters with my sister about Amma's visit to Muscat and how it would have been nice if Appa could also have been there, an idea started taking root in my mind. I had a diplomatic passport, which I would need to surrender on my return to India after the deputation. Getting a tourist visa would be much easier with my white passport. If I shelved the idea of buying a car, I could easily make a trip to London, and take in the sights on behalf of Appa. Already, my friends and I were discovering a lot of hassles we would have to go through to export a car to India. Customs duty was prohibitive. Cars here were left-hand drive models, while in India, the traffic, imposed as it was by the Brits, required a right-hand drive vehicle. I decided to explore the London option instead of a car. Besides wanting to see London for my father's sake, my own interest had been piqued after hearing stories of stately buildings and beautiful parks from Sunil. The underground rail system was another attraction.

And there was this small possibility that I could ask Glynnis if she would please show me around in London—after all, she was a local, wasn't she? Well, it turned out she wasn't. When I gently brought up the idea with her one day, she laughed her trademark laugh.

'London? Harry, I have never been there! I am a Llanyrafon girl, you know that, don't you? The only city I have been to outside of my little town is Liverpool! You could add Manchester, if you consider I flew to Oman from there, but I have never been to the town centre there—only to the airport! Why, I haven't even been to Birmingham, what to talk of London! Harry, London is 250 miles from my home, probably 300. I don't believe anyone in my family has ever been to London! If you promise to take me with you and show me around

London—I bet you have already read up everything about London—I would be happy to go with you.'

This was a shock to me! That she was willing to go with me to London was exciting alright, but I couldn't believe that she—in fact no one in her family—had ever seen London! I realised it is the same with all of us—she is British, so we think she must have been to all the big places in the UK, just as an American or Britisher thinking every Indian must be visiting the Taj Mahal whenever they felt a bit bored! How easily we take things for granted about people!

As it happened, I did visit London, but without Glynnis. And without anyone else, for that matter. The reason was short and simple: Army-leave policy! I was disappointed as I boarded the Cathay Pacific flight.

10

The Unexpected Cup that Cheered Me —and 800 Million Others

U nlike poor Columbus and poor Captain Cook, my trip to London was a breeze. I didn't have the disadvantage of language those two gentlemen had, and maps were sort of more accurate than in their times. My Pakistani friend Moin Khan had arranged my flights and accommodation.

'Bed & Breakfast, Doctor Saab,' he explained, 'is a kind of family-run hotel where you get a small room to sleep in, and a sumptuous breakfast to start your day with. Eat your lunch and dinner outside, but make sure you tuck in really well at breakfast. Food is really expensive in London, so take a fruit or two from your breakfast table when you set out,' he advised.

'I have booked you in with a Pakistani British family that runs a B&B in South Kensington, a posh part of London, close to a lot of museums and all such things. The place is very close to the Underground Tube station, bus stops, etc. You can ask them for guidance—Mr and Mrs Latif are a very nice couple,' he added.

As it turned out, that was an understatement. The couple went very much out of the way to make me feel at home. I landed in Heathrow airport one fine afternoon in June 1983. Taking advantage of the excellent signages at the airport, I was able to find my way to the underground station within the airport complex, buy a ticket from one of the many machines to South Kensington where I got off, luggage and all. Here again, I didn't need to ask anyone for help—this suited me, as I was a bit diffident, unsure of my pronunciation. There was a map of the local area, and I was easily able to spot my destination—just a few minutes' walking distance from the station. I dragged my suitcase along the neatly paved road and reached the address Moin had given me. When I knocked on the door, a tall, handsome Pakistani chap opened the door and enquired, 'Yes, how can I help?' in a very British accent. When I told him my name and that I was Moin's friend from Muscat, he looked amazed.

'*Kamaal hai, Doctor Saab* (It's amazing, Doctor),' he said, switching to Urdu and helping me with the luggage.

'Moin Bhai had written you would be coming, but I expected a phone call asking for directions and all that. But you are already here, right at our door. This is really brilliant!'

I was given a special room with an attached bathroom—called "en-suite" for some inexplicable reason. A nice shower and some tea and biscuits so thoughtfully provided for in the room (thanks to my Muscat experience, I already knew about teabags), I decided to hit the sack for a much-needed snooze. Later, Mr Latif, the owner, helped me make a local call through his private switchboard.

I got through immediately to Dr Meera, (Meera Akka to me) my sister's classmate from her medical college days. Meera Akka was very close to our family during her student days, with my parents playing the role of local guardians for her, as her own parents were in far off Baroda. I had written to her about my plans but had hesitated to ask if I could stay with her. The moment I announced my name, Dr Meera let off affectionate steam at the other end of the line.

'You silly donkey, I got your letter just three days back; how am I supposed to reply? And how dare you even ask for permission to stay with me? Did I ever write for permission to Appa and Amma (she always addressed my parents as if they were her parents, too) for all those weekends I used to spend with you guys? Why, I even spent the entire winter holidays once at your home, not wanting to travel to my parents' place in Baroda, so that Lalitha (that's my sister) and I could do some combined study! And you try and act formal with me, eh? Wait till I see you; your earlobe is going to get a lot longer, I promise you. Where are you anyway now?'

She paused, making me admire her lung capacity. I knew her as a pathologist, but maybe she ran marathons when she wasn't busy looking through microscopes or through the innards of dead bodies. Couldn't tell. I told her instead where I was. This led to another barrage of scolding, at the end of which she summarily ordered me to pack my bags and come straight over to her place—which I learnt was some 30 minutes and two Underground changes away.

I had already paid for a week of accommodation, so I simply avoided getting into a discussion on the subject with Akka. Mr Latif told me how to navigate my way to Akka's place in the exclusive suburb of Hampstead. I had picked up a free map of the underground network at the airport. Mr Latif's place had such maps everywhere— lobby, breakfast hall, the landing of the stairway, my room, literally everywhere, though the bathroom, to be fair, was free. There were any number of walking-tour maps, tourist information pamphlets etc., too, all over the building. I helped myself to a few and taking leave of Mr Latif and his very pretty wife, set out to find Meera Akka's place.

I found the place very easily in a broad street full of houses on either side, without any gap between dwellings. And for all I knew, I was probably back in Mr Latif's neck of the woods—the street and the houses, all two storeyed, all with sloping, red-tiled roofs, looked exactly the same as the one I had left behind. Even the kind of flowering trees that lined both sides of the street were very similar. (Years later, I would find that the same monotonous pattern was replicated all over England and Wales!) I tentatively knocked at Akka's door.

There was some more scolding when Akka realised I had not brought all my luggage along. But in all this, there was no mistaking her affection for me. Her two kids, both girls, were kind of assessing me while all this exchange was going on. Sneaking in a word here and a word there, I managed to tell Akka about how my trip had all been planned to the last detail by a friend back in Muscat, using teleprinter communication for all bookings, including the B&B at South Kensington. But she would have none of it—I had to come over next morning—she pointed out her own graciousness in giving me time until next morning, and that was that.

I was unsure of what Mr Latif would say if I cancelled my booking. B&B though it was, the money involved was not small. Akka read my mind quite easily. She asked for the contact number and dialled it right away. Her chaste Urdu, an oh-so-soft tone, and a bit of tweaking of facts here and there (I am seeing my cousin after 15 years, she said, practically choking on her emotions), and of course, the innate goodness of Mr Latif all led to the expected result—I would be charged only for today and tomorrow, provided I checked out first thing in the morning after breakfast. The girls seemed really happy to hear that this newly arrived Hari Mama would be staying in their house for a few days. I think they were starved of company, with both parents away most part of the day, and mid-term holidays around. I was already something of an expert with kids—and they both took to me instantly.

Akka had the TV on when I entered their home, and some BBC reporter was rounding up the day's news by the time we finished all the phone calls and things and sat down to eat some truly tasty Dosas. It was then that I realised how truly fortunate I was: the TV reporter rounded off his bulletin by reminding viewers about the final match of the ongoing Prudential World Cup cricket tournament to be played at the Lord's Cricket ground the next day—between the mighty West Indians and minions (He didn't say the word but meant every bit of it), India! Oh my God, I thought, how hard I had tried to avoid being able to see this match by insisting on staying at the B&B! The disastrous start by the Indians in the ongoing World Cup series had been extremely depressing, and no one had even imagined they would make it to the finals. Now that they so fortuitously made it to the last encounter, the fact that the West Indies were already two-time champions, had absolutely no effect on the hopes of so many millions of Indians, in India and abroad, for a favourable outcome.

In retrospect, I now realise how this one game changed the face of cricket in India forever over the succeeding years. Today, India is the undisputed driver of all-cricket related issues in the entire world; the BCCI (Board of Control for Cricket in India) is the world's richest cricketing body, helping young people realise their cricketing dreams. It is the ultimate destination for all things cricket, including for teams like England and Australia who monopolised cricket for decades before this particular event.

Of course, my excitement had nothing to do with these facts—all this was yet to come in the future. But for me—and for the 800 million Indians like me back home, cricket was even then the only religion—the undisputed unifier across faiths, class, caste, or creed. It was the most potent, enjoyable, and widespread addiction!

I seriously considered asking Akka if it was okay for me to go to the B&B right away and come back, bag and baggage. But it was already late in the evening, although I was totally surprised to see the sun shining bright so far into the evening. Akka merely said that I was to be back next morning before the match start time of 11 a.m., and that I had better bring some sackfuls of luck; India was going to need it. She would have to go to her hospital in the morning but expected to be free after lunch. The girls would be home, and thankfully, knew how to operate the TV! I couldn't wait for the match to begin. I left for South Kensington after spending some more time talking to Akka and her two adorable kids.

So it was that I put my mission of fulfilling Appa's dreams on hold, at least until after the match tomorrow. I knew he would understand. He would have quoted Bernard Shaw's "eleven fools playing in the middle and eleven thousand fools watching" comment no doubt, but he was not fully free of the cricket bug, absolutely no one in India was. (And to think that the man who really weaved the magic of cricket around all Indians from 5-year olds to 85-year olds, Sachin Tendulkar, had not yet entered the arena!) I had a hurried breakfast and checked out of Mr Latif's B&B.

I desperately wanted to find someone to discuss the game due in the next few hours, but wasn't sure of Latif—after all, he was a Pakistani, he would be more than happy to see India lose. I had just about entertained such ugly thoughts in my mind, when Latif ambled up to me, to help carry my luggage.

He said, 'Doctor Saab, today is a big day! The world thinks West Indies is the greatest cricket team, and I agree, but we should never forget that even an elephant can slip. And if it falls, it may not be able to get up at all! Let us hope India gets to bat first and puts up a nice score. If they get 260-280, these West Indian fellows will panic, I am sure. I think this new captain of the Indian team, Kapil Dev, is a great all-rounder. And you have the greatest batsman of all in Gavaskar. I get the feeling India is going to be champion today. *Hum sab ki duayein aap ke saath hai* (All our good wishes are with you).' He shook my hand warmly. *I might as well be stepping out on to the cricket pitch,* I thought. Instead, I stepped out on to the street looking deserted that early Sunday morning, luggage in tow.

As I walked the short distance to the underground station, I was full of remorse. I had carefully avoided looking Mr Latif in the eyes, lest I reveal my unworthy thoughts. I was truly ashamed. Mr Latif was one hundred percent like me. Somebody drew a stupid line, and so he became a Pakistani and I, an Indian. That's all. But that line had become so deep rooted in our psyche that I failed to see that sans the tag of nationality, Mr Latif was just the same as I was. *I should be all the more ashamed,* I thought, *having already had the pleasure of friendship with so many other nationals, including many Pakistanis, in Muscat.* Why, I was walking the streets of London only because Moin, of Islamabad, Pakistan, had planned my trip so meticulously. And Ashraf! He had taught me the basics of squash; he, an acclaimed expert and I, a miserably unwieldy beginner. Yet, he had never once talked down to me—in the squash court or outside. Lost in such self-deprecating thoughts, I reached the station. My education in humanity was being reinforced on a daily basis.

At Meera Akka's home, the kids opened the door the instant I knocked and appeared truly delighted to see me. We chatted about this and that, and I was delighted to find that both were learning classical Carnatic music. They obliged me by singing a song or two, and I was impressed by their adherence to pitch. The kids were really talented. The elder one, Ratna, made a nice cup of tea for me, and as I sipped it, chatting with the girls about Muscat and London, my eyes kept darting to the clock on the wall.

Finally, the match started after a lot of fanfare, including the national anthems of both countries. *Fauji* (Army-man) that I was, I automatically stood up in attention as the Indian national anthem was played—the kids immediately followed suit! India was to bat first—I hoped Mr Latif's prediction would ring true. But those hopes were shattered in less than five minutes of start of play—India's leading batsman, Sunil Gavaskar, was out in the very first over!

The others seemed woefully out of touch, unable to handle the breakneck speed with which the huge West Indian pacemen bowled. Indeed, on more than one occasion, some of the Indian batsmen almost had their neck—and a few other parts of their anatomy—broken, such was the menacing speed of the Caribbean bowlers. Yet, there were moments of brilliance from the Indian batsmen, and we heartily cheered each run, each boundary scored by them. But despite our fond wishes, all India could put on the board was a paltry 183 runs, about a hundred less than what Mr Latif had predicted as a challenging score. The commentators seemed to think so, too—they predicted it was all over for India, and it was just a matter of how quickly the West Indians mopped up this ungainly target. Although it hurt a lot to hear India being described as "minions", "weak in all departments of the game", etc., I knew that the comments were true. India had never made it to the finals in the World Cup series so far, and more importantly, had never beaten West Indies in this new format of the game.

What had started as an experiment in Melbourne a few years back, when three days of a regular match between Australia and England was washed out, had now become an accepted new format of cricket. In that match, the authorities, aware that two remaining days would not produce a result, had decided to go for 40 overs a side match. Australia had won the contest, and people all over realised the joy of having a format with an assured outcome. The International Council for Cricket, the snooty, all-white organisation which controlled cricket around the globe, condescended to have 60 overs-a-side match as a regular feature from then on. The match played in Melbourne had followed the Australian pattern of eight balls an over, but the 60 overs' match would follow the English pattern of six balls an over.

While the ICC dragged its feet over the rules and regulations, an impatient, enterprising Australian called Kerry Packer started a privately funded organisation—the World Series Cricket. He was considered a real maverick when he suggested that bright-coloured uniforms replace the traditional white slacks and shirts, that games could be played under floodlights (Day-Night Matches, he called them), and that teams and players would be remunerated based on their collective and individual performances. Till then, cricket was a leisure sport, with more fun than money for participants. It needed players to hold on to a proper job on the side to make both ends meet. Even at the time of this present world cup final match, all the Indian players were employees of banks, railways, and other accommodating government organisations, and their remuneration hardly covered their passage to England. Other than national pride, there was not much by way of incentive—at least for the Indian team—to win the world cup. I wasn't aware of it then, but that evening would change all that for ever and ever, and take Indian cricket to unimagined heights of fame, glory, and money.

The West Indians had started their innings after the break. The commentators were going on and on about how it was going to be a mere formality, with the mighty West Indies most likely to make mincemeat of the Indian bowling attack, and so on. One English commentator in particular kept on harping on the theory of "rank outsiders" India about to get a solid thrashing from the likes of the great Vivian Richards, Clive Lloyd, and other greats in the Caribbean team. He kept coming back to his pet theory of India never even deserving a final berth, what to talk of winning the Cup. He expressed his incredulity at the gumption of the Indian Captain, Kapil Dev, having said in a pre-tournament interview that he and his team were here to win the World Cup. The said commentator could simply not get over this.

He asked the only Indian representative in the commentary box—the erstwhile Indian wicket-keeper batsman, Farokh Engineer, to comment on the audacity of the Indian Captain. Engineer, ever the witty one, simply reminded his colleague that being audacious was better than attempting to be clairvoyant. The match was not over yet, so it would be best to see if Kapil Dev was being confident and audacious, or merely daydreaming. I wanted to get into the television set and wring the neck of the chap who was putting India down every few seconds. The feeling was, of course, made worse by the realisation that with just 183 on board, India had a Himalayan task ahead of them, to say the very least. India had not even lasted their full quota of 60 overs. West Indies, therefore, merely had to score about three runs an over and the Cup would be theirs—yet again. And history showed that most West Indian batsmen did not believe in singles and doubles—they dealt in fours and sixes. The atmosphere at the start of the second half of the match was thus gloomier than the typical English weather outside, at least from the Indian perspective. I wondered if the rain gods could be invoked to save the day for India—but they would have to oblige tomorrow as well, as a reserve day had been kept for the finals, should play be interrupted.

Thus, it was that we—the two kids and I—sat down to watch the proceedings, a prayer on our lips, and a lot of fear in our bellies! Our prayers were answered in the very second over—West Indies lost their first wicket! But there was no time to celebrate—in walked the most formidable batsman of the time, Vivian Richards (later to be 'Sir' Richards). And not without reason.

His very presence at the wicket sent chills up the spine of bowlers across the world. As he ambled over to the batting crease, I stepped up my prayers. But even before my prayers could register themselves with the Gods, Richards hit the very first ball he faced for a four. West Indian supporters in the crowd welcomed this with a huge shout, while the motley Indian crowd in the stands was shocked into silence. This silence continued over the next few overs while Richards thrashed every bowler, despatching ball after ball to the boundary with disdain.

The Indian pantheon of minor and major Gods runs into millions—and one of them seemed to have listened to my prayers. I am being rather naïve here, I know—surely, the Gods were being bombarded with similar prayers by many millions of my fellow countrymen, who easily outnumbered the Gods! An unbelievable thing happened. Viv Richards hit the gentle paceman Madan Lal for what seemed like a six. But the ball covered more distance vertically than outwards—and running crazily to his side, Kapil Dev took an almost impossible catch—and held on to it. This catch is the stuff of legends—I believe it is permanently etched in the minds of every single Indian cricket fan of those days. If I close my eyes now, I can see it crystal clear in my mind's eye and hear the shocked silence of every single spectator (and commentators, too—especially the loss of words by the villainous English commentator), to be replaced in a few seconds by an uproar from the Indian fans that would have reminded all Britain of its Roman gladiator days. There was much rejoicing in Meera Akka's home, too—oh, in all this melee, we had hardly noticed her having come back—and she declared this was a great time for a cup that cheers.

At three down for 57 runs, the battle with Vivian Richards had been won, but the war with the West Indies was far from over. There was Clive Lloyd—the captain—no mean batsman himself, and a whole lot of other formidable batsmen to follow, to wipe out the remaining 130 odd runs. We had to keep our Gods engaged through intense prayers—there was not a moment (or a run) to lose! And boy, did they oblige!

The great West Indies had not yet notched up 80 runs on the board and they were already six wickets down. The Indian team sensed blood—in an unexpected turn of events, the hunted were suddenly hunters. The body language of the team was suddenly very different. They were willing to give their best in the field to cut off the boundaries, and the twos into ones. The West Indies, not used to defeats at all, had probably underestimated the Indian team. Kapil Dev had led from front, with that incredible catch to dismiss the one man who could have single handedly taken the match away from India. While the West Indian tail enders—all of them over six feet in height and built to size—were eminently capable of taking their team across the finish line, the sudden surge of self-belief in the Indian bowlers and fielders was more than equal to the occasion. But for a brief hiccup in the middle, the Indians chipped away at the West Indian wickets steadily, and the cricketing giants of the day fell well short of their target, all their wickets folding up for a mere 140 runs. Surprise, surprise, the West Indians also did not bat their full quota of 60 overs. Indeed, they were all out for 52 overs, two less than what the Indians had managed to bat for!

It was perhaps the most unexpected victory in the world of

international cricket, and I believe it still remains so. The poor commentators, who had been chiding India for attempting the impossible, had to summarily eat their words. Of course, they did that with the typical attitude of persons incapable of being dignified in defeat.

'Rank outsiders India have caused an impossible upset' was, I recall, the most complimentary remark on offer. But I didn't care. No one did, not in Meera Akka's home, in the streets of London, and all over the world, where Indians lived. In India, there were national level celebrations—from busy politicians to the common folk in villages, people were dancing in frenzied delight. This was a night to remember, savour, and recall—again and again. Children born long after the event would be told increasingly anointed versions of the story—my children have grown up on my own "personal" version, in some of which, I even managed to place myself inside the Lord's cricket ground!

The whole experience was totally draining of our emotions, and the scene in Meera Akka's home could have been mistaken for a funeral, so many tears were shed unabashedly by all of us. It is only proper that I add a word or two to the already long passage above. Suddenly, the cricketing world sat up and took notice of Indian Cricket. The increasing availability of television (the Indian government started placing television sets in community halls all over the cities and countryside), an improving economy, corporate sponsorships, all led to the Board of Control for Cricket in India (BCCI), becoming, over the next few short years, the richest sports body in the whole world. Cricket—already a very popular sport—has become firmly established as the uniting fibre of the country, a religion that cuts across all religions. It remains so to this day.

11

Appa's England

Although cricket dominates memories of my visit to England, I did many other interesting things while there, many for my father's sake, some out of my own interest. I learnt a lot, too, professionally, culturally, and socially. Among the first things that caught my attention was the fact that unlike back home in India, or for that matter in Muscat, where the days and nights were pretty much equal, here in England, the days (in summer) were unusually long. It was rather confusing for me, initially; I had to hit the bed because it was bedtime, rather than because outside conditions of light and dark dictated it. But bright light or not, most shops in the city shut down by 5:30 p.m.!

What a waste of shopping opportunity, I thought. I was so used to stepping out from my home in India around ten at night for buying essentials! Having said that, there were many admirable policies as well. For instance, the day India won the World Cup, I insisted that we go out to eat. This was agreed upon enthusiastically by the girls, and promptly shot down by Meera Akka. She would not have me wasting money eating out, she said. Besides, she had already made the traditional sweet dish, *payasam*, to celebrate India's historic win! Could I buy them something? No, was the retort; all major stores would be closed, anyway! Pleading with her, I managed to convince her into letting me buy something for the kids. The next afternoon, we travelled by Underground to Oxford Street, and I had my first

212

encounter with the famous Marks & Spencer's stores. The sheer size of the store, with its myriad floors dedicated to women's clothing, men's apparels, etc. was daunting.

But I was (relatively) loaded with moolah, coming as I was from Muscat. After much persuasion and discussion, I was allowed to buy a pair of jeans and tops for the kids. Akka, of course, flatly refused to let me buy anything for her. We walked about the great shopping place full of huge stores, the likes of which I had never seen before in India, Muscat, or Dubai. I took in all the evidence of a flourishing capital economy, feeling sorry for India, the original source of wealth for England, in more ways than one.

When we returned home, Ratna was horrified to find that her jeans were too loose at the waist. Veena, the younger kid, was lucky. I was disappointed. I offered to go back to the store, but Akka said no need, we could exchange it for the right size the next day at a branch of M&S near her home. This was the first time I had ever heard of buying an item in one place and exchanging it at another! I was amazed at the customer convenience available in London—and as I was told, all over Europe and America. I wondered if we would ever see such facilities in India.

London's incredibly complex, yet extremely efficient Underground Tube system, its double decker buses, and the predictable accuracy of their service were other things I could never get over. I realised India was indeed rather backward in so many ways. And it really hurt. Perhaps, such a country as mine was not expected to excel in other areas like sports, and perhaps that explained the incredulousness of the English cricket commentator. His rude comments were still rankling in my mind, but I had to accept that as a country, we in India were not giving much for people to admire. That hurt like hell as well.

But nothing came even close to making me feel small, and sad, as my visit the next day to the University College Medical School to see Akka's department. Her department with all its fancy equipment and spotlessly clean labs was impressive enough. When she left me in the Anatomy department with an introduction to one of the demonstrators, I was allowed access to a large TV with a video player—not unlike the one I had bought in Muscat. I was shown a bookshelf full of video cassettes. I selected one on a rather difficult topic—Peritoneal Reflections, under the category "Abdomen". I was all by myself in the room for the next hour and more.

I was stunned by the clarity with which the subject was presented by the speaker, with accompanying video animations. This is a subject which most medical students find impossible to master, because visualising the development of the peritoneum—a nebulous layer of sheet like material that invests the entire inside of the tummy and simultaneously covers the organs—is never easy. The video made all the difference. There were so many other topics I would have loved to see, but obviously not that day, not even on that trip. Again, I had mixed emotions—happy to be able to see such nice things, sad that such facilities were not available—in the early 80s— in a single medical college in India.

I had other pilgrimages to undertake: a visit to the Royal College of Surgeons in central London. This was less satisfying than I expected, entirely due to my fault—I was rather diffident, unwilling to ask anyone for help, and all I did was hang around in the common areas, look at some portraits of great surgeons, and quietly slink away. No doubt it was a reflection of my sense of deficiency. But it did have a positive side to it.

I was determined more than ever to crack the FRCS Part-I exam. I had applied for taking the exam at the Royal College of Surgeons in Edinburgh—partly because I somehow felt everything about the English College was more intimidating than the Scottish one, and partly because I very much wanted to visit the College in Edinburgh, as most of my surgical heroes happened to come from there. I wanted to spend time seeing their portraits in the College Hall and was sure their very gaze would inspire me to become a good, competent surgeon. When I mentioned this to Akka, she told me something I have not forgotten since then.

She said that she had been appointed a senior lecturer at the University College soon after coming to London, because she had all the necessary qualifications and many years of experience behind her. When she was assigned students to supervise, she expected to carry on from where she had left off in India.

'But Hari, believe me; in the initial days, I was rather disappointed with the students—they would ask the most obvious questions about reading histology slides, for example. From staining of slides to what magnification of the microscope to start with to what routine to follow in reporting them, I had to practically spoon-feed them. I used to think that my students back in Delhi were far more independent in comparison. But a few months down the line, I would walk into my office, and find that one of my postgraduates had prepared a preliminary report about a particular slide—and going through it, I would get this feeling of relief that I had not insisted on reporting it first—I could hardly add or delete a word! The reporting would be so methodical, so thorough, such was the sense of commitment almost all my students showed.

Well before their qualifying exams, they would be as good as me, or better—way better, in the case of some of them! And here I was, with more than twenty years of experience in the field. Hari, that is what training is all about. Never be afraid to clarify the silliest of doubts while you train. You are allowed, even expected, to ask silly questions as a trainee. But not after you get the qualification and the stamp of a senior! Remember that.' I do, to this day. And I encourage students to ask questions, however ridiculous it may seem to them—often, such questions from a greenhorn student would make me think and look up relevant literature. Perhaps, that was the most enduring of all my experiences during that first visit to the UK, the idea of constant learning, reflection, and self-improvement.

I spent a few hours visiting the Piccadilly circus, Madame Tussauds,

Sherlock Holmes's fictional address in Baker Street, and the famous Hyde Park speakers' corner, which was one of Appa's favourites. I looked up the places where P G Wodehouse's famous Drones Club was meant to be, and sites mentioned in Charles Dickens' Oliver Twist, especially Bethnal Green, which showed no signs whatever of the impecunity of Dickens' days. I made the sacred journey by bus to Stratford-Upon-Avon, Shakespeare's birthplace. This was exclusively for my father.

He would have shown equal reverence to this site as any holy temple in India, had he been able to make it. I looked up to the skies, my eyes misty, hoping Appa would be watching from up there somewhere, seeing what I was seeing on his behalf. I was glad Meera Akka or her kids were not there with me on that trip—I was an emotional mess, and being by myself with thoughts of my father was a very private moment. As always, when thinking about his demise, I heaved a sigh, remembering his oft repeated quotation, "It might have been."

12

Honorary Membership of a Cult
—and College

I took the long journey by overnight train to Edinburgh soon afterwards, reading my books all through the night. London in June is passable, temperature wise. Edinburgh was something else, as I found out when I got off the train. It was very windy and very cold. There was a tourist information centre at the station, where Akka had advised me to get help with cheap accommodation. Sure enough, the young man at the counter was most helpful. He gave me a form to fill out and asked me to wait while he tried to match my needs with available accommodation. About ten minutes of sitting and shivering later, he called me to the counter.

He had booked a B&B for me and gave me directions to get there. He added that I had better hurry, because the position would be held by the B&B owner only for an hour. I thought it a bit unfair—didn't they want my custom? Why offer the room, then? Somewhat upset, I decided to go there, anyway—it was only a ten-minute walk away, and I could easily drag my luggage; it wasn't much. At any rate, I had not much choice. In time, I found the address and knocked on the door. It was opened by a middle-aged lady, who said a somewhat surprised sounding, 'Hello, there. How can I help you?'

I said I had been sent there by the Tourist Information Centre at the station.

She looked puzzled. 'And what was the name, again?' Again? I hadn't as much as started on my initials till then.

I said, for better effect, 'Dr Harikrishnan.'

She looked absolutely startled by this information. She turned towards the inside of the house and shouted, 'Sophie, come here! Look who is at the door—it is Harrikrishna.'

I was even more perplexed! I didn't know any Sophie, and didn't expect anyone in Edinburgh, Sophie or otherwise, to know me. A roly-poly young woman with pink cheeks appeared at the door, had one look at me, and said, 'Oh! My good God.'

And mother and daughter (that's what they turned out to be) burst into unstoppable laughter, in the midst of which, my luggage was taken from me, and I was very warmly welcomed, into the dining area, with Sophie actually holding my hand! Then came the explanation.

The senior lady said, 'I am so sorry, Mr Harrikrishna—sorry, Doctor, is it? Hope you didn't think me rude, making you wait at the door. You see, they rang up and said they were sending a Harrikrishna, and I said to Sophie, "Oh, no, not one of them noisy baldies again, singing at all odd hours; what will I tell our other guests?" And here you are, full of nice, thick hair and all that, and such a pleasant young man you seem to be. Please pardon me. Some nice and hot tea to start with, Sophie, please, before we sit this young man down for breakfast. It is pretty cold outside.'

Thus did I survive a rejection by the B&B, all because my innocent parents decided to give me a name which would club me with others who, in their pursuit of Lord Krishna, decided to adopt the very same name for their cult! At any rate, same name or not, I hardly had the time to disturb the other guests in the B&B. Post breakfast and a shower, I set out to explore the city. I bought a long-term passion of mine—a corduroy jacket with a leather patch over the elbows—ever since I had seen Sean Connery wearing one of those in a movie, I had wanted to own one. And where better to buy such an iconic jacket than in Sean Connery's birthplace?

That, and a St. Michael tie I bought in Edinburgh remained with me for many, many years, hardly the worse for wear. I checked out the Royal College premises on Nichols Road, in preparation for my exam the next day. The great surgeons of the past century and more stared down rather severely at me from their huge portraits, almost admonishing me for intruding into their domain. I then wandered around to the Edinburgh Castle, where I sat along with a few, very old locals and stared at the even older castle. The rest of the day was spent studying hard for the exam, with my moods swinging from pure elation to total depression, depending on whether I got my answers right or wrong.

The next day was spent almost entirely at the College of Surgeons. We had the written MCQ exams to begin with, followed by "tables"—where we were quizzed in Anatomy, Physiology, Pathology, Clinical Surgery, and Operative Surgery. It was a totally draining experience, to say the least. Then started the suspense-filled period of waiting for the results. When they finally called out my name and announced I had cleared the Part-I exams, I was relieved more than elated. It was an achievement to be proud of—the College boasted of just about 15 to 18% pass percentage. But somehow, I was not sure of my emotions after the event—I felt rather intimidated and unwanted—I am sure it had a lot to do with my rather new surroundings and lack of familiarity with the UK lifestyle, but frankly, I would have happily accepted a fail result, as I would have then had a kind of closure!

Now, when I rang up Akka at her home to convey the good news, the enormity of my undertaking dawned on me—she pointed out that I would have to somehow find a way to come over to the UK, somehow find a job, and clear the final exam, the Part-II. This was the norm in those days, and I could hardly see myself making the necessary arrangements to come away from the Indian Army for a prolonged period. This suddenly made me realise that my own three-year tenure was coming to an end very soon, and I was now suddenly impatient to get back to Muscat and pack my things and go back home to wherever the Army HQ decided I was fit to be posted.

13

Time to Pack for Home,
and a Hard Choice to Make

I picked up a few touristy items to give as gifts to people at the FBH, and for the kids of my civilian friends in Muscat. I also remembered to pick up some dark chocolate for Glynnis—I knew she was fond of them. Armed with these, and saying my goodbyes to Meera Akka and her kids, I left one grey afternoon for Muscat. My last act before going to the airport was a quick stop in front of the Lord's cricket ground entrance—the taxi driver very kindly agreed to click my picture. I would treasure this photograph for years to come. It would help me recall the best thing that happened during my triumphant trip to the UK—more than even my passing the Primary FRCS exam.

These twin achievements were the main topics of discussion from the moment I was picked up at the airport by Sunil and continued to be the staple topic in most conversations for many days afterwards. Even Glynnis was not spared my ball-by-ball recounting of the match, although I consciously toned down my choice of adjectives and expletives, for fear of offending the Brit in her. She actually seemed to enjoy it all, her laughter, especially the way her eyes twinkled when she laughed, making my heart skip a happy beat or two. At this rate, I thought, I would need a personal cardiologist around, if I were to have a lifelong association with this wonderful girl.

However, a somewhat depressing thought kept drawing my attention. We were into the month of July, and sadly, September loomed dangerously close. All my pretensions of wanting to go away back to India in the shortest possible time after landing in Oman nearly three years back were gone. The frequent revisions in my prayers to the Gods above now stood at 'I am okay to leave anytime (in September, not earlier, please) but if you want to keep me here for a few more weeks…' Like Professor Higgins, I had become rather accustomed to my lifestyle in Muscat. Besides, I had my own Eliza Dolittle in Glynnis—a sophisticated version from the beginning, no doubt—and I was truly getting accustomed to her company. I was quite confused about my feelings for her. I had no doubt I liked her a lot—but how about her? While I was fairly confident of her fondness for me, I knew that was not quite the same thing as her being in love with me—and by extension, being willing to cement our relationship and become an Indian wife. For that was the only option I could see ahead of me for both of us.

With my Indian passport, even my Primary FRCS qualification would not get me more than a visitor visa to the UK, so it would have to be Glynnis who would need to make the hard choice of moving to India. Besides, I had a permanent commission in the Army. The thought of quitting the Army was anathema to my very upbringing. And I could not even conceive of a "you there, me here" type of arrangement with Glynnis, unlike Sunil, who was very clear that he would put his relationship with Kristine behind him when he left Oman (and his "relationship" with Kristine was far more intimate than I had ever allowed myself with Glynnis).

I was agonising all the time. How to bring this up with Glynnis? Neither Sunil nor Deepak even made an attempt to see my viewpoint. They simply laughed it off as being stupidly sentimental. 'Jab tak idhar hain, enjoy, Boss (Make the most of your time in Muscat),' was their casual philosophy. I turned to my own personal philosopher, guide, and friend—Suresh. He was quite candid.

He said, 'Quite frankly, Hari, you know it is not going to work. If you try to quit the Army after this lollipop posting to Muscat, I can assure you the Army will not take it nicely—in fact, you will neither get your release, nor will you get your specialty training—you will have one punishment posting after another, friend. All organisations tend to be selfish. You will be labelled a traitor, and personally, I think they would be right. So don't even dream of that option. As to her willing to move to India, well, stranger things have happened. But don't merely imagine things. Put it to her squarely, and get a firm yes or no.

'These Brit girls are unlikely to dilly-dally—I bet Glynnis will be quite frank with her plans and decisions. Assuming she agrees, all related issues—like objections from your mother, family, why, even the Army's acceptance of your marriage to a foreign national—all these can be overcome in time. If she says sorry, have the grace to shake her hand, exchange a kiss or two, maybe, and accept it.

'A year after going back to India, especially if you get into the Surgery course, you will be eyeing some pretty young girl there, or your mother will put up a panel of irresistible beauties for you to marry. But don't be an ass and leave things unsaid—more than you, you need to consider Glynnis' feelings, whatever they are.' Buddha could not have expressed it better, I thought. But Suresh's *bhashan*—except for that traitor bit—made sense, as always. I knew that much. What I did not know was how to go about the whole thing with Glynnis.

As always, Glynnis helped. We found ourselves in her room one evening, and shaking as I was in the beginning, I rushed through all that had to be said before she could even guess what was coming. I added for good measure that I would accept it if she were to say I was stupid to have been presumptive about her feelings for me, but that I would beg her to please listen me out. The wonderful girl that she was, she never once interrupted me.

I know I must have gone round and round the same things a few times, so at one point, she politely asked, 'Harry, can I say something now?' I went silent. Glynnis came over and gave me a long, tight hug. I savoured the moment like never before.

Then she said, 'That hug is to tell you how much I love you, but it is also a substitute for a nice kick I feel like giving you for even doubting that my feelings for you are casual. So don't you dare talk any more nonsense! I know you will be getting back to your regular Army life soon, and I understand how things will be for both of us once you leave. I am going to have to stay on here for a few years more, Harry, to take care of my commitments back home. Not all Brits are born rich, you know! Let us make the most of your remaining time here in Muscat, okay?' And that was that. There it stayed, our friendship or relationship or whatever else one can call it.

Although the outcome was perhaps the most natural, sensible thing, it really hurt. I tossed and turned in bed that day, and in the end, sent in a specially worded request to all my favourite Gods. Could they let me stay on in Muscat for a little longer? It wasn't greed for money, I made it clear to them; it was more about being able to spend a few extra weeks with this really lovely girl. *Hope you all understand my reasons*, I added, looking heavenward.

14

The Bonus

The Gods understood! Indian Gods always smiled a kindly eye on lovebirds. By the end of August, I had all my LO related work neatly filed and ready to be handed over to the next incumbent. I had already identified one of the dental officers who had joined in the beginning of the year. He was a smart, handsome young Sardar, rather over-qualified for his young age, suave, and diplomatic to boot. I had no doubt he would get the approval locally and in Delhi. So, I shot off official letters to all concerned—The Deputation Cell at Army HQ in Delhi, Col. George at FMS HQ, and the Indian Embassy. In the letter to Army HQ, I made a polite enquiry about the incoming batch.

Around 15th of September, we had still not heard anything from Delhi about our replacements. Sunil and Deepak were quite sure the Army HQ had forgotten about us and wanted to explore if deputationists could buy property locally! As for me, I had no intention of buying any property in Muscat. I had actually even given up on my idea of buying a car. Calculations done with the help of local agents told me that a car bought here would cost almost twice the cost of one in India, even if those available here were better models.

Rumour had it that a Japanese company, Suzuki Motors, had already signed a contract with the Indian Government for manufacturing cars in India. So why bother with the hassle of taking one from here, customs duty and all? On the other hand, there would be a fair bit of waiting in India even after booking a car, and the current waiting time was close to two years! I was therefore in two minds—should I or should I not buy a car?

As always, Suresh nailed the issue. He had been exploring, too—in fact, his repatriation date had already been confirmed a few months back. I, as the LO, had passed on the news to him. But the FMS had taken up the matter with the Indian Army HQ to retain him for six months to oversee the expansion of the Dental Centre at UAG hospital, and so, he was slated to leave for India in December.

He said he had done all the research related to taking a car versus buying one in India. He had found out that the customs duty, at 160%, was on the CIF value of the car—the cost (at the point of manufacture), insurance (at 1% of the cost value) and freight (from country of origin to country of purchase). Apparently, he had done the math for a Toyota Starlet—a sleek, air-conditioned (both warm and cold air conditioning, unlike most models coming to the Middle East with only cooling facility) hatchback. It was a smallish car, he said, but a 5-seater, nonetheless. If we owned a car for even three months, there would be some trade discount and some depreciation, which would bring down the total customs duty significantly.

Suresh's stamp of approval was good enough for me, and without as much as thinking for a moment, I agreed. He wanted to buy the car in Muscat, and was coming to buy it next weekend, he said. I suddenly got all excited and made sure I had the necessary money (about 1700 Omani riyals) ready—I simply would not send home any money for now. I was buying a car without any worry about the source of the money for purchasing a car—something I would have been unable to dream of in my erstwhile Indian conditions.

Come the weekend, we both simply walked into the Toyota showroom in central Muscat, Suresh picked a silver-coloured Starlet and I settled for a gleaming metallic blue colour, and that was that. Both cars would be delivered, number plates, registration papers etc., included, to my location on Sunday, the first working day of the week. Just like that!

I was to drive both cars every now and then, till Ramesh came over in the beginning of December to do the export formalities for his car. I was now fervently hoping we would be allowed to stay till December at least—it would be so much easier to do all the necessary paperwork if I could combine it with big brother Suresh. But he would not let me be complacent.

'What if your letter of repatriation came tomorrow?' he asked.

We had already finished our three years, and if the letter came, it could mean moving back in rather quick time. So, he wanted me to keep all the paperwork ready—and in his usual way, he made a couple of phone calls—he had friends everywhere, even in Muscat where he had hardly served! Within a week (no letter came from the Army HQ in that time, and none of us complained!) my papers were all ready, except for the date of export. The local agent came to survey my other belongings and declared that a single container would take all my household effects and the car. However, he advised making wooden crates for the fridge, TV etc. for safe transportation.

15

Killer Ice Cream

If my initial days in Muscat were a drag, the latter part of my stay there was crowded with excitement, some of them unsolicited. Young Amarjit, who was to take over as LO from me, had been recently joined by his wife Anita, a bubbly, fun-loving girl. She was lean and thin and had this peculiar habit of coughing whenever she laughed out aloud. I found that rather funny, but obviously never mentioned it. She was instantly popular with everyone in the FBH fraternity.

I was happy—this would sit well with Amarjit's duties as LO in the coming months. Anita had a weakness for ice creams that was comparable to Kristine's. At the drop of a hat, she would want to visit the Softy Ice Cream stall in Ruwi. The place was extremely popular with all of us, and Anita had been introduced to the shop's menu within a couple of days of her arrival. She and Amarjit were often part of our group when we went to town. One weekend, we all had gone out for dinner, and sure enough, on the way back, Anita wanted to have her favourite strawberry softy ice cream. None of us objected, of course, and we all had a round of our choice flavours.

The conversation turned into some kind of challenge about which flavour was the best, and young Anita decided to play judge—by tasting another flavour. Amarjit protested, but she would have none of it. She was but halfway through her second ice cream when she started coughing her funny cough after some joke. Except, this time it was far from funny—she went from coughing to gasping in a matter of seconds.

Amarjit, ever the loving husband, suddenly asked, 'Sweetheart, where is your inhaler?' Turning to us, he said, 'She is asthmatic you know, that's why I was telling her not to overdo the softies.'

In between gasps, Anita informed us that she had forgotten to bring the inhaler with her! She was getting worse with every passing minute. I took an instant call.

'Deepak, I will take Anita and Amarjit with me to FBH. You drive Amarjit's car back to the hospital,' and without as much as waiting for his response, rushed the couple into my car—luckily, it was parked right where we were standing—and drove off. I was not sure if my decision was the best, but I didn't pause to think.

The Softy shop was about 30-odd kilometres from FBH. Luckily, at that late hour, traffic was light, and more importantly, there were no police patrol cars about. I drove like I have never done before or since, way above the speed limit, hazard lights on, while Anita was gasping away, turning more and more blue by the minute. How she held on till we reached FBH and rushed her into the casualty, shouting for help, I honestly do not know. All of us were really scared, poor Amarjit most of all. Within seconds, though, the competent nurses on duty managed to put her on an oxygen mask and give her intravenous deriphylline*, and poor Anita, who was understandably scared stiff, recovered, her breathing returning to normal pretty soon. Naughty girl that she was, she tried to look unfazed. When I asked her how she was, her answer made all of us go into fits of laughter. 'I think strawberry flavour is better than butterscotch,' she declared!

---

* Modern day drugs like albuterol were not available in those days at FBH.

16

India Pakistan, Bhai Bhai

I f my experience with Mr Latif in South Kensington had broadened my thinking, what followed was to seal my views on friends and foes. We were discussing the packing issues, those of us who were getting ready to leave—we were going to be six in all, leaving together as soon as the signal came from Delhi.

The ship would set sail from Muscat, stop at Karachi, and then go on to Bombay. It would take anything from 30 to 60 days to reach Bombay, where we would have to go for clearing the customs. For an additional fee, the agents would be happy to clear the customs themselves. We were only taking "used" household goods (anything with a purchase invoice of over six months would be considered used goods), and we were all diplomatic passport holders. The agents would clear the customs and despatch the goods in the original container by road to wherever we would be posted. That was all very good, but the actual packing had to be done by us (as in, through our own arrangement—the customs agents would not be able to do that).

I had a moment of inspiration. I called my squash coach from Thumrait days, Ashraf Khan, and asked him for advice.

His first response was one of anger, for I had promised to keep in touch, and hadn't. After giving me a mouthful, with free use of chosen Punjabi expletives, he said he was grateful to Allah that at least, if He was going to send his friend away to India, it meant there was an opportunity in that separation to be of some help.

He said he would send one of his colleagues from the local ordnance workshop in Muscat to inspect my goods and take care of everything. After the packing materials were in place, Ashraf would fly over to Muscat to personally supervise everything. And the payment for the boxes and packing and all that? He said the payment would be in the form of a series of Squash matches, and I would have to score at least one point against him in each match! This was a rather tough ask—my track record against him had been a very clean 0-9 in every game I had played with him, and post-Thumrait, Squash had been far away from my mind! *A cash payment would have been so much easier!*

As it happened, I did score a point or two against Ashraf, although only he and his Allah will know whether the point was gifted or earned! Ashraf's junior had come over the very next day, and having merely cast an eye on the things, had gone off without as much as a chat. In a couple of days, a big Bedford truck came over, with a whole lot of ply boards, and a number of Jundy boxes (Army issue iron trunks—usually supplied to all soldiers or Jundys). Next day, a couple of carpenters came after working hours, armed with tools, and over the succeeding week, I had crates made specially for each of the big items. They left a few wooden boxes, too. These were machine made in a matter of minutes, as I was allowed to see for myself in the workshop.

I was really a lucky chap, privileged to have a friend like Ashraf. We had jokingly agreed that if we ever met across the firing line in a war between our countries, we would shoot the other bugger without hesitation. But we equally fervently agreed that both of us would pray really hard that we never meet under such circumstances.

Ashraf said he had only one major regret in connection with our friendship—that I was not a Muslim: he would have loved nothing better than to give his dear sister's hand in marriage to me. And one look at her photograph, I realised that even if I had been a Muslim, I would have still had to ward off any number of competitors to get to her—she was one hell of a strikingly beautiful girl.

The others preparing to leave for India had made similar arrangements through their connections, and we were all mostly packed—except essentials (like TV and VCR player and toothbrush) by end of November. Still, there was no news from India about our repatriation. Had they really forgotten us? Would we have to unpack and strike a local deal with the FMS? These were the happy points for discussion at mealtimes, but we knew it was a matter of time before the official recall letter came.

Meantime, we decided we would make the most of our time in Oman. Sunil, Deepak, Banerjee, and I decided to put our Omani driving licence to good use. We hired a huge Chevrolet Impala, a monster of a car with a boot that could easily have challenged the container we were hiring for our luggage. At least that was my view about the boot of the car. Sunil had a more romantic view—he said, rather wistfully, that he should have gone for this car rather than his Toyota Cressida. Reason? The boot could take a comfortable double bed, he said, leaving the rest to our imagination!

The car was hired for the entire weekend, and we went driving all over and around Muscat, taking turns. Sunil and I were given a couple of hours—albeit grudgingly—to take our "girls" for a private ride, which was really nice, as both Glynnis and Kristine seemed to love it, especially when we had the hood drawn down and let the wind blow our hair all over. Boy, was that fun! Even more fun was when the girls gave us both really tight hugs when we stopped for ice creams!

17

Home Bound at Last

About two weeks after our jaunt with the Impala, Suresh landed up from Salalah. A couple of days later, he was off to India for good. As I dropped him off at the airport, I realised what a wonderful friend I had gained in him—he was always there when I needed him. He had bailed me out of terrible situations like with my car accident, he had had a role to play in the turnaround of my association with Dr Sivanesan, but above all, he had given me excellent counsel regarding my relationship with Glynnis.

I wondered what kind of a fool I would have made of myself in all such things but for his big brotherly help. And never once had he expected the smallest favour in return from me. People like him, Major Kuriakose and Ashraf, I felt, were the reason the world still continued to be such a wonderful place. My father would have said such people were the reason the Gods still sent down life giving rain and sunshine. I was really going to miss him terribly.

And then, suddenly, the inevitable happened. One day, I got a call from the embassy and went over to collect a bunch of letters—the top of the bunch was a letter about our batch's posting orders. I had drawn a Regimental Medical officer's post in an artillery unit in Jhansi, which was pretty okay, all things considered. I was aware of a medical college in Jhansi, so I would have access to clinical material, even some classes, to prepare for my surgery course. The others had fairly reasonable postings as well. We had had a fantastic tenure abroad; we were more or less sorted financially for the foreseeable future and had no right to complain about where we were being asked to go. I knew I would be restless till I started my Surgery training, and Sunil would be keen to get going as a medical specialist as well. The others were content with their lot, as well.

It is a mark of our collective integrity that soon after we received our posting orders, we unanimously turned down an offer from Brigadier Ward, the DG-FMS. He called us all to his office and said that should we choose to quit our commission in the Indian Army Medical Corps, a position in the next rank—Ra'aed (or Major)— would be waiting for us. He expected us to make a commitment about the tentative time frame in which such an arrangement could be put in place. He, Col. George, and everyone else in the FMS HQ and elsewhere, were extremely happy with our performance, he added, declaring that we were the best batch of deputationists he had seen in many years.

He had a special word for Sunil and me—Sunil for having cleared his MRCP, which entitled him to apply straightaway as a medical specialist in the Omani Army, and me, for having cleared my primary FRCS—I would of course have to clear the finals too to be appointed a full-fledged surgeon. We were all taken by surprise at this offer of a job in the next rank, with all its advantages of a proper house, extra pay, and so on, but were not hooked. Not even one of us—even Sunil, who had so much more to gain than any of us— showed any weakness. After exchanging a few words amongst us in a matter of seconds, we—I, as the spokesperson for the batch— thanked the Brigadier for his generous words and the offer, but we had been lucky to get this life-changing posting because of the Indian Army, and we now owed it back—a lot. All of us were permanent commissioned officers in the Army and had no intention of biting the hand that had trained and fed us and honoured us with a foreign posting. We intended to serve out our commission with sincerity and dignity.

I could see that the DG and Col. George were both disappointed. We were, after all, easy fits in the scheme of the FMS—but I could see that Col. George was inwardly proud of our decision. He said it in no uncertain terms in our farewell party a few weeks later. As for us, we were very proud of our decision, to the last man. When we shook hands later that day, there was a collective sense of duty and honour. We were truly worthy soldiers of the greatest military force in the world.

18

Excitement till the End!

Some interesting things happened in the few weeks we still stayed on in Muscat. One was of special importance to me: Lalgudi Jayaraman, the legendary Carnatic violinist, visited Muscat a month before I left Oman for good. The moment Gopal and Lalitha told me this, I decided to make the most of this golden opportunity of getting to know this extraordinary man—front-ranking violinist, singer, composer, musicologist, teacher par excellence, cultural ambassador—the ultimate definition of a complete musician. I already knew everything about his musical career. I now had a chance to know the man up close. I decided to find out everything about his upcoming journey. I met with the organisers and offered them all help since I was staying closest to the airport.

'May I have the privilege of receiving him and transporting him and his illustrious young son? (Now a famous violinist himself, the flag bearer of his father's fiddling technique.) May I please be involved in everything related to this visit?' They agreed readily.

I even did a test drive of the route from the airport to the hotel where he and his team were to be put up, and the route to the concert premises. And did I get into trouble in the process!

There was a Sultan's Armed Forces Training Unit—SAF-TR—midway between the main army campus and the main part of the town. The Chief Medical Officer there was an ex-AMC officer by the name of Raai'd Shivkumar. Shiv and I knew each other well. Since the CMO was almost equal to the CO of FBH in hierarchy, he was treated on par with other Muqaddams. This meant he had a brand-new Toyota Crown issued to him—perhaps the flagship car of the Toyota Company. Having driven once during our trip to Dubai, aware also that I could never afford to buy such a car, I decided on the next best option. I wanted to impress Sri Lalgudi Jayaraman with a swank new car, and so I went and begged Shiv to loan it to me for a few days. Decent soul that he was, he agreed readily.

Deepak had come along with me on this mission. When we left SAF-TR, we decided to go check out the car, and look up the parking arrangements etc., at the Indian School, which was to be the concert venue. The approach road to the school was somewhat narrow, and as I negotiated the wide-bodied car through the entrance gate, I realised I could not go in, as there was a large truck blocking the way. I had to reverse into the road to let the truck pass. I think I miscalculated the turning radius a wee bit. There was a sudden thud, and I realised to my horror that I had backed too far back and hit a low wall at the back.

Deepak, ever the reliable friend, started discussing the possible ways in which Shiv would torture the two of us for damaging his brand-new car. I cursed freely, and somehow managed to go back and forth and extricate the car out of the narrow space. We stopped a little ahead to assess the damage. A cursory inspection revealed no damage whatsoever. Not for nothing was this Toyota's best model! Totally relieved, we decided to beat a retreat. We chatted on the way about the pros and cons of driving a huge car with VIP guests—what if I did something silly with the great artiste in my car? How terrible it would be for me, trying to impress him? Better sense prevailed, and we decided we better quietly return the car to Shiv before I did more damage. We went back to Shiv's place, and just before going in, had a look at the back fender just in case we had missed something.

The fender was fine, but the silly number plate was missing! And it was no ordinary number plate. All Army issue cars had the Sultan's crest embossed on them! How in heavens was I going to explain this to Shiv? He would skin me alive! This was no casual mistake! We realised the damn thing must have fallen off when I hit the kerb wall at the school entrance. Deepak and I hurriedly got back into the car and drove back to the school—some 20 km away. All the way up, I was reciting one prayer after another, begging each and every God I could invoke to please, please let the number plate be right there, near the school. How come we never saw the damn thing? What sort of a silly car has such loose number plates? How could Toyota be so casual about such an important aspect of their car? Suddenly, I wasn't very impressed with Toyota's efficiency—it was so easy to put the blame on them than accept my own poor driving skills!

We reached ground zero, parked a little distance away, and went looking. Nothing! The number plate was nowhere to be seen! My heart sank. What if some local urchin had taken it home as a souvenir? Worse, what if some police patrol had found it lying on the ground? Omani jails loomed large in front of my eyes—Deepak had earlier assured us the food there was good, but now that he also might need to go as a visitor, he kept a stoic silence when I talked about being arrested for losing a Sultan's crest embossed number plate. We really panicked. And then, as always, one of the Gods smiled.

As we were about to give up, wondering what to do, Deepak spotted a ray of sun suddenly reflecting off something in the muddy road. It was the Sultan's Crest!

'Oh, my dear God!' we both cried, and kicked all the dust and mud off the place, and there it was, the entire number plate, covered over by dust from passing vehicles, but totally intact! The two of us hugged each other in our relief. We agreed that this called for a trip to the temple to say thanks. The temple itself was closed, but we parked—safely this time—stood at the doors to convey our thanks and beat a quiet retreat.

Shiv was a bit surprised when we returned the car and didn't seem very convinced that we found the car unwieldy. I wonder if he saw anything more in our faces, but he didn't say anything, and let us go, saying I could take the car after the artistes arrived, if I so wanted. Thanking him profusely, we slinked off from there before the temporarily fixed number plate decided to fall off again!

In the event, I used my standard issue Corolla to great effect. I was one of the few with the recently introduced National Panasonic Camera, a monster of a gadget. The camera itself was huge at about 18 inches; the recording deck was another heavy item that had to be carried along everywhere; the original variety of six inches long video cassettes necessitated a separate bag to keep spare tapes at the ready, and an ungainly flashlight was a must for recording in anything but bright daylight. Without hesitation, I offered to record his three concerts—two in the local Indian school, and the third, a chamber concert at the home of his friend where he and his team had been put up. After each concert, I would go home and copy the entire thing in real time into another tape for him.

Since the concerts were evening affairs and usually three hours long, I lost much sleep at night. But I didn't mind it the least little bit. The last concert was the toughest—he was catching a flight early morning next day, so I had to copy the original, and reach it to him at the airport. I managed all this without the slightest sense of discomfort; reaching it at the airport in the wee hours of the final morning was a cinch, experienced as I was with handing over letters to people for posting in India! My reward was the great maestro, a living God in his days, calling me by my name. And a handwritten letter in a handwriting as beautiful as his music, after he had reached Madras.

But there was something else even more special: I had become bold enough to ask him for a special *farmaish* (request) when he started the chamber concert. Ever since I had heard his *Thillana* in Sivaranjani raga, I was in love with that piece. I asked him if he would play that for me.

He said, most nonchalantly, '*Adunala enna? Vasiccha pochu*

(Why not? No problem).'

I was thrilled. I positioned myself at the far end of the room, recording the concert, enjoying every bit of it, but not losing sight of the available tape left for recording. I was therefore stopping the recording after each piece, waiting for the informal comments and questions to pass before starting the recording at the exact moment he started the next item.

At the fag end of the concert, he asked his friend's permission to close the concert. That gent, who was an old-time companion of the maestro, said, 'Sure, play my favourite *Thillana* in Desh ragam and finish.' Without as much as looking at me, Lalgudi started playing the Desh Thillana. I was mechanically recording the piece, but my heart was broken, because this was the moment of personal glory I had been waiting for—Lalgudi playing *my* request. Alas, he had chosen to go by his friend's choice.

I switched off the recording after he finished the *Thillana*, inwardly hurting to the point of crying. And in doing so, I sadly missed what would have been the most memorable words in my entire life: Lalgudi was saying, 'Breaking usual tradition, I will play one more Thillana before Mangalam—this is a special one for Hari.'

Oh, what an honour! What a treat—and here I was, machine switched off to save video tape! How stupid and stingy could I be? I hurriedly started the recording, but Lalgudi was done with his talking, and was on to the Sivaranjani *Thillana*. This tape is still in my possession, one of my most treasured memorabilia from my three Muscat years. I never miss a chance to bring this topic into discussion every time I am with musically inclined people!

Just a week before we were to leave, another exciting thing happened. The Indian embassy invited us deputationists to attend a dinner arranged for the visiting Indian cricket team. This was the same victorious team that had won the World Cup a few months back, and they were in Oman to promote cricket as a sport by playing a friendly match with a team from England. I had the pleasure of shaking hands with the great Kapil Dev, captain of the team, Sunil Gavaskar, the undisputed batting legend of those days, and Mohinder Amarnath, the man who with bat and ball, had helped India achieve an unlikely milestone at the Lord's cricket ground. Nothing could have been a fitting finale to three years (not forgetting the bonus of almost six extra months) of my life-changing experience in Oman.

19

A Tearful Farewell

On the 5th of April 1984, our deputation finally came to an end. Our personal effects had already been despatched by the forwarding agents—some of us were having our effects sent by air to Delhi because of an ongoing strike at Karachi Port. Some others decided to take their chances, as the cost of transportation by ship was much less than that by air. We had all had our various private and combined farewell parties, hosted by our military and civil friends. I am sure all of us must have gained a few kilos, we were constantly hogging good food followed by better desserts! I was invited by most of my civilian friends—an indication of my status as an eligible bachelor. I also had my private time with Glynnis, as I am sure Sunil did with Kristine. Deepak, poor chap, was running short of time, as he had to spend private moments with quite a few fans! The others had their own special farewells, too.

My time with Glynnis did not go very well. Glynnis cried a fair bit, making me feel rather guilty. I did not have the courage to take on the world by making her any promises, nor was I able to accept a simple end to a happy relationship full of fun and mirth. Glynnis undoubtedly brought out the best in me—I know for sure that despite the chance commonality between Dr Sivanesan and me in matters of music, my ability to withstand his association, and retain my love for surgery, was entirely due to Glynnis' constant encouragement. I could have so easily drifted away from surgical training, just to avoid the initial unpleasantness, but I would have regretted it later for sure. More for my redemption than any other reason, I pointed out all this to Glynnis as she buried her beautiful face on my chest and sobbed away, rather loudly at times, softly at others, but wetting my new T-shirt all the time! She refused dinner and took her leave, saying she would drop by to say goodbye in private next morning. She wouldn't be able to come to the airport to see me off, she said. She would surely make a mess of herself by crying in front of others.

This was a setback, alright. I had already boasted to the others that I would be making my own arrangements to reach the airport—naturally, with Glynnis driving me there in her car. I begged her to reconsider, without telling her the additional reasons, but she was firm. She left me after a long and lingering kiss, smearing more of her tears on to my cheeks and lips, and ran to her room without turning back. I really felt sad, realising how much I had enjoyed her company all this while.

My typical South Indian upbringing, and an unduly deep sense of morality had prevented me from exceeding self-imposed limits in my relationship with her. But more than once, especially when she came to spend the weekend with me in Bid Bid, I had come pretty close to sleeping with her. Later, when we were much more relaxed in our friendship, she had told me that she would have certainly not minded my advances, but that she respected my values. What a girl! I was the world's leading fool, letting go of a fine girl like her. But I realised it was not the time now to try and reverse things, with my flight just a few hours away. We had exchanged our postal addresses and made promises to keep in touch. *Maybe*, I thought, *just maybe, one day.*

Friday morning dawned bright and sunny (meaning, hot as ever!) and I finished packing my toothbrush and sundry last-minute items after an early breakfast all by myself in my room. A whole lot of friends—Omani officers, my Pakistani mates, Sri Lankan staff nurses, and of course, other deputationists and contract doctors dropped by to say their farewell. Glynnis did not show up, which made me feel acutely sad for some reason. I had reluctantly confessed to young Amarjit, the new LO, that my planned transportation had failed; could he please drop me off at the airport? As the newly appointed LO, he was more than willing to oblige his predecessor.

He turned up well before our agreed time of 11 a.m. We had just put my luggage into his car's boot, when all of a sudden, Glynnis turned up! Without speaking a word, she started to remove my luggage from Amarjit's car. When I asked her gently what she was doing, she burst into another bout of crying, saying she couldn't stay away! As she put her arms around my neck and sobbed away louder than ever, young Amarjit politely shifted my luggage to her car. Glynnis, ever the good human being, offered to let him come with us in her car, which thankfully he refused. I knew I had passed the LO's baton on to a sensible chap! Our cavalcade of two cars made its way to the airport, where, to my surprise, there were at least twenty-odd people, children included, who had turned up to say bye. Some of them—Lalitha for one—must have entertained fond hopes of fixing me up with one of her family girls, for sure! I could see some element of surprise in them as I alighted from a car driven by a white girl. I tried to look nonchalant, saying hello to this person, ruffling the head of that kid, and so on. Of course, it didn't last very long. Little Indu asked the question on everybody's mind.

'I know her,' she declared, pointing at Glynnis. 'She is your girlfriend, no? You came with her to Uncle Sid's house. Are you married?' Well, she couldn't have put it any better!

As I fumbled for words, Glynnis, as always, rose to my rescue.

'No, sweetheart,' she said, with a bright smile. 'We aren't married—he is running away to India, see?'

But even as some of my civilian friends were beginning to relax, Glynnis burst into sobs yet again, much to everyone's discomfiture. She moved away, leaving me to face a barrage of questions in Tamil from Lalitha, Shanthi, and others.

Siddhant, ever the gentleman, said, 'Go and comfort her, Hari, she is obviously very fond of you.'

It was all a big mess, but luckily, we were short on time, and the others had already started to move into the terminal building. I said my goodbyes to all the loving civilian friends who had treated me like their own, hugged the kids, and turned to say bye to the folks from the hospital. In front of everyone I knew and many I didn't, Glynnis gave me a big hug, sobbing all the time. Luckily, she didn't kiss me— I guess that would have probably meant a jail term for me, may be for both of us—Glynnis was intelligent enough to know that.

On that terribly confusing note, I passed through the double doors into the Departures hall, a heavy sense of sadness choking me as the doors shut me off from three years of wonderful stay in Oman. I realised I had forgotten to take a picture with all my friends from the hospital and civvy street before entering the terminal. I would have very much loved to, but I consoled myself. Every moment of the past three years and more had been etched in my mind, to last my entire lifetime. I joined the rest of the chaps at the check-in queue.

Epilogue

Our first year in Oman seemed never ending—at least for me—my father's passing away, the unsettled feeling due to frequent change of workplace, the really depressing initial days with Dr Sivanesan all made it look like a jail term with no end in sight. But things improved, and the monthly pay slip was certainly something to look forward to. The second year was quick, but the third year passed in a mere flash! By the end of the third year, all of us were praying collectively for some reason—any reason—for an extension to our stay in Oman by a few more months, weeks at least, before we packed and left. Such was the transformation brought about by beautiful Oman and its incredible people.

How did this come about? With all honesty, I can say that this was not merely the lure of a sizeable tax-free income. No doubt the financial benefits were palpable—most of us were from ordinary backgrounds, children of middle-class parents whose main desire was to give their kids a good education. But I doubt if any of our parents ever thought we would have a windfall such as this deputation. Speaking for my own father and mother, I can firmly say no, they didn't. My father wanted me to join the Army for two reasons—as a Gandhian and a true nationalist, he wanted me to join the armed forces to serve the country. I knew that he was extremely proud of my commission in the AMC.

The other reason had to do with stability. A government job meant an enduring source of income, however poor that income may be in comparison to the private sector. All four siblings in our home were urged to take up government jobs. No doubt he would have been proud of me had I made a name for myself in a foreign land, but for my father that was hardly ever in his plans for me or his other children. The money I earned in Oman was thus an unexpected bonus, never craved for, but gratefully accepted, nevertheless. It changed the course of my life, including in many ways that of the rest of my life, in ways unimagined.

To this day, though, I regret that the man who nurtured me without in any way pushing me, did not live long enough to enjoy the benefits of my extraordinary good luck. That regret will live with me as long as I live. Yes, I derived immense satisfaction by taking my mother to Muscat for a short period. But even she would have preferred a single day's visit with her husband in exchange for her own good fortune. Of this, I have no doubt whatsoever.

In the eighties, India was still a truly third-world country. Life was very different from what today's generation takes for granted: without grudging their good fortune in any way, I want to emphasise that we lived in the pre-television, pre-mobile phone, pre-internet, why, pre-computer age, with all its limitations, unthinkable in today's world. Making a landline phone call was a major achievement, leave alone owning a phone connection. Unlike today, where anything made anywhere in the world is available readily in the Indian markets, even chocolates, printed plastic bags, etc. were a craze for those who had people visiting them from "abroad".

In addition, the absence of social media meant that we were totally insulated from other peoples and cultures of the world. The few Hollywood movies that acted as a window to the outside world merely gave false impressions of life in far-off places, which could just as well have been on another planet. Those who had the benefit of a sneak preview were so smitten by it, they stopped belonging in India, and certainly didn't qualify to belong in the West. In that respect, our deputation was like an umbilical cord, allowing us a limited freedom for a specified time, but reminding us constantly of our roots. Looking back, I feel we deputationists were the luckiest of all—we got to see the world outside of India, and yet were not lured silly by it.

But we came back richer, not merely in terms of bank balance. I can easily say that the learning that we all picked up—in terms of other cultures, languages, people, and their customs—had made better individuals out of us all. We learnt to respect the differences amongst people from different parts of the world.

Oman was a happy meeting point of cultures and practices from the East and the West (Kipling got it all wrong, foolish man): we had an admixture of Indians, Sri-Lankans, Bangladeshis, Pakistanis, Indonesians, Filipinos and Singaporeans rubbing shoulders with Middle-Eastern Arabs, West-Asian Arabs, Europeans (mainly British, but a fair number of other nationalities from Eastern parts of Europe as well), and Americans. Omanis themselves were of three types: locals, Balochis, and the Afro-Arabs from Zanzibar. I would think that Oman could be the right place to start teaching humankind how to live in harmony with different peoples and learn to peacefully coexist. In this, the role of the ruler, His Majesty Sultan Qaboos bin Said, cannot be overemphasised. It was his benevolence that allowed peoples of different religious beliefs, customs, and lifestyles to coexist. In the three years plus of our stay in the country, we did not feel even remotely alienated. Be it at work or in the marketplace, we had an instant sense of belonging from Day One.

The Omanis are a proud people, with a very strong sense of nationality, but it did not stop them from accepting the idiosyncrasies of the many other nationals who chose to make Oman their home, some temporary, some long term. This could not have happened without State support. And the State was Sultan Qaboos.

He was a visionary in the truest sense. Col. George, like almost everybody else I came across in Oman, thought the Sultan worthy of worship. Col. George would repeatedly say no one deserved the Nobel Peace prize more than His Majesty. Forty years down the line, every individual who has had some association with Oman feels the same. I think some of that goodness of the great leader, and his wonderful subjects, must have rubbed on to us. Acceptance of fellow humans was the greatest gift Oman gave me. I certainly returned home a more mature, tolerant man, free of petty prejudices. Those three Muscat years are forever part of my very being now.

Of the three Muscateers—Deepak, Sunil, and I—two had fallen happily in love but returned empty handed for different reasons. Deepak perhaps had the most sensible approach—enjoy the temporary friendship without losing sight of reality, the reality being an inevitable end to our association with Oman and its residents. We all knew this, we had been briefed about all this even before we left on our deputation, but the heart is not bound by Army Rules and Regulations!

I hurt a lot for a long time, whenever I thought of Glynnis and what might have been. Sunil was far more candid. It surprised me to learn that it was he who had plainly told young Kristine to lay off when our return to India was nearby. I was shocked and disappointed with him, because he had taken his association with Kristine—quite possibly with her consent—to a different level. Well, that's proof of the differences in attitudes amongst people of similar backgrounds! All the more reason for people from different countries to be tolerant of one another. Professionally, we had all gained a lot—Sunil perhaps the most, for he was a full-fledged MRCP; I, with my extensive exposure to practical aspects of surgery (and in some measure, to my Part-I FRCS diploma), while Deepak had gained enough knowledge about general practice and administration to make it to the very top rank in the years after we all returned home.

The best part was that we were rooted enough in our *Indian-ness* to count our blessings and carry on home. Our gratitude to the Army

Medical Corps for this life-changing opportunity was genuine, and we were determined to give of our best to the Corps and Country. I continued to pray to my private Gods—thank you, God, for this wonderful innings; now, could you please look into helping me carve a career in surgery?

I must confess, though, that at times I would slyly add, *maybe, dear God, after I fulfil my obligations to the Indian Armed Forces, you could give a wee bit of a thought about getting me back to Oman?* Will He, will He not? As always, the Gods only smiled back at me from the pictures I prayed to. I had no option but to wait and see....

Acknowledgements

Although the cover mentions my name as the author, it is no secret that a huge amount of contribution from innumerable people was needed to make this book possible. When the idea of the book occurred to me, almost everyone I talked to encouraged me wholeheartedly. I owe a big round of thanks to all of them.

This book has been dedicated to my dear sister, Lalitha. She was my role model and was most influential in everything I did in my life. Her love for me was total and unconditional.

My wife Veena, son Kartik, and daughter Jotika have been urging me to write for many years now. This is a reflection of their love for me, and I am grateful for that. But when the first draft took shape, all three went about it with their editorial toothpicks! But for their persistent editing, I think this book—no doubt a horrible version of it—would have seen the light of day long back. I have no regrets with the delay they imposed, though—their contributions were invaluable and insightful. As was the support from Abhi and Anup, my children-in-law. Thank you, family.

Sanjana, my grandniece, volunteered to do the wonderful sketches that have really lifted the readability of this book. A very special thanks to you, dear Sanjana! I strongly believe you have a career in this field.

My parents and three siblings, having paved the way for me, would have no doubt derived immense satisfaction at this effort of mine. Wish you all were here, but I am content in the knowledge that you would have wholeheartedly approved. Also nodding approval from his celestial abode, I am sure, is my dear friend and schoolmate Niranjan, author of many books, and a great source of inspiration to me. Thank you for the wonderful times, and for teaching me the power of perseverance.

I can say without any hesitation that my writing has been heavily influenced by all the reading I have done in my life. My choice of words has been subconsciously moulded by authors like P G Wodehouse, Charles Dickens, Mark Twain, James Michener, Vikram Seth and Amitav Ghosh. I owe them, their style and wisdom, my most sincere respect and eternal gratitude.

Heartfelt thanks are due to the real persons who feature in this book under aliases—forgive me any slip-ups or mistakes, dear friends; you know that my love for you goes much deeper. We had a great deal of fun together and learnt a lot in the process. I hope you all will have fun going through this book, essentially one of our reminiscences.

To Raghu Chikkup and Kasthuri Chikki, Vinod and Meera, thank you for your wholehearted support and encouragement, as always. To Gopal, Ramani, and Nanu, my dear friends of some five decades, thanks for the thoughtful inputs. You will notice I have incorporated most of your suggestions. What I have not included merely reflects my vanity, not any disrespect to your valuable comments. To my other friends, especially Ramani-Uma; Madhavan-Shobha; Raju-Latha—all I can say is that your encouragement is a sign of our deep and long-time bonding, which so easily overrides my shortcomings. Other friends who gave suggestions have chosen not to be mentioned by name, but I am equally grateful to them all the same.

Major Gen. Naidu, AVSM VSM, thank you, Sir, from the bottom of my heart for your valuable time and comments. Lt. Gen. V Ravishankar, VSM, reminded me of some interesting incidents—

thanks a lot for that, Ravi. I think that added a fair bit of spice to the book!

A special round of thanks to Col ATK Rau for showing the way with his own book "Yesterday's Train to Nowhere", (a book really worth reading after you finish this one!) and for introducing me to the Inkfeathers team. I am very lucky to have landed the support of Uma, Anush, and others at Inkfeathers Publishing with my very first book. You are doing a great job of promoting Indian origin authors like me, and I salute you for that.

The Indian Armed Forces, and the Army Medical Corps provided the opportunity, and Oman provided fertile ground for these experiences. This book would not have been possible but for them. No words can adequately acknowledge my indebtedness.

Finally, thank you, dear reader, for picking this book up to read. Each one of you, while hopefully getting a few moments of happiness while reading this book, is also helping some budding Carnatic musician somewhere, for every rupee earned from your contributions will go for encouraging them in some way or the other.

Harikrishnan,
Bangalore, May 2022

Glossary

1. Akka – Sister in many Indian languages
2. Aloo Puri – A typical Indian dish with potatoes and fluffed wheat bread
3. AMC – Army Medical Corps
4. Appa – Father
5. Babuji – Father
6. Bhai Saab – Brother (respectful way of addressing almost any male)
7. Bhashan – Lecture
8. BHQ – Short for Brigade Headquarters
9. Bilkul – Very much or Exactly
10. BM – Brigade Major. A very important administrative position in the Brigade Headquarters.
11. C.O. – Short for Commanding Officer, the top man in any Army unit
12. Chadhao – To adorn
13. Chhappad phad ke – Hindi equivalent of "when it rains, it pours". Literally Translated, it means when God decides to give you, He will break the roof above your head to pour riches down on you.
14. Dak – The army term for post/letters
15. Dao – Traditional dagger or sword
16. DDMS – Short for Deputy Director, Medical Services

17. Dhoti – A type of sarong wrapped around the waist
18. DR – Despatch Riders
19. Farmaish – Request
20. FRCS – Fellow of the Royal College of Surgeons (a UK Diploma)
21. Funda – Basics, Motto
22. Ganesha – Indian God who removes all obstacles
23. Ghat/ Ghati – Pier
24. Gora – Common term used to refer to White people
25. Hamdulillah – With God's grace
26. Hb – Haemoglobin, an indicator of the oxygen carrying capacity of blood
27. Head Clerk Saab – Respectful way to address the senior most among clerical staff
28. HQ – Short for Headquarters
29. Jaise the – Hindi term for 'as you were'
30. Jhanda – Flag
31. Jhandewale – one who carries a flag
32. Jonga – Jabalpur Ordnance and Guncarriage Assembly vehicle, a kind of largish Jeep, originally made by Nissan Corporation for the Indian Army
33. Kahwa – Arabic coffee
34. Kaif haal ak – Arabic for 'How are you?'
35. Keen-Kumar – Indian term for overenthusiastic
36. Khanjar – Traditional Omani dagger (ceremonial)
37. Khareef – Monsoon
38. Khubs – Arabic flat bread
39. Kopuram (also, Gopuram) – Tamil term for a temple tower
40. Kullu Zen – Arabic for 'All's well'
41. LFT – Short for Liver Function Tests
42. Mangalam – Refers here to the end piece in a traditional Carnatic concert

43. Masala – Spices or spicy

44. Mataji – Mother

45. Mauth – Dead or Death in Arabic and Hindi

46. Mess Havaldar – The person of non-officer rank who is in-charge of the administration of an Officers' Mess. He works under the supervision of the Mess Secretary

47. Mess Secretary – Officer in-charge of the Officers' Mess in any military unit

48. Moksha – Emancipation or enlightenment, used in most Indian religions

49. OPD – Short for Outpatient Department

50. OT – Short for Operation Theatre(s)

51. Pakodas – Indian snacks made with various ingredients, like flour, lentils and vegetables

52. Panditji – Respectful for Pandit or priest

53. Panga – Argument; confrontation

54. Payasam – A tasty Indian dessert

55. Povva – Slang for influence

56. Prasadam – Food or other items offered to God

57. Raga/Ragam – Indian term for melody

58. RMO – Short for Regimental Medical Officer

59. Rota – Duty schedule

60. Saab – Indian version of 'Sir', as a respectful form of address

61. Sabah al khair – Arabic for 'Good Morning'

62. Samosas – A deep fried Indian snack made of flour with different fillings

63. Shurta – Omani for police

64. Sloka/slokam – A Sanskrit term for traditional Indian verse adhering to a particular metre

65. Tabeeb – Omani for doctor

66. Thalis – Typical Indian meals

67. Thillana – A Carnatic musical piece mainly used for facilitating classical dance

68. Vadai malai – A garland of doughnuts usually made of lentils.

69. Vaikuntha/Vaikuntham – Celestial abode of the Gods; what devout Hindus aspire for at the end of their lives.

INKFEATHERS PUBLISHING

We love creating beautiful books for you!

Come be a part of our ever-growing community of writers. Grow, write, and publish with us!

Scan here and get to know us better.

Connect with us on socials. We'd love to hear from you!

     Inkfeathers Publishing